EVITA

EVITA

The Woman
With the Whip

by Mary Main

DODD, MEAD & COMPANY • **New York**

Library of Congress Cataloging in Publication Data

Main, Mary Foster.
   Evita : the woman with the whip.

   Published in 1952 under title: The woman with
the whip: Eva Perón.
   1. Perón, Eva Duarte, 1919-1952.
2. Politicians--Argentine Republic--Biography.
3. Argentine Republic--Presidents--Wives--
Biography. I. Title.
F2849.P37M3 1980   982'.06'0924 [B]
ISBN 0-396-07834-6   79-27288

1 2 3 4 5 6 7 8 9 10

Foreword

The spectacular success in London of the musical *Evita* by Tim Rice and Andrew Lloyd Webber, and its debut in New York, have been the occasion for the reissuing of this book, which was first published in 1952, the year of Eva Perón's death, while her husband Juan was still in power. It might seem surprising that someone as ruthlessly destructive as Evita should have been considered a fit subject for a popular musical, but Evita was the product of her own fantasy, a fantasy in which she so steadfastly believed that, in the end, reality surpassed her wildest dream.

If this book should serve to recall the real Evita, the woman obscured by rumor, scandal, and the glamour of a musical, I shall be grateful. Successful and unscrupulous as Evita was, she was a profoundly tragic figure; but the tragedy was not hers alone. It was the tragedy of a whole people, for she and Perón set in motion those forces which were to destroy their country. No, it is not for Evita that Argentina should cry! It is for all those Argentinians who have, since her time, and in increasing numbers, mysteriously disappeared, and whose deaths remain unaccounted for. It is to the memory of these *desaparecidos* I dedicate the new edition of this book.

Mary Main
Stamford, Connecticut
1980

Publisher's Note

This book was first published in 1952, shortly before Eva Perón died, and is being reissued because of the renewed interest in her life. When the book first appeared Mary Main wrote it under the pseudonym of María Flores to protect her friends and relatives living in Argentina. For this edition she has added a foreword and an epilogue; otherwise, the text is essentially the same as in the original book.

Buenos Aires

I was born and brought up in Buenos Aires, and I have of
it those childhood memories that hold the power to re-
awaken all five senses to old ecstasies. I have known its tempo
quicken from the clop of horses' hoofs on cobblestones to the sigh
of cars on asphalt avenues and turn to the anxious pattering of
feet that herd up subway stairs and into offices.

There was a time when the gossiping of women servants under
the languid trees of the plaza was as soothing as the croon of doves
to the gleaning ear of childhood, a time of long, whispering siesta
hours and of rooms shuttered against the heat, or against the dust

that filmed the city before the storm, before the wind itself came booming in across the plains to drive children, like cattle, crazy with delicious restlessness. The First World War was half a world away and in another time than ours.

But the ripple of its upheaval reached our becalmed lives at last and it was not against the dust that windows were shuttered and doors barred. An old man stood guard over us with a dueling sword and the ladies gathered in my mother's drawing room twittered like startled birds at the sound of gun-firing in the streets, or whispered in shocked voices of a President[1] who seemed to think the working people had a reason and a right to disrupt our lives with violence.

By the twenties the violence had subsided, and life became as sleek and opulent as the Rolls and Daimlers that glided slowly round and round the Rose Garden in Palermo Park, the ladies in the high tonneaus inclining their heads to their acquaintances, which was then the fashionable exercise on Thursday afternoons. A time of five-course dinners and calling cards, of mornings spent in choosing the material for a gown, and of lifetimes spent over coal ranges in windowless kitchens. Our President then wore a frock coat and not a uniform. I saw him once, a portly, bald-headed gentleman stepping out of a car with his top hat in his hand and, with youthful exuberance, I exclaimed, "Why, there's the *Pelado!*"[2] and he turned and gave me a courtly little bow, to my dreadful confusion. Twenty years later I was driving down Avenida Alvear with a friend and, when the traffic slowed, he nudged me and said, "Look, there's Perón in the next car." I leaned forward to look at the fleshily handsome man in the white-coated uniform, shaking my head a little disbelievingly, and the President-elect, seeing my uncertainty, grinned genially and nodded and tapped himself expansively on the chest. Between those two gestures, the

[1]President Hipólito Irigoyen.
[2]President Alvear was known as the *Pelado,* or Baldy. His friend Irigoyen was known as the *Peludo,* the Hairy One, the name given to the little armadillo that hides in his hairy shell.

bow and the grin, between the top hat and the uniform, an era had passed away.

In the thirties, when the government was seized overnight, we were more astonished than alarmed, for we had thought ourselves as stable as England in Gladstone's day. We were not to be confused, you understand, with smaller South American states where revolutions were an accepted part of politics. And the new decade seemed to confirm us in our respectable commercial wealth and comfortable security, for it was a decade of material progress, a time of modern apartments with bright-tiled electric kitchens, a time of cocktail parties and of bridge, and there was more grumbling about maids who "did not know their place" than about the government's encroachment upon liberty. Strangely it was then the President[3] himself who was the champion of our civil liberties; the city was already touched by fear, for there were rumors that he was held a prisoner, that he was being poisoned. I once passed the house where he lay dying, an obese and almost blind old man, and as I approached a guard stepped forward and told me brusquely that I must keep to the far side of the street.

Then came the time when we woke in the night to hear the clop of hoofs as mounted police patrolled the empty streets, and sometimes we saw the crowds that stroll down Calle Florida in the afternoons scattered by trucks loaded with armed men. And almost without violence, in a rich and peaceful country, we found ourselves under a dictatorship.

I had left Buenos Aires shortly after Perón was first elected President and I returned again in 1951. The old leisurely way of life was quite gone as it was gone elsewhere in the world, and at first glance the city seemed more prosperous; on almost every block the debris of new building cluttered the narrow sidewalks, and handsome avenues had been opened up with monumental government offices along the way. The flower shops on the corners were as full of exotic color as before and bouquets of roses and

[3]President Roberto M. Ortiz.

gardenias were still hawked for a few cents in the street. Calle Florida, closed to traffic in the late afternoons, was as crowded as the dance floor of a *boîte* and the crowd as polyglot and full of sleek well-being as it had ever been. On the surface the social life seemed changed only in speed; it still revolved about cocktail parties and clothes, week ends at a country club or an *estancia,* and talk was all of rising prices, of quick money to be made, of golf scores and the scarcity of butter and of the good old days when cooks earned fifteen dollars a month and did all the laundry in the house; but it had the high note of conversation quickly changed to trivial matters to hide a deep and common preoccupation. There were small touches that gave a nightmare flavor to frivolity; the finger to the lips and nod towards the taxi driver's listening back, the red crosses smeared on certain doors and, at night, the floodlit billboards in a city almost dark and, on them, the two names that were not to be spoken out aloud. All this belonged to a sub-life of secret fear which touched us all, for there was no one who had not had some friend under arbitrary arrest or who did not feel possessions and livelihood to be under threat. Yet in the midst of this social and business life this fear had a quality of fantasy; only for a few did it have immediacy; to the rest it seemed a deviation from the reality of business and bars and clubs. But the hold the threat had over everyone was revealed by the insistence with which the conversation turned, in private but often with indiscretion, to rumors of violence perpetrated or revolts to come and to gossip of *her.* The thought of her was at the back of every fear, for she had become the symbol of this new uncertain and apprehensive way of life, and the obsession that she had become to most was shown by the energy with which they belittled her influence and power. Only those who were actively opposed in politics to the regime could speak of her with restraint and dignity, if they would speak of her at all.

I saw her first at her most beautiful. It was at a gala performance at the Colón Opera House and I stood in the crowds pressed close behind the double row of military cadets that lined each side of the entrance steps. The crowd was of office girls, shopkeepers, with here and there a small family group, and they waited not so much with eagerness as with avidity. There was no mention of her name and no chat or badinage as one might have expected from such a gathering; it was a crowd without unity or friendliness. Whistles and peremptory orders and a bustle of uniforms up and down the carpeted steps, and she came, a slender, pale-haired, dark-eyed woman passing with the swiftness of flight, her spreading dress and satin cloak all rose, embroidered gold and deeper rose. She paused a moment to shed her smile this way and that, and then sped on, the President and all his ministers at her heels.

I came once upon a small crowd gathered in the evening street, outnumbered by the police who held it in check. There was a line of police cars along one side of the street and on the balcony above them electricians were setting up floodlights trained on an entrance opposite, which was papered with portraits of the Peróns and Peronista coats-of-arms. This crowd was all of poorer women, domestic servants from the apartments around, one old peasant woman with her shawl clutched under her chin, a brawny-armed working girl dressed all in black with the face of a medieval fanatic, and a few shopkeepers leaning in their doorways with arms akimbo. Here again there was no mention of her name, no talk at all until a young girl with a friendly, frank expression came up and asked quite loudly why everyone was gathered there. No one answered her so I told her that we were waiting to see the President and his wife who came every week to give a talk in this school for young Peronistas. "Huh!" she said. "In my country we don't make all this fuss. We can see our president down on the beach or playing pool any day we like." There was a slight movement as if the little crowd had drawn away from us on every side. "Your country?" I asked. "Uruguay," she answered, her pleasing frankness changing to belligerence. "We have something there that you don't have here in Buenos Aires and that's freedom!" There was a deliberate challenge in her voice but no one answered her. She laughed and shrugged her shoulders and moved off, and the little crowd was silent, avoiding each other's eyes.

A jeep shot up to the floodlit entrance and two young men bounced out; they might have been twins with their padded shoulders and black lacquered hair. One carried a sheaf of arum lilies and the other a vase of roses and a bowl of sweet peas, and they darted into the school with the officious haste of amateurs preparing a stage for theatricals. More police arrived and began to herd the crowd further back; the old peasant woman refused to budge until they took her arms and pushed her back. Two cars drove up and Eva stepped out of one into a bevy of men. In the floodlit entrance she paused for an instant and turned her glittering smile towards the crowd and then was gone, followed by the faint pattering of clapping hands and by the old woman who, eluding the police, plunged desperately after her, only to be caught and led away before she reached the door.

Each time I saw Eva it was the same; the silent crowd who, even if they worshiped her, seemed afraid to speak her name aloud except in chorus and at command. Her name, with Perón's, was stenciled on every wall, her portrait smiled in every public room, in every room of every railway station, every post office and every school, in shops and in business offices; the sight of her was inescapable, the thought of her haunted the whole town.

One

I am a woman of the people . . . E. P.

So much scandal and so many rumors have circulated
the drawing rooms and cafés of Buenos Aires around the
name of María Eva Duarte de Perón that the story of her life had,
before half its natural span had run, assumed the cloudy proportions of a myth. No one—certainly no woman—in the history of
South America has been the subject of so much speculation and
controversy or the object of such hatred and such fanatic adoration
as she. The mention of her name has been enough to evoke an intensity of emotion that made objective discussion of her impossible;
those who had known her best had lost or gained too much by knowing her to speak impartially; those who praised her did so with such

13

fulsome servility that the listener was less persuaded than nauseated; those who criticized her, much as they might disclaim prejudice, betrayed their hatred by the vehemence with which they accused her of every perversity. And added to the emotions of loathing and devotion that distorted discussion of her and, of course, often at the root of both, was fear. Not a question could be asked, or answered, without a mental glance over the shoulder to see if one was overheard. She might be flattered in public or vilified in private, but any serious inquiry into her character and life set up at once the devious mechanisms of fear; those who were against her were, quite rationally, fearful that even a well-intended interlocutor might publish information that would unwittingly bring retribution down on them; while those who supported her did not dare to advance the mildest criticism, since even a lack of enthusiasm might have been interpreted as *desacato* and, as such, "disrespect," was punishable by three years' imprisonment.

Eva Perón herself did nothing to disperse the clouds of misinformation surrounding her. She forbade all mention of the past, other than the fact that she was of humble birth, and she destroyed what records she could lay her hands on—and there was not much in Argentina that was beyond the reach of those acquisitive white hands. It would seem that she would have had us believe that she rose, resplendent as the phoenix, as the wife of Juan Domingo Perón from the ashes of the 1945 revolt. And the picture of herself that she presented to her public in her prime, that charming picture of a Lady Bountiful dedicating her life to humble folk, was not a millimeter nearer to the truth than the most scurrilous of the stories that abounded.

The truth about Eva Perón has been obscured by greed and hatred, vanity and fear, so that in writing about her now one feels compelled to offer some sort of apology, not to the subject herself who is beyond the reach of misinterpretation now, but to the reader who may look for documentary evidence and a definitive biography. Such a biography can be written, if ever written, only long after the fury and the fanfare are forgotten, and only one thing is certain of it—that the story will be even more remarkable than all that is known of her now.

María Eva Duarte was born in Los Toldos, a small pueblo in the province of Buenos Aires about two hundred miles west of the capital, on May 17, 1919. No one who has not seen such a pueblo can imagine the dreariness of it. It lies like a worm cast on the platter of the plains, its squalid little buildings crumbling back into the dust from which they have been built. Dust lies everywhere, a foot thick on the unpaved road where a passing troop of cattle raises a white cloud that for a while stagnates in the hot air and then settles slowly on the earth again. Dust seeps into the small houses whose pink and yellow plastering has faded to the dun of dust; the grit of it settles on the food and on the clothes and on the skin and teeth and in the very heart of man. Dust and silence everywhere, a deathly stillness broken only by the mongrel dog crossing the road to scratch itself or an iron windmill that clanks as it turns which way to the wind. Flies buzz above offal cast out in a yard and men's voices are raised in momentary anger, or a woman scolds at a whining child.

Earth and sky are huge. Around the pueblo lie the vast, rich plains—seven to eleven feet of black topsoil—where the wind stirs a happy whispering among the young corn or lifts a cloud of yellow butterflies out of a field of flowering alfalfa. Ovenbirds' nests are clamped to fence posts and *bien-te-veo* birds balance precariously on the topmost strand of barbed wire. And over it all, encompassing as a cup turned down upon a plate and dwarfing the pueblo and man himself to insect size, is the great dome of the sky. By night it is more glittering with stars than northern skies, by day of the most serene, ineffable blue—until the ink-dark storm clouds mass on the horizon and hail and rain come galloping across the pampas to turn all this dust into a slough of mud that, in those days before the roads were paved, isolated one pueblo from the next.

It was in such surroundings, where man and his works seem so

15

small and earth and sky so large, that Eva's mother, Juana Ibarguen, grew up. She was a pretty, coarse, lively girl of Basque descent. She had little if any education, for her family was poor—her father was a coachman, it is said, and perhaps he drove one of those hearselike vehicles that used to take the rich folk from the railway station to their *estancias* in the days before cars. In such a pueblo as Los Toldos there were few opportunities for an ambitious girl; if she had a slice of property she had hope of buying herself a respectable marriage; if she had a pretense of education she might become a schoolteacher or a post-office employee. With neither, and if she had any wish to retain a semblance of respectability, she must earn her keep as a servant girl in the house of some rich landowner in the neighborhood where, if she were not seduced by the master of the house himself, she ran a very good chance of being so by one of his sons or employees, and then married off to some peon who needed a woman to cook for him and help him in the fields. For a girl to remain virgin beyond her fourteenth year was the exception and too many of them ended by setting themselves up as prostitutes in some squalid rancho on the outskirts of the pueblo.

But for a pretty girl there was yet another way—to find some married man who liked her well enough to support her in a secondary establishment. This did not by any means preclude the necessity of earning money from casual customers but it did at least offer a temporary security and even some sort of standing in the community, this depending on the wealth and position of the man, and might eventually become as stable a relationship, and almost as respectable a one, as marriage.

Juana Ibarguen found herself such a protector in Juan Duarte, a man of moderate means who came from the not too distant town of Chivilcoy where he already had a wife and family. The dual domesticity he set up did not imply any unconventionality on his part; the situation was so common that it would have surprised only the most strait-laced among his acquaintances and caused indignation only among his legitimate family back in Chivilcoy.

To be faithful to his wife would have been more unusual, and he was a conservative sort of man.

His relationship with Doña Juana, as she came to be called from courtesy, lasted more than a dozen years, over the births of their five children of whom María Eva was the youngest. He seems to have felt some responsibility towards his unlawful brood; if he did not live with them he did at least visit them frequently, and he did not disclaim his paternity, for they freely used his name and Eva's godfather was a friend of his.

It was at the time of his death, or, rather, of his funeral, that the small Eva first came to the front of the scene. When Juan Duarte died his family in Chivilcoy, with an understandable lack of charity, refused Doña Juana's request that she and her children should be allowed to attend the funeral. In Argentine culture funerals have a deep family significance; for Doña Juana to be present would have meant a formal acknowledgment of her relationship with the dead, an acknowledgment that the Señora de Duarte must have been as anxious to avoid as Doña Juana was greedy to procure. Doña Juana appealed to Eva's godfather and it was through his intercession that a compromise was reached—Doña Juana's children, but not Doña Juana herself, were allowed to attend the funeral.

Elisa, the eldest of the family, was about eleven at this time, Blanca nine, the only boy, Juancito, five, Arminda, three, and little Eva about two. She was small enough to be carried into the room in her godfather's arms but old enough perhaps to resent the airs of her *papito's* richer and more established family and to be conscious of their hostility. Even at the age of two it is a shock to discover that your father belongs to another family.

The little girls, even the smallest of them, must have been hastily rigged out in mourning, black smocks and long black stockings and new black shoes perhaps, and a band of black crepe for Juancito's sleeve. These were formalities which not the poorest or the most irregular family would wish to avoid. Eva was a small, quiet, sallow-faced child with thick dark hair. Perched up there on her

17

godfather's arm she had the advantage of her brother and sisters; she could look over the heads and shoulders of the more welcome guests at her father's coffin and stare down at her half-sisters with the implacable animosity of childhood in her dark eyes.

The year or two that followed the death of Juan Duarte were ones of privation for Doña Juana and her children. She had no legitimate means of support and she had to cast about to find a new protector for herself and her small family. But she was a woman who knew how to please men and who was clever and unscrupulous in the way she handled them, and she met and captured the fancy of an Italian who kept a small restaurant—an eating house would describe it more accurately—in Junín, a town some forty-odd miles away. If he had any other family they were not in evidence, and he moved Doña Juana and her children into his house in Junín. Although the financial improvement in their life was not so great— Doña Juana had to take in lodgers to make both ends meet—it must have seemed to the children when they moved to Junín that they were moving into the metropolis itself. Here there were two-story buildings, railway stations and hotels, cobbled streets and a plaza with a bench or two, a few shops that sold calicos and cottons and cheap gaudy silks; some of the women wore high-heeled shoes instead of the rope-soled *alpargatas* that were the common foot-wear of the countryfolk; not all the men wore the voluminous cotton *bombachas* that make such comfortable riding breeches; some of them wore city suits even if in summer the jacket was exchanged for a cooler pajama top. Once or twice a week there was a movie show in a dingy hall and, as well as the high-wheeled sulkies that came rattling off the dust onto the cobblestones, there were the Fords and Chevrolets that came to fetch the mail for the *estancia* folk and covered the sidewalks and the houses with a cloud of dust.

The house the Duartes lived in was the classic house of Argentine towns—indeed they moved into another later that was its twin —built in the shape of an F, the top of the F being the front of the

18

house whose two balconied windows and narrow front door gave directly onto the sidewalk. The row of bedrooms behind the *sala* in front had no windows, for they backed onto the house behind, but each had three doors, two opening into rooms on either side and another, with slatted wooden shutters to it, opening onto the patio around which the rooms were built. The patio was shut off by the wall of the neighboring house and divided in the center by a larger room which was meant to serve as a dining room and cut off the front part of the house from the kitchen quarters at the back. Since Doña Juana must have given the front rooms to her lodgers, she and her children most probably lived in the "dining room" and the rooms at the back. Perhaps there were a few plants set about in tubs in the patio and, at the back, a small garden with a lemon tree and an iron windmill that supplied the house with water. Junín had been built on the plan set out for all Spanish colonial towns, in blocks a hundred meters square which until lately distorted the shape of all Argentine houses. The houses are inconvenient—one must walk through the bedrooms or out in the patio to get from one room to another—ugly, and give no possibility of privacy.

Although the Duartes must often have been short of money it is unlikely that they ever went hungry. In the country in those days a pound of tenderloin cost less than ten cents—it was never tender because the steer was slaughtered as soon as it was driven in to the butcher's and sold while the flesh was warm. The children did not go hungry but their meals were as monotonous and as unappetizingly served as the rest of life. The staple dish was *puchero,* a watery stew of meat and sausages, root vegetables and rice, served first as soup and then as the main dish of the meal. There were great dishes of Italian pasta on which a hungry family of six could feed themselves for twenty cents and, even for the youngest of the family, plenty of red wine at ten or fifteen cents a liter. No need for children to go hungry, but of a balanced diet few mothers, and certainly not Doña Juana, had ever heard. Milk was regarded with suspicion—with reason—and if a child had colitis she was

19

given tea to drink. It was more difficult for Doña Juana to provide her children with the white smocks that are the uniforms of all schoolchildren, boys and girls alike, in Argentina and which effectively cover the makeshift garments that the poorer children wear underneath, and the leather shoes that they had to wear sometimes instead of the cheaper *alpargatas* to show they were not the children of a peon, and the big white bows the girls wore on the top of their heads for fiestas.

The household was a noisy one. Doña Juana would scream shrilly at her daughters; neither she nor her children had ever learned to control their tempers or their language, and the Argentine woman's voice is the shrillest in the world. Juancito, being a man, or almost one, would expect his mother and sisters to be at his beck and call; he would run wild out in the streets, come home long after dark and refuse to account for his absences. There was no order or discipline in the household; the youngest children were allowed to sit up until their elders chose to go to bed and to witness any scene that might take place between Doña Juana and her protector or her other visitors, and hear in endless reiteration the details of it afterwards when Doña Juana explained to her eldest daughter or to her friends the reason for her rage. There was certainly no intimate secret of her mother's life of which Eva was not very soon aware—she was such an unobtrusive little girl listening to it all with her sharp ears and watching it all with her sharp eyes, and only occasionally drawing attention to herself by a fit of what seemed to her family unjustifiable rage.

In the evenings or on Sundays when the boarders were at home there was a great deal of flirtatious giggling, horseplay, and some pretty little scenes of affection put on by the mother and her daughters for the benefit of the men but which, since they as frequently witnessed their quarreling, must have failed to convince.

But beyond what entertainment the girls could make for themselves, beyond, in fact, the practice of their arts upon their archenemy, man, there was nothing in the town to provide them with interest. At school they learned their lessons by rote, repeating

20

them after their teacher in a singsong chorus; there was no library or bookshop in the town; there were no country excursions or picnic spots, only the straight dusty road that led over the horizon, not infrequently adorned with the carcass of a horse or cow left for the maggots and the ants to scavenge. The girls might walk down to the railway station to watch the Buenos Aires train come in— and the soul-destroying boredom of life in the pueblo is testified by those lethargic little groups of men and women that still collect at every wayside station to watch a train run through. Or on summer evenings they could stroll arm in arm with their girl friends, half a dozen of them stringing out across the path, round and round the plaza. This evening promenade had conventions which could not be flouted, even by girls with so irregular a homelife as the Duarte girls. The girls circled in one direction and the young men, in smaller groups, in the other. The girls acknowledged the young men only with a flurry of chatter and giggling among each other as they passed. The young men addressed their remarks at, not to, the girls. If a young man's fancy happened on a girl in green, "How sweet she will be," he would say, "when she is ripe!" Or if it fell upon a girl in pink, "Pretty as a rose—but I am afraid of thorns!" A type of wit made proper by long wear.

The younger children were all at school now. Elisa, the eldest, was the only one to finish high school and she had a job in the post office and an admirer among her mother's boarders. Doña Juana's friend had gone off to Buenos Aires to try his luck in an obscure little restaurant only a block or two from the Casa Rosada —the pink Government House—on whose balcony the youngest Duarte girl would one day step out to receive the applause of the people. Doña Juana seems to have been able to inspire considerable fidelity in her friends, for he allowed her to stay on in the house he owned and he returned from time to time to visit *la vieja,* as he called her with a deprecative sort of affection. Since she had by now a number of friends in Junín his absence could have left no great gap.

The townsfolk were, in general, too simple and too familiar themselves with poverty and illegitimacy to turn up their noses at the Duarte family. There were some certainly who would not allow their daughters to associate with the daughters of Doña Juana—for what a son might do a mother had no recourse but prayer; and at school there must have been girls who would have nothing to do with the Duarte girls, for no one is more sensitive to measures of respectability than the adolescent. But on the score of their illegitimacy they would have received no very great affront. To the sentimental Argentine a child is a gift from God no matter how it is got, and some twenty-eight per cent of Argentine children are gotten illegitimately.

Eva did not finish her schooling; she got no further than the primary grades, perhaps because of the family's financial insecurity, perhaps because of her own not very robust health. She showed no particular aptitude for school learning but she did enjoy and take as prominent a part as she was able in any small festivity at school. She already had a liking for those emotional displays of patriotism which took place on any national holiday when the little girls, all dressed in freshly starched white smocks and with white bows like butterflies on the tops of their heads and blue and white rosettes pinned to their young breasts, marched up and down singing with shrill untunefulness paeans in praise of the glorious *patria*. Even in those days a narcissistic nationalism was inculcated in the Argentine schoolchildren and, perhaps to compensate for their remoteness from the world, they were taught that their nation took as large and bright a place on earth as the sun did in the sky. They sang:

> *And the free people of the world reply:*
> *Hail to the great Argentine nation!*

But Eva's real schooling was in her home and this was a hard, untender nursery for the dreams of youth. She was taught from the beginning that life was a struggle for survival in which the prizes went to the toughest and the most unscrupulous; that she could afford to give advantage to none and that man was her natural enemy or a fool whom a clever girl could exploit. There was nothing known to her of tenderness between the sexes, much less of romance or even honest companionship. The relationship between man and woman was a struggle in which one or the other must become the victim and the dupe, so that communication between the two was based on insincerity and deceit. A wise woman simulated indifference or passion according to which best suited her ends; a foolish girl, who allowed her emotion to get the better of her and softness to invade her heart, ended as a drab with a string of children and no man.

Eva learned her lesson well although she was not a forward sort of child. She was a quiet, thin little girl, unremarkable in looks, with long, dark hair and a pale, almost sickly complexion. There was nothing about the child, except perhaps her intensity and her tantrums of rage, to betray the dreams of grandeur by which she was obsessed. She spoke very little of the ambition that consumed her, for she could not bear to be held in ridicule, but she was sustained by the belief that one day she would be great and rich and beautiful. In the book[1] which she published late in 1951, in which she pretends to explain her mission in life, she claims that in early childhood she was appalled at the discovery that most people in the world were poor and that she felt an enormous indignation at the injustice of poverty. Her indignation has a ring of sincerity; but it is likely that it was directed against the injustices from which she suffered herself, for she must have hated the shabby clothes that she was forced to wear and the shoddy house where they lived and the too easy familiarities of her mother's friends. To have wanted to escape so fiercely, so desperately, she must have hated her life, her family, and her very self.

It is perhaps essential to the understanding of Eva Duarte's background to realize how divorced the people of the pueblo— whether it were a hamlet like Los Toldos or a modest township

[1]Eva Perón, *La Razón de mi Vida.*

like Junín—had become from the country life surrounding them. Many of these pueblos were like tiny incipient slums set in as rich an agricultural district as any in the world. The wealth that stretched on every side of them, the golden fields of corn, the slow-moving herds of champion Hereford, the magnificently muscled shire horses, the high-ceilinged old *estancia* houses shuttered against the summer heat and buried among mimosa, eucalyptus and acacia trees planted a generation or more before—all belonged to the landed aristocracy of Argentina, the oligarchs, who have become Eva's most bitterly persecuted enemies. Very little of the enormous wealth these *estancias* brought in found its way into the pueblo; there was little exchange of any sort between the people on the *estancias* and the people of the pueblos. Even the small *estancias* formed independent communities of their own and the larger ones—and some ran to more than twenty-five thousand acres —had chapels and schools and hospitals of their own. The owners of these *estancias*—and sometimes half a dozen huge estates might be owned by one family—spent their money and leisure in Paris, educating their sons at Harrow or Winchester. Sometimes they would return to live for a while in their great family mansions in Buenos Aires and their starched and begloved children could be seen playing sedately in Palermo Park under the eagle eye of an English nannie or a French governess. Their families were so inter-related and their estates so vast that they had come to regard the whole country as if it were a family estate to be administered, sometimes conscientiously and with benevolence, but always for their own convenience. They regarded the people on their property as part of their property and they were as convinced of their own unassailable superiority as the mastodons must have been of theirs.

Perhaps the only time in the year when they came in contact with the pueblo was at Christmas time when the whole family would arrive by train to spend the summer on their estate. Before their arrival the *estancia* would be in a ferment of activity; there were always new servant girls to be engaged—for this silly girl had got herself pregnant or that one had been caught stealing a handkerchief—and these the housekeeper would try to find from among the families who worked on the estate, for the girls from the pueblo were not to be trusted and had "ideas." There were horses to be groomed, fences to be painted, rooms to be aired and sometimes the major-domo and his wife would drive into the pueblo in the Ford or the Chevrolet, or the sulky if the roads were bad, for some necessity they had forgotten to order from the city; only what had been forgotten or what was needed in an emergency was bought in the local town. Trunks and packing cases and servants would begin to arrive by train, and then, at last, the main body of the family with the *patrón* dressed already in baggy white breeches in expensive imitation of the countryfolk, and shedding a Jove-like condescension on all around. And with him his señora and a great number of children and aunts and cousins and governesses.

Little Eva must often have been witness to such an incursion, for the arrival and departure of the train was a daily event in their monotony which the Duarte girls were not likely to have missed. She must have stared, much as slum children stare in the zoo, with a sort of hostile astonishment rather than envy at the little oligarchs whose starched suits and dresses had wilted in spite of their governesses' care and whose tempers had worn ragged on the hot, dusty journey from town. But the rich children would have looked at Eva with no more interest than they gave the cur the major-domo had hastily booted out of their way and certainly not with the sympathy they felt for the pedigreed fox terrier Papa had brought from England for breeding purposes. It was, they had been taught, all a matter of breeding, and there was as fixed a disparity between such children as the Duarte children and themselves as there was between the starved cow dying by the roadside and the blue-ribboned and unweaned bull who had his own valet and his hair crimped for the Rural Show.

The *patrón* and his señora would very often take a benevolent interest in the families who worked on their estate; they frequently stood godparent to any child born on the place, if the *patrón* was not in fact the father. But their charity seldom extended to the pueblo whose only convenience for them was its railway station and its post office. At most some rich elderly widow might rebuild the little church—with more thought for her own soul than for the souls of those who worshiped there—or endow a nun's school; but nothing was done for the entertainment and liberal education of youth.

In Argentina there is almost none of that modestly well-to-do class of farmers who will drive into a local town to do their shopping once or twice a week and whose increasing affluence becomes reflected in the amenities of the town. It is the wives and daughters of such farmers, demanding silk underwear and fashion magazines, that are the lifeblood of the rural town. The peons on the *estancias* and the sharecroppers who worked on them would sometimes drive into the pueblo with their families but in most cases they were too poor, too rustic and, very often, too precariously established, to gain the respect of the townsfolk; they came to gape at what the town had to offer and had not the sophistication to demand more.

Isolating the pueblo further were the great distances and the unpaved roads which after rain became impassable to anything that did not move on legs. Only in the thirties did one pueblo become linked to the next by ribbons of cement which, like those little Japanese sticks of fiber that swell in water into flowers, blossomed steadily with filling stations, roadside eating houses, and small country homes. In the twenties the only dependable link with other towns and villages and with the city was the railway. But the cosmopolitan culture of the capital did not reach the people of the pueblos who prided themselves on their *criollo,* that is, native, way of life and who had always regarded the Europeanized city man with a rustic's half-envious distrust of the unfamiliar. They had forgotten, or had never realized, that the *carnaval* they celebrated with such *criollo* zeal in every hamlet had come to them from Europe.

In Junín, as in every other pueblo, the carnival season was the one reliable break in the monotony of the year, monotonous as it was itself in its horseplay and time-honored jests. Small boys would put on masks and plague their elders in squeaky falsettos; young men would squirt sickly scented water at the girls leaning on balconies who would retort with coyly thrown colored streamers or handfuls of confetti; or some old woman, remembering the more lusty carnivals of her youth, would rush out into the street with a bucketful of water and drench the passers-by, and then dash, cackling with laughter, into the house again. In the evening there was a procession with bevies of girls—and, no doubt, the Duarte girls among them—dressed as flowers or gypsies or Columbines and followed by young men who, in the guise of devils or Harlequins, had become more boldly personal in their remarks.

More truly *criollo* were the fairs that brought, besides the ubiquitous carousel, a fortuneteller and a quack doctor selling herbs gathered in the north and guaranteed to cure a childless wife or lovelorn maid, and country musicians who made the older women gather up their petticoats and snap their fingers and cry, *Jota!* to their accordions and guitars.

Only occasionally a group of players or musicians from Buenos Aires passed through the town, the tawdriness of their costumes and the poverty of their performance invisible to such bedazzled eyes as Eva's.

She was fifteen now and like so many of her age she dreamed of going on the stage. One of the girls in the town had gone to the city and become a radio star—or, at least, had had an audition. And in the city there was money, men were rich and women had beautiful clothes. Eva began to scrape acquaintance with any theater group that came to the town; perhaps she was really taken in by their loud talk of triumphs in the capital, or perhaps she saw them only as her first step on the road to wealth, but when a young tango singer came to Junín with his guitar and began to court her, promising her a job on radio and heaven knows what else besides, she was more than ready to listen to him. She was not quite sixteen when she eloped to Buenos Aires with him, leaving her mother

Two

From each year I keep the memory of some injustice that roused me to rebellion, rending me inwardly. E. P.

Eva Duarte was born in that brief period of Argentine democracy that followed on the Saenz Peña law of 1912 which had given the country the secret ballot and, for the first time in its history, the possibility of honest elections. Hipólito Irigoyen, the great and tragic Radical leader, brought an end to the reign of the oligarchy who had, for more than eighty feudal years, grown rich on a monopoly of land. For a lifetime Irigoyen, in hiding and in exile, had conspired to bring about electoral reform. The habits of conspiracy remained with him after his success, for, when the party's delegates came to beg him, with tears in their eyes, to accept their nomination for presidential candidate, he received them singly

29

and in a darkened room. He steadfastly refused the nomination—
he had sought no personal power or wealth—until they threatened
to disband the party. Unwillingly he accepted but would not take
any part in the campaign and shut himself away in his *estancia*.
When he was elected President in 1916 the men of Buenos Aires,
porteños as they proudly call themselves, took the horses out of his
carriage and fought for the honor of drawing it, while from the
balconies women showered him with blessings and flowers. Neither
Perón nor Eva ever received a more moving ovation from the
porteño crowd.

Irigoyen's greatness lay in his idealism and his lack of self-interest; the tragedy of his life stemmed from his mysticism and his
naïveté. He expected his colleagues to prove as incorruptible as he
was himself and he was convinced of his own divine mission to
destroy the evil forces that oppressed the workingman. Under his
government the first laws alleviating the workingman's lot were put
into effect but, as if this relief weakened the dam that had held
back resentment and bitterness for so long, a great wave of violence
swept the country, aggravated by the propaganda of German agents,
who hoped to delay the shipments of food to the Allies. The first
years of Irigoyen's presidency were marked by strikes that par-
alyzed the transport system of the whole country for weeks and
for a while turned Buenos Aires into a city of shuttered windows
and silent streets where no man dared show himself abroad by daylight for fear of the sniper's bullet—and among the snipers were
some of the city's playboys who found this a more exciting pastime
than shooting partridge on their fathers' *estancias*. There were a
thousand killed in one week that has been known since as the
Tragic Week. Eva was born at this time when Labor had begun to
stretch its muscles and awaken to its strength.

But at the end of his six years' term Hipólito Irigoyen, who had
become more obsessed by the idea of his divine mission as he became more disillusioned by his colleagues' dishonesty, imitated the
system he had conspired to displace and nominated his own successor to the Radical candidacy. Until Perón changed the constitu-

tion no Argentine president could succeed himself, but it had been the custom of the retiring president to nominate a candidate to follow him. Irigoyen's choice fell on Marcelo Alvear, who was his close friend and himself a leader among the Radicals, and whom he expected to manipulate until he himself could return to power in the elections of 1928. But Marcelo Alvear was no puppet; he was a man of the world, traveled, wealthy and although he was no outstanding liberal—the Argentine Radicals were perhaps less liberal than the English Conservatives—he had an honest respect for the Constitution. He saw that the law was kept and he kept it himself. Under his efficient leadership and with the help of the post-war boom, the country enjoyed an orderly prosperity it had not known before, nor enjoyed since, and began to regain the respect of the world which Irigoyen's isolationism—the old man seemed to want to shut his country as well as himself away in a darkened room—had lost. But the friendship between Irigoyen and Alvear was broken, and the Radical Party split with the most tragic consequences. When the 1928 elections came it was an embittered and aging Irigoyen who was returned to the Casa Rosada on a flood of votes.

At seventy-six Hipólito Irigoyen was not the man to guide his country, enormous as was its potential wealth, through the difficult years of world depression. He was almost senile and more and more he shut himself away from his fellow men and isolated his country from the world. He had recalled the Argentine Ambassador from Washington, and for two years the country was not represented there or in any conference of world affairs. He trusted no one, not even those most close to him, and waiting documents piled high on his desk, for he would allow no signature but his own and would sign nothing until he had read every word. In his anterooms ministers and officials and unpaid government contractors kicked their heels, waiting for interviews that were almost never granted. The great crusader had become a senile old man who had to be kept hidden lest his wandering wits and his weakness for women become the common knowledge of his enemies. His government collapsed almost before the revolution broke out.

On September 6, 1930, General Uriburu marched his forces from his headquarters at Campo de Mayo into the city and took possession of the Casa Rosada without encountering opposition. The Casa Rosada is a large rococo building of a grubby strawberry pink; it stands with its back to the river, facing Plaza de Mayo where the Revolution broke out on May 25, 1810, and has symbolically taken an important part in all revolutionary movements since, perhaps because it stands on the site of the old Fort of colonial days; it houses the presidential offices and state banqueting and reception rooms.

Uriburu declared that his action had been taken in response to the people's demand; but, although it was true that the revolution was a popular one, the discontent of the people had been used as an excuse for a military coup planned well in advance.

A mob, shouting insults against the man they had so lately venerated, broke into Irigoyen's house and destroyed his papers and his furniture. Earlier a friend had discovered the old President, ill and deserted, and had carried him off to safety. He was imprisoned for a while and then released to live out his life in the most humble circumstances with the only two women who had not deserted him, his natural daughter and his secretary. But when he died the people's fickle gratitude returned, and tens of thousands came from all over the country to sleep on park benches so that they might take one last look at the man who had championed them. The narrow stairway of his apartment house was jammed night and day by this humble pilgrimage and half a million mourners thronged the streets and balconies to watch his coffin carried by.

By that time the country was learning that a military coup paved the way not for a restoration of civil liberties but towards a military dictatorship. Uriburu had opened the way for Perón. Backed by an oligarchy who wanted at all costs to reduce the workers to their former state of servitude Uriburu canceled the elections he had promised, declared a state of siege, banished Alvear to the penal colony in Ushuaia and outlawed the Irigoyen bloc from taking any part in government. It was among his fellow officers that Uriburu met with opposition and, although he bribed the younger officers by paying off their outstanding personal debts from government funds, he was forced by the Army to hold elections in November 1931. The Radical Party, the only one that could offer a powerful opposition, had split; Irigoyen's followers, still banned from taking part in government, refused to vote; those who had followed Alvear —he was still exiled in the south—voted with the Conservatives and the Independent Socialists, and elected General Agustín Justo as President of Argentina.

Here one may see the start of that pattern which the Argentine military have used with increasing and disastrous effect since. Making an excuse of popular unrest, the military stage a coup under the direction of a general who is not too unsympathetic to the crowd and then, with a pretense of free elections, replace him with a man of their own choice.

It was during Justo's presidency, a period of great prosperity and as great corruption in the capital, that Eva Duarte came to Buenos Aires. She came with the conviction that she would succeed. Her declared ambition was to become the leading actress on the Argentine stage, an ambition which must have seemed to her companions as ridiculous as if she had announced that one day she would be the First Lady of the Land, for she had no talent, no experience, no unusual beauty, little education, no money or influential friends, and not very good health. Their laughter, much as it must have angered her, probably did nothing to discourage her, for she had already that obsession of greatness that is impatient of even the friendliest criticism. She was at an age when fantasy plays a great part in the life of the most unimaginative girl, but her dreams were not the melancholy little romances of so many adolescents. They were not so much an escape from life as the very dynamo of her existence. They were her only satisfaction in a life that was sordid and disillusioning. Her favorite reading betrayed the secret of her

33

heart; she read with avidity a magazine, still in vogue among romantic little girls, called *Para Ti,* which published Cinderella stories of success and glamorized the lives of such great women of history as Queen Elizabeth and Josephine.

If she fed her heart on dreams, her body had less regular fare. The guitar player had left her, and for the small part she had on radio she received a salary of only fifteen dollars a month—scarcely enough to feed a growing girl even in the land of meat and wine. She might have starved if she had not been able to cadge meals in the unappetizing little restaurant run by her mother's still faithful friend.

She was close enough now to the life of luxury she coveted. She could see the impregnable matrons of the Argentine aristocracy with their demure and exquisitely groomed daughters drive by in their Daimlers to the opera; she could sniff the air outside those restaurants in whose lighted windows crackling chickens and ducks turned slowly on a spit; she could walk down Calle Florida past the haughty windows of the Jockey Club—beneath which one day she was to have a fish barrow set up so that the aristocratic nostrils within would have real cause to curl—and stare at the gowns displayed one at a time as if they were jewels in the expensively small shops. Oh, she was close enough to it now—and as excluded as if she had never left Junín!

In spite of her obsessive lust for recognition Eva showed no intention of working to become an actress; she had no understanding of what being a great artiste involved. She expressed a puzzled sort of contempt for those in her profession who had achieved success through hard work and envied them not their talent but their position and openly wondered why they did not make better use of their "opportunities." In whatever activity Eva engaged it was not the work but the impression that she created that was of prime importance to her. It was as if a woman in baking a cake cared not in the slightest how the cake turned out but cared only for the pretty picture she made of domestic busyness—after all, one could always run out and buy one at the bakery if guests

34

arrived! It was a lack of understanding and not of wits that stood between Eva and a legitimate stage career. She did nothing to improve her acting, her diction or her vocabulary, which was limited, although she could have done so as she later proved. She had an ear for mimicry or a tune and an excellent memory—she often knew the parts of the stars by heart; but she used her memory to docket the names of those who might be of use to her or the faces of those who had slighted her. She seems to have been unconscious of any lack in her education or her understanding, or at least unwilling to admit, even to herself, such a lack. What small parts she was given—and without influence she was never given any but the smallest part—she overdramatized, perhaps compelled to do so by her need for recognition; she spoke her lines too rapidly and with a monotonous lift at the end of every sentence—a delivery taught at school and which she used later in her more emotional speeches when it gave a note of hysteria to her words.

It was not by application to the stage but by intrigue that Eva meant to succeed, not by study and self-improvement but by the clever manipulation of others; indeed, her upbringing had shown her no other means of getting on in the world and she used her influence over men with a ruthlessness and energy that might have made of her a great actress had she applied them to the pursuit of her art.

The women of the theater and radio world were not unkind to her; they saw no threat to themselves in this undernourished little sparrow of a girl who subsisted so precariously on the fringe of their profession. Even to them—and they had all started young enough —she seemed very young, and she could assume a little girl air that reminded them of young sisters they had left at home. To their not too critical eyes she had the appearance of a *jeune fille* when she was dressed up. She helped the older actresses sometimes when they had to make a quick change between acts, using this as an excuse to hang around the dressing rooms when she had no business there, and she did so with an appearance of willing friendliness that made them ready to take her with them when they went out to eat or lend her clothes when her own were in rags. In kindly elder-sisterly fashion they advised her to find some decent fellow who would make a home for her and for whom she might feel some genuine affection. But Eva had no affection to give to anyone; she could pretend to love or passion or friendliness but perhaps the only real emotion she could feel was hate. It is doubtful if she felt any gratitude towards those who befriended her, for she discarded them quite callously when they could be of no further use. Once, when she thus discarded the friendship of a young actress who had been kind to her when she first came to the city and whose beau she had appropriated, an older friend reproved her for her heartlessness.

"You have to use your head, not your heart, if you want to get on in the world," Eva retorted.

"You may get on by using your head," answered the other, "but you will never learn to be a good actress unless you use your heart."

But Eva laughed.

That Eva should expect to succeed solely through the manipulation of others, that she should use her sex as a weapon, was not only the result of her home life and her upbringing but was natural to the culture of the society in which she now found herself. The Argentine woman had been exploited just as much as the peon and only in cases of great wealth or unusual strength of character had she been able to escape from the position of inferior dependency to which the men in the family had consigned her; in most cases such dependency seemed so usual to the women themselves that the thought of any freedom frightened and shocked them. Argentine men—and by no means only Argentine men among South Americans—regarded their women, sometimes respectfully, as mothers, wives, virgin daughters, or mistresses; too seldom did they regard them as individuals as intelligent as themselves. This attitude towards women may be seen in Argentina today when many of the Opposition and the military disapprove of Eva Perón not so much because of the corruption and illegality she has encouraged but because she is a woman in a position of great power.

36

The Argentine woman had, at that time, no vote; she could not get a divorce, and still cannot, unless she went abroad for it; she and her children and her property were in the hands of her husband, who had in most cases been chosen for her by her family. A married woman was expected to stay at home and raise a large family; it was a matter for boasting if a man got his wife pregnant on the honeymoon. A woman who remained single stayed at home as companion to her mother, who, because of her daughter's singleness, often regarded her as if she were mentally retarded; or she was offered the equally ungrateful position of unpaid nurse and governess to her nephews and nieces. Only among the middle classes in the city was a changing economy making it possible for a wife to go out to earn her own living. A poor man was, of course, always willing for his wife to go out to work as long as her earnings went into his own pocket.

It is significant that the word used colloquially for "wife" is *mujer,* "woman," which can apply equally to a man's mistress; for marriage, which did not liberate a woman enough to allow her to walk into a restaurant with a man who was not a relative, did nothing to restrain a man in his pursuit of other women. It was the rule rather than the exception for the Argentine who could afford it to maintain a secondary establishment, often on almost as permanent a basis as the first; neither one nor the other impeded him from finding transitory pleasure elsewhere and often he maintained a *garçonnière,* bachelor's rooms, for that express purpose.

Men's constant preoccupation with the pursuit of woman was implicit in the atmosphere of Buenos Aires—it has decreased during the last decade or, at least, become less overt. Even the most modest of women, were she not anile, was subject to persistent attentions if she went out in the streets alone; or if she took a seat in a tram car or one of the micro-omnibuses that in the thirties had begun to infest the town like cockroaches, the man who sat next to her would shift an elbow or a knee until it came into contact with hers and, if a church or funeral were passed, he was quite ready to make the sign of the cross with his other hand without relaxing for a moment from his pursuit! It was as if the attentions he paid to women were as habitual to him as drawing breath and the individuality of the woman no more important than that of air.

Although a wife did not have the discomfort of meeting her husband's mistress socially—a man did not choose his mistress from the same social strata as his wife—she was usually aware of or suspected his infidelities; she had been brought up to expect them. If she were a woman of wealth she swallowed her resentment as best she could—only rarely did she retaliate in kind, for the risk to her reputation was too great—and sought solace in her family and the Church and good works. With all the weight of a large family, and sometimes a woman could count five hundred relatives, and the parish priest behind her, she often gained considerable influence and had a hand in running her husband's estate and, if she were fortunately widowed young, might end as a formidable matriarch determined that her granddaughters should be as respectable and as unhappy as herself. She had the consolation, and perhaps it was a considerable one, that her position as wife was unassailable; if she could not get rid of her husband neither could he get rid of her, and, even more comforting to her ego, her repeated pregnancies made her an object of interest to friends and strangers alike and of envy to less fortunate women, who would sometimes ask to be allowed to touch her so that they might catch the "infection." Pregnancy in Argentina has an importance, a dignity, and, one might say, a glamour, that it lacks in some countries. The wife of the small business or professional man was less likely to be resigned; she had perhaps earned her own living before marriage, and might continue to do so, as a teacher or government employee, and she demanded a semblance at least of fidelity from her husband and, in some cases, might insist on a divorce from Montevideo or Mexico. The very poor, having no money for the luxury of legality, were frequently not officially married at all.

It is not surprising that the Argentine woman should so often have regarded her sex as her only marketable commodity, whether she were the daughter of an oligarch whose guaranteed virginity went down to the highest bidder in a cloud of Brussels lace and with the blessing of the Church, or the little servant girl who got herself an imitation gold watch by smuggling the butcher boy into bed or a woman of the port whose prices ranged from a peso up. And the woman who earned her own living, however determined she might be to do so respectably, could not escape the consciousness that the men with whom she had dealings valued her as much for her amorous potentialities as they did for her business ability; nor, however she resisted, could she entirely escape the temptation of using herself as barter.

In such an atmosphere it was only natural that Eva should adjudge her opportunities by the use that she could make of men; and it was also to be expected that she should have no feelings of friendliness towards those whom she meant to use, since the relationship was not one of honest convenience but was based on contrivance and subterfuge and all the hostility that that implies.

Eva has often been called a *resentida,* a resentful one, by her enemies. She had two real causes for resentment against society: that she was born poor in a country of great wealth; and that she was born a woman in a society made for man. The fact that she was a woman made it more difficult to escape from poverty; it was almost impossible for her to escape except by the use of man. And those very men who were so ready to seduce an unprotected girl like herself with gifts or money or lies, if they were necessary, were as ready to defend the honor of a daughter or a sister—was it not valuable family property?—at the point of the sword. It would have been surprising if Eva had not hated the men who regarded her so lightly and the women whose virtue seemed of so much more importance than her own.

Eva herself referred briefly to these years as her "career as an artiste." She did not deny her theater past and boasted of her humble origin, but she gave no detail of either; she spoke only in the vaguest generalities of the past. In those interviews she granted to the press when she became a radio star she was indefinite and sometimes contradictory. She said that she had a part in the old Teatro Comedia and then went to Radio Nacional, or again, that she worked first with Radio Prieto and then with Radio Argentino and that the Liceo gave her her first chance on the stage. Probably she no longer remembered, or no longer cared to remember, the vicissitudes of those days. She went from one small part to another, eking out her living by posing for cheesecake and advertisements. Once she went on tour with a theatrical company which was stranded in the provinces and it was she who used her charms to persuade the authorities to give them permission for a performance. It was a dreadfully precarious existence that would have broken the spirit of anyone less tough or unscrupulous. During those years and always with the certain—to herself—goal of her success in view she amassed a horde of acquaintances. It seems now that she must have had a phenomenal gift for attracting the attention of influential men and making use of them. Her gift was an unwavering self-interest and an unabashed hardihood. Undismayed by the snubs she received she would push herself forward into the attention of anyone who might conceivably be of use to her, and, because even effrontery can be appealing in the very young and pursuit is always flattering, she gained the attention she sought. And once she had gained that attention she did not readily let go of her victim but pursued him in person and by mail until the last drop of usefulness had been squeezed out of him.

It was in 1940 that her persistence in cultivating useful acquaintances brought its reward. She caught the attention of a radio program sponsor, a wealthy soap manufacturer. She had been earning no more than thirty-five dollars a month from her radio career; now her salary went up to sixty dollars and she was earning as much again from a walk-on part in the Teatro Nuevo. From this time on she began to appear with regularity on the radio, her salary leaping ahead with each new friend she acquired. Her radio sponsor introduced her to a friend of his—also in soap and also the sponsor of a program—and she changed her allegiance as easily as she slid from one costume to the next.

It was about this time that she moved into an apartment in Calle Posadas, a cobbled, tree-shaded little street tucked discreetly behind the fashionable Avenida Alvear. With a more comfortable life and regular food Eva's health improved and she came back from a holiday in the hills of Córdoba looking as plump as any little bride ready to put on weight as soon as the first baby arrives. At this period she overdressed in an adolescent fashion, clinging to the bows and bangles that would have been more suitable to her early teens—she was in her twenties now—in what seems rather a pathetic attempt to cling to a childhood she had never enjoyed. She was no longer the quiet little girl she had been when she left Junín; she had become an extremely voluble young woman, ready to become emotional over trifles and readier than ever to fly into a tantrum. There seems to have been nothing very remarkable about her at the time except her vitality and perhaps the suppressed intensity of her ambition.

Once she was established in her apartment in Calle Posadas— it was by no means an unfashionable building or district—her circle of acquaintances began to shift. Her sister Elisa had become the intimate friend of a Major Arrieta and it was probably they who first began to bring officers from the military barracks at Campo de Mayo to the not very discreet little parties that Eva gave. The military were everywhere now and it was wise to cultivate them. Yet Eva did not entirely abandon her old friends who might still in an emergency be of use to her and who could supply her with those little bits of gossip which could be so useful to her in her career. She still hobnobbed with the messenger boy from Radio El Mundo over a cup of coffee in the milk bar across the street.

Eva could not have been unaware of the growing influence of the military in political affairs. In 1943 a military coup had ousted President Castillo, the Fox, and put General Ramirez in his place; a Colonel Imbert had taken part in the coup and was rewarded with the Directorship of Posts and Telegraph, an office that carried with it the control of radio stations. This in itself was enough recommendation for Eva and she had heard the rumor that General

Ramirez, the Little Stick, was only a figurehead and that the real power was in the hands of a group of colonels. She deserted her manufacturer of soap and began to cultivate Colonel Imbert.

The contact proved a useful one. In January of 1944 the northern provinces of Argentina were shaken by an earthquake that destroyed almost totally the old Spanish colonial town of San Juan. Fissures appeared in the streets that swallowed man and beast, broken water mains flooded the ruins, the Cathedral roof caved in and killed the members of a bridal party gathered there—there were in all some 3,500 killed and 10,000 injured. The disaster was one of those which by sheer magnitude and suddenness shocks a whole nation into spontaneous acts of generosity; the hospital and supply trains and planes sent by the government were reinforced by jalopies and sulkies of the neighbors from miles around who came to gather up the children left orphaned and destitute. In the emotional fervor of philanthropy that followed on the tragedy Eva saw a heaven-sent opportunity for self-advancement; it is very possible that she identified herself with the homeless and the destitute—she had been homeless and destitute herself—and that her emotions were in some degree and temporarily at least sincere; but not for a moment did she overlook the advantage to herself. She persuaded Colonel Imbert, and by this time he was easily persuadable, to allow her to plead for the victims over the radio. There was to be a monster rally at Luna Park, a stadium usually reserved for bouts of boxing and catch-as-catch-can wrestling, organized by the people of the theater and radio world to raise a fund for the relief of San Juan. Eva threw herself into the campaign for the fund with all the extraordinary energy of which she was capable. It was the first public exhibition of that compulsive and compelling drive of hers which made her achievement possible.

Eva attended the rally at Luna Park with Colonel Imbert. The stage was crowded with theater and movie stars and with military uniforms. Eva's quick eyes picked out a tall, genial-looking colonel who was talking to the lovely actress Libertad Lamarque. It is possible that Eva had seen him before—he and Colonel Imbert knew each other well—and certainly he compared very favorably with Colonel Imbert who was short and stout. But Eva would never have allowed herself to be sidetracked by mere looks. She had heard of this colonel who was becoming familiar, not only to his fellow officers but to *porteños,* as the strong man among the colonels. She went up and greeted Libertad Lamarque who in turn introduced her to Colonel Juan Domingo Perón. With a lack of guile that must have seemed incomprehensible to the scheming Eva, Libertad Lamarque turned away to speak to other friends. In an instant Eva had taken the vacant seat at the colonel's side and for the rest of the evening did not budge.

Three

And I said to myself, each time with more strength: Yes, this is the man. The man of my people. No one can compare with him. E. P.

When Eva Duarte first met Juan Domingo Perón his name, familiar enough already to his brother officers as that of a man with a future not only in the Army but in the government, had only lately become known to the man in the Buenos Aires streets who associated it vaguely with the sinister-sounding G.O.U.— Group of United Officers—a society of military elite said to be the power behind the government.

Juan Domingo Perón was born on October 8, 1895, twenty-four years before Eva Duarte, in the small town of Lobos in the southern part of the province of Buenos Aires. His father, Don Mario, had a modest position in the local courts, and his mother, another Doña Juana, was what is known in those parts as a *chinita* —a little country girl with Indian blood in her veins. Don Mario was a gregarious fellow who took a lively part in the local fiestas and country horse racing, and was as nimble in dancing a *pasodoble* as he was quick to pick up his guitar for a song. He had no great influence on the lives of his two small sons, Juan Domingo and his elder brother Mario, who spent their infant years in the house of their paternal great-uncle, Dr. Perón. The old man's medical title may have been only one of courtesy but he was a well-known and substantial figure in the neighborhood.

When Juan Domingo was about five years old his parents took him and his brother Mario to live in the territory of Chubut, in the bleak Patagonic region of southern Argentina. It seems to have been the promise of a government grant of land that led Don Mario to leave the fertile pastures of the provinces for those inhospitable parts. Their new home was little better than a desert where the grit-laden wind blew night and day, year in, year out, making a faint and maddening tapping on the corrugated iron of which the shacks were built. The discovery of oil had not yet brought any traffic to the country and almost their only neighbors were the isolated Scottish sheep farmers who had not so much emigrated to a new land as taken up part and parcel of the old country and transplanted it in a new continent. This was no sort of life for the convivial Don Mario and one day he went off, leaving Doña Juana to cope with the farm and the upbringing of two small boys as best she could. She was not so easily discouraged—and in that cold, stony, rainless land only the toughest could survive; she sent the two boys off to a rural school and got a man in to help her with the land. Their father did not appear on their horizon again but old Dr. Perón had not forgotten them, or, at least, he had not forgotten little Juan Domingo who seems to have been his favorite. When the boy was going on ten he packed him off to Buenos Aires to live with a schoolteacher aunt and get a better education for himself.

Doña Juana and her elder son continued their toil for existence in the south; the land had by this time become their own. Later, when a prudish governor of the territory passed a law ordering all couples who lived together to get married, Doña Juana married the man who had helped her work the land. There seems to have been some uncertainty as to what had become of Don Mario. As soon as he was of an age to get married the younger Mario set himself up in a *boliche,* the poorest sort of roadside pot-house; the place where he had chosen to live was utterly barren and solitary but it came to be known in time as the Flowery Window, for no sooner did some vehicle appear like a solitary ant on the horizon than the heads of his three pretty daughters popped anxiously over the window sill.

There is some controversy as to whether Juan Domingo was a star pupil or a very ordinary scholar indeed. The truth is that in Argentine schools pupils were, and are even more so today, judged on their parrot ability to repeat a lesson word for word and to copy it down in a flowing hand without a blot on the page. Letters written by Perón in his early forties are in such a copybook hand and both in writing and content show the naïveté of a schoolboy mind —an appearance of simplicity with which he has often misled his enemies. Certainly he did well at the military academy, where he went when he was sixteen, for he was all that a Prussian-influenced officers' training school could wish; he was tall, handsome, athletic and genial, and he had a mind very ready to accept machine-made ideas and ideals. He made a fine-looking second lieutenant when he graduated in 1915.

Juan Perón embarked on his military career just at the time when Hipólito Irigoyen first became President, and his first action was seen during the strikes and riotings that disrupted the city at the end of the First World War. In one case it was Perón's own voice that ordered the troops to open fire on the strikers; it seems unlikely that he or his senior officers had received instructions to do so from the government, for, in another instance, while allowing the military to mount guard over threatened railway property, Irigoyen had ordered that they should not be issued live ammunition. In

1945, when Perón proclaimed himself the champion and blood brother of the workingman—his "beloved shirtless ones"—a new generation, that had forgotten the blood that had been shed in 1919, was ready to acclaim him.

During the presidencies of Irigoyen and Alvear, Juan Perón was working his way up in the Army in an unspectacular fashion. He was hard-working and ambitious but not brilliant; he knew better how to make use of the knowledge of others than how to acquire knowledge for himself; he wrote a number of pamphlets on military technique, but the material was unoriginal and he was accused once of actual plagiarism. In 1928 when he had reached the rank of captain, he married Aurelia Tizón; Potota, as the family called her, was a schoolteacher, a pleasant, simple girl with some pretense of culture. The marriage seems to have been a happy one; at least old Doña Juana approved of it—she must have traveled up from the south sometimes to visit her successful son—for she wore a brooch of Potota's miniature pinned to her breast, which said a good deal for the young schoolmistress's tact, for she could have had very little in common with this tough old woman from Patagonia. The Tizón family affirm that Juan Domingo was a good-natured, indulgent husband and he must have been proud of his talented little wife who not only drew and painted in the most genteel fashion but could translate English military textbooks for him. This first marriage presents a picture of uxorious suburban contentment. The pity was that the young couple had no children; the greater pity, that, in 1938, Potota died.

During the ten years of his first marriage Juan Perón had only once stepped forward onto the stage of political events; when General Uriburu marched on the Casa Rosada and supplanted the senile Irigoyen, Perón marched with him at the head of his company and mounted guard on one of the nearby streets whose name, ironically enough, he himself years later changed to Calle Presidente Hipólito Irigoyen in honor of the old man he had helped to depose. Perhaps in this bloodless action Juan Perón first drew the attention

48

of his seniors to himself. Later in the thirties, with the rank of lieutenant colonel, he was sent as military attaché to the Argentine Embassy in Chile. The Chilean government asked for his recall on the charge of espionage and the two Chileans accused with him were sent to jail. It was after his return from Chile that he found himself widowed.

Perón genuinely mourned the death of his young wife. Friends of that time testify that he refused for a while to seek consolation elsewhere, as it was taken for granted that he would immediately do. He devoted himself entirely to his career for the next two or three years. By nature he was ideally suited to peacetime Army life. He was handsome, gregarious and good-humored; he was not witty but he had a way of turning a situation to his own advantage with a gesture or a joke; he was a good horseman and an expert with the foils, although he never seems to have made use of this skill to vindicate his honor as many Argentines still do; he enjoyed food and drink and, when he recovered from his grief, the company of pretty women; above all, he enjoyed popularity. To the simple he might easily appear to be the best and cleverest fellow in the world; his boasting was not without charm nor was he as simple as he liked to appear. If his bragging were challenged he was ready to explain with a laugh that, of course, he had never meant to gull his listeners, that his bluff was for others more naïve than present company; he had the knack of putting himself in cahoots with his audience. But his natural self-indulgence was stiffened by ambition and his appetite for work.

From before the First World War, while England cultivated her trade with Argentina, Germany had set out to woo not the people of Latin America but the armies, and was sending over military missions and inviting impressionable young officers to return the visit in Berlin. The Germans had seen that in the young republics of South America, where the laboring classes had been kept too much in subjection to count, as yet, as a political force, the governments, if not actually placed in office by a military coup, ruled only by courtesy of the armies. This cool policy won the Germans a passive partner in Argentina during two world wars, a base of operation for their agents and a new seedbed for their ideology. The Argentine Army, in uniform, in exercises, in weapons and in theory, was modeled on the Prussian Army, and from the day Perón entered the military academy, he was under the influence of German authoritarianism, blunted but made not much less destructive by the indiscipline of the Latin temperament. The groundwork for his development into a dictator had been prepared—and there were a hundred others as equally prepared if circumstances had not elected him—but it was not until after the death of his wife, when he was sent to Europe on a mission, that his desire for easy popularity was given direction and turned into the megalomaniac's lust for applause. In 1939 he was sent to study the tactics of modern mountain warfare in Europe and, since the Army was so influenced by Germany, it was through the countries of the Axis that he traveled. He was as convinced as were his superior officers that Germany would emerge triumphant from the war; he had an enormous admiration for the outward show of power and efficiency and very little understanding of the strength that may lie dormant in the spirit of unmilitarized peoples. He regards all men as venal and appeals to them primarily through greed and self-interest.

It was while he was with the Bersaglieri in Italy that he conceived for Mussolini not the wholehearted admiration of a professional soldier for an acclaimed leader but rather that sort of half-envious admiration that one mountebank has for another greater, temporarily at least, than himself. He has himself said that Mussolini's error was that he was not ruthless enough and that he, Perón, would not fall into the same mistake. Like many men who are not as simple as they appear he believes himself much cleverer than other folk. That he studied Mussolini's methods and profited by his study is evident from the use he made of them later on.

But it was the weakness, the greed, and the mistakes of others as much as his own foresight and contrivance that gave Juan Perón his opportunity. President Justo, under some pressure from the Radicals, had named Roberto M. Ortiz as the candidate to succeed him and in 1936, in some of the most fraudulent elections the country has ever known, Ortiz was elected President. The military had given their support to Ortiz in the belief that he would be no more than a figurehead, for he was an enormously fat gourmand suffering from diabetes. But Ortiz had been a close friend of Alvear's and was a man of high principles and integrity; no sooner was he in office than he began to clean up the corruption and fraud that had flourished during Justo's term. Thus he made enemies for himself, not only among the military who had put him into office but also among the conservative oligarchy who feared the results that a working democracy would have on the laboring classes as much as did the militarists. Ortiz might have, by weight of his own personal prestige, withstood the machinations of his enemies—the public had begun to applaud him when he appeared in the street—but his health broke down. In 1940 his condition had become so serious— he was almost blind—that he had to delegate his powers to Vice-President Castillo.

Ramon S. Castillo was an astute little lawyer known as the Fox, who was quite outspokenly anti-democratic and who believed that fraudulent elections were necessary in a country whose people were not sufficiently educated to be allowed to vote. For some months Ortiz, although in retirement, was able to put a brake on the Vice-President's anti-democratic policy by insisting that his retirement was only temporary and that he would shortly return to duty; but the Conservatives appointed a committee to certify that he was permanently disabled. It was when this enormously fat, blind, and bereaved old man—he had recently lost his wife—was making a last stand for civil liberty in his darkened library—darkened because of his eyesight, and not, like Irigoyen's room, from some compulsive secrecy—surrounded and spied upon by enemies who rejoiced at his increasing infirmity, it was at this time that Juan Perón returned from Europe. He found the Conservatives abetting the military in the suppression of political freedoms; the Radicals, who were the only party strong enough to have opposed the military, divided against themselves; an acting-president with strong anti-democratic leanings and no personal following—and a dying President.

Perón was sent up to the Andean province of Mendoza to train Argentine ski troops in the pattern of the Bersaglieri. But he was able to put into practice more than the theory of mountain warfare that he learnt in Italy.

Some of the younger officers in the Army had for some time been discontented with the leadership of their generals not in Army affairs but in the political field and a secret society of officers was organized, the G.O.U., or *Grupo de Oficiales Unidos,* whose articles of faith stemmed straight from Nazi ideology. In a communiqué issued confidentially to its members in 1943 the G.O.U. asserted that it was the great destiny of the Argentine Army to set the nation at the head of a unified South America—they allowed the United States at least temporary monitorship of the north!—taking as their example Hitler's titanic struggle to unify Europe; that civilians must be eliminated from the government—since they could never understand the grandeur of such an ideal—and taught to work and to obey which was their true mission in life; and that to accomplish the necessary sacrifices an inflexible dictatorship was necessary. All this talk of destiny was red meat and wine to many a young Argentine officer raised on narcissistic nationalism and with all the insecurities of immaturity under his swaggering uniform. It was not difficult for Perón with his genial personality, the glamour of his European trip still around him and his firsthand knowledge of totalitarian methods, to take a leading part in the organization of the G.O.U. and to become the center of its intrigue.

Membership of the G.O.U. was very soon to become almost obligatory for every officer in the Army—of the thirty-six hundred officers, all but three hundred joined—but some, when pressure was brought to bear on them, resigned their commissions rather than accept its dictation. It is said that the committee of the G.O.U. had in their possession the signed but undated resignation of every

52

officer on its lists; whether or not they had this means of blackmail, it is certain that no officer could expect promotion, even that which was his due, unless he followed the directives of the G.O.U.

In Buenos Aires, Castillo, the Fox, was becoming daily less popular. Provincial elections had become so scandalous that the public, resigned as they were to political dishonesty, had made a general protest. Nor were the military any too pleased with their protégé who, for all his pro-Fascist sympathies, just to please the Conservative landowners had named Patrón Costas as his successor. Patrón Costas was himself a man of property and known to have British and American sympathies.

On June 4, 1943, the Army again marched into the city from Campo de Mayo; the only resistance encountered was when the Naval School was reached, where in a futile attempt at defense nearly a hundred naval officers and young cadets were wounded or killed. Castillo, protesting at first that he would resign for no one, fled with precipitate and undignified haste aboard a gunboat standing out in the river roads, his cabinet ministers scrambling after him.

This coup had been organized by General Ramirez, Castillo's Minister of War, who had played a somewhat oblique part in the proceedings and allowed himself to be put under arrest in the Casa Rosada. It was his co-conspirator, the venturesome and buoyant General Rawson, who led the troops into the city and proclaimed himself head of the provisional government from the balcony of the Casa Rosada. But Rawson was too democratic and honest a man for his brother officers to make use of him and too ingenuous a politician himself to make use of them. Within two days he was persuaded to retire and General Ramirez took his place.

In this opera-bouffe performance neither Juan Perón's name nor his person was in evidence, but when Ramirez formed his cabinet Colonel Edelmiro Farrell was announced as the new Minister of War. Ramirez and Farrell and Perón had all been closely associated in Mendoza in the organization of the G.O.U. Farrell, appointed by his friend Ramirez as Minister of War, made his friend Perón chief of the Secretariat of the War Ministry. Neither he nor General Ramirez could have had any conception of what went on behind the smiling face of the man who was of so much use to them; certainly Perón himself did not betray his ambition. They were both mediocre men who understood nothing of the responsibilities of government and very little of the wiles of politics. Ramirez was a reactionary and an anti-feminist—he was henpecked at home—and his stiffness earned him the nickname of the Little Stick. Farrell, on the other hand, enjoyed the company of women and liked to strum on his guitar and sing to them. Juan Perón could play with both of them as easily as a child plays with plasticine.

But Perón has never been a hotheaded man; his overcaution might have been his ruin later had it not been balanced by the audacity and vigor of his mate. He decided with foresight that the backing of the G.O.U., on whose personal allegiance he could not count, was not enough to guarantee him security. Making use of what he had learned in Italy—and of this lesson he would not have boasted—he angled for a position in the National Labor Department. Organized labor had had so brief a spell of influence in Argentina after the First World War that its potentialities as a political instrument had been almost totally ignored and Ramirez was glad enough for this obliging colonel to take over what seemed to him no better than a chore. Perón was the only one of the military who realized that a regime could not stay in power indefinitely with only the backing of the Army.

Later in the year, when Ramirez announced that his government was no longer a provisional one, Farrell was named Vice-President as well as Minister of War and the Secretariat of Labor and Public Welfare was formed with Colonel Perón at the head.

Perón had begun to be recognized as a man with a future in politics; he had slipped into position so discreetly in the barrage created by his associates' activities that no one knew quite how he came to be there, or what his politics were, or in what direction he was likely to move. It was at this time that he met Eva Duarte and, like two celestial bodies whirling at great speed through space, they were caught in each other's orbit and continued on their fantastic career together, held by a mutual necessity that allowed neither that one should be totally eclipsed by the other nor that they separate.

Four

*I held the lamp that illumined his nights; warming him as best
I could, covering his shoulders with my love and my faith.* E. P.

Much has been said of the "romance" between Eva Duarte
and Juan Domingo Perón, and romantic the relationship
was, if not in the accepted Hollywood sense, at least in the sense
that it was akin to fiction and appealed to the imagination. In her
book[1] Eva asserted unblushingly that she fell in love with Perón
because his cause, that of the working people, was her own. She said
that the poverty and suffering of humble people had long caused
anguish to her heart but that she had resigned herself to the injustices of society until that "marvelous day" on which she met Perón
and recognized in him a leader superior to others.

[1]*La Razón de mi Vida.*

"I put myself at his side," she wrote with that self-abasement which characterized so many of her public utterances. "Perhaps this drew his attention to me and when he had time to listen to me I spoke up as best I could: 'If, as you say, the cause of the people is your own cause, however great the sacrifice I will never leave your side until I die.'" Of his response she writes: "He accepted my offer. That was my 'marvelous day.'"

The book is, of course, propaganda written for the most unsophisticated readers, with an express and almost complete lack of data, and has only an unintentional connection with the truth. But it is no more fantastic than the stories of her enemies who attributed her influence over Perón to blackmail, erotic practices and even witchcraft. There is perhaps a simple explanation for their mutual attraction, for if not love there was certainly a passionate infatuation on his part and on hers a stronger motive than expediency. The bond was there and though it may have been strengthened later by their mutual usefulness—indispensability, you might say—it was forged in the common experiences of childhood. Both were born to the drab poverty of pueblo life, both came from families whose financial and social status were insecure, in both cases there may have been the resentment engendered when one parent cannot take part in the social life of the other. From these parallel backgrounds sprang two characters dissimilar in many ways but each with a driving ambition, the desire for recognition from a world which from the beginning had slighted them. It was this, their own cause and not the cause of the people or magic practices, that drew Eva and Perón together, and it was necessity that held them to the end.

Eva did not find her way entirely clear with the susceptible colonel when she first caught his roving eye. He had been seen about in the company of a pretty young thing whom he had introduced on more than one occasion as his daughter. However, when his brother officers planned a party for their wives and daughters and invited him and the "Señorita Perón," he was forced to admit the truth of the relationship, a confession which seems to have been more embarrassing to his friends than to himself. The girl was very young and simple and no match at all for Eva, who was twenty-four at the time and had been neither young nor simple since baby-hood. Some stories have it that Eva threw her rival bag and baggage out of Perón's apartment when he, surely with more guile than guilelessness, brought them together there and then went out; and it is consistent with a certain aspect of Perón's character that he should have allowed two young women to fight for his possession and then accept the winner as his love. But whether the story is true or not, Eva was not a woman to tolerate any rivalry; she made a clean sweep not only of the other women in his life but of any little keepsake that might have reminded him of women in his past —and there is a sentimental streak in his nature that would make him treasure such keepsakes. She got rid of everything that might recall his wife and, it is said, went so far as to snatch Potota's miniature off the indignant bosom of her mother-in-law.

It was not long before Eva and Perón set up housekeeping together in an apartment in Calle Posadas, next door to the one where she had lived before. They made no secret of the relationship; they spent week ends up the river together, had parties in their home and every morning a conscript from Campo de Mayo would tote a can of the Army's fresh milk up to the apartment where sometimes it was the colonel himself who opened the door.

During the next year and a half Eva's life bloomed into one of extraordinary activity; one of the most remarkable aspects of her character is that, having so lately emerged from near-starvation, she was able to seize on her opportunity and make so bold and determined a use of it. The mistakes she made came from over-confidence and impatience, never from timidity.

No sooner was she seen about in the company of the colonel, who was now chief of the Secretariat of the War Ministry and head of the National Labor Department, than a career was opened up for her in radio and on the screen, and the little girl who had had to hang around studios and ogle managers very soon had them running after her for her signature. Radio Belgrano raised her salary to fifteen hundred pesos a month—only about three hundred and seventy dollars but more than six times what they had been paying her the year before. Very soon they had signed her on to appear daily in a soap opera program called *My Kingdom for Love* and to give talks on Wednesday and Friday evenings on a program that was called *Towards a Better Future,* impassioned little sermons on such subjects as *Motherhood, Patriotism* and *Self-Sacrifice.* This was the first sign of Eva's interest in moral uplift as a means of self-advertisement; whether she had public appeal or not it was convenient, so Jaime Yankelevitch the director of Radio Belgrano evidently decided, to give prominence to this young woman who exercised so much influence over the influential colonel—and he raised her salary again. Before the end of 1945 she was appearing regularly on the three largest Argentine radio stations, Radio Belgrano, Radio El Mundo, and Radio Estado, and she was making thirty thousand pesos—seventy-five hundred dollars—a month. By that time the colonel's political future seemed assured.

In the films Eva's success was not quite so spectacular. She herself had said that radio was the best medium for her art—which, for propaganda, it was—and that she had very little interest in stage or screen. But she had had at one time at least dreams of a fabulous Hollywood career, for she had once approached a visiting American film producer with the suggestion that he might launch her in Hollywood, a suggestion he turned down with derision after he had seen her act; which may in part account for the difficulties of American film distribution in Argentina since. It is not surprising that she had no success in the films, for not only could she not act, but at this time, before her hair was dyed, she was unphotogenic; but now, with the good will of the colonel in mind, the San Miguel Studios signed her on for a small part in a film called *The Cavalcade of the Circus* in which Libertad Lamarque was to star. Eva's "artistic" temperament made her very difficult to work with; she evidently resented her comparatively inferior role, for she quarreled with any actress who had a better part than herself, and turned up at the studio at her own convenience. Lamarque scolded her for keeping the whole cast waiting but Eva, who could accept reproof from no one, only flew into a tantrum. But as the colonel's political influence became more overt and her relationship with him continued secure, she was signed on to star in three more films for which she was to get nearly four thousand dollars apiece. And it should be remembered that in Buenos Aires the equivalent in pesos represented a much greater purchasing value than the dollars would have done in New York.

It may seem strange that Eva, with the dramatic use that she made of the platform later, should never have had any success on the stage; but not only was the theater audience a much more sophisticated one than the audience that listened below the balcony of the Casa Rosada, but the part she played on the platform was one she had created for herself, not one based on a true understanding of character but one that was acting out the fantasies of her own dream life.

Eva's name was now beginning to be known beyond the circle of her military and theatrical acquaintances. Her photograph began to appear first on the back pages of radio and movie magazines and very soon on the front pages and covers not only of those but of women's magazines as well. The history of her development during those months is in these photographs and the clue to her pretenses lies in the accompanying interviews. At first she posed, with a wide-eyed look of innocence, in the frilly blouses and pinafore dresses of adolescence; her thick, dark hair was worn with curls piled on top of her head and hanging loosely to her shoulders; but the girlish picture is spoiled by the thickness of her lipstick and the too heavy and ornate jewelry she wore. She was plump, almost lumpy-looking at this time and she had not yet learned to hold herself erect, so that you seem to see in these photographs a glimpse of the stout, coarse matron she might have become had she lived out her life tranquilly in Junín. In later photographs she appears in a satin housecoat, still with her pile of dark curls but already with a look of sleek opulence about her, and against an overcrowded background of gilded Empire furniture and rococo ornament. It was probably for her first star role on the screen that she dyed her hair to the reddish blond with which she first blossomed into the full, ripe role of the affluent demimondaine. For her public she spoke dreamily of her love of sentimental waltzes, of Greer Garson films, and of flowers and books. Her true career lay in radio, she said; the stage and screen took up too much of her private life. Although, of course, there was no mention of the colonel in these interviews, she spoke coyly of giving up her career for "home life," and, more frankly, of having so much faith in her future that she was ready to jettison her artistic career altogether— what exactly she meant by "her future" she left her audience to guess. She confessed to being "a tranquil woman, a homemaker, one who loved family life" but, with a charming pretense of feminine weakness, she admitted to a passion for clothes; perhaps she was rather extravagant, she conceded, but her wardrobe was not "showy," only "complete." She liked jewelry, she said, but was not "moved" by it; her real weakness was for perfumes, of which she had a great collection, and which she blended to suit her mood. There was, she said demurely, no mystery at all about her career, which was, she added without a trace of humor, fortunately in the ascendant.

But it was not of her artistic career of which she spoke, meteorlike as that had suddenly become. She had discovered a more profitable and exhilarating field for her talents.

Since the military coup of 1930 there had been increasing governmental restrictions on the import and distribution of such goods as newsprint, raw film and auto tires, restrictions that began with a view to curbing opposition. Any firm known to be in opposition to the government, and many who were not, was likely to find itself short of some necessary import, unless, of course, it was ready to pay for immunity from embargo. For parallel with this system of restriction, which so invited corruption, there had grown up a whole bureaucracy, each man with some official title or other and each with a profitable side business in engineering the evasion of the very restrictions he was employed to impose.

Eva sailed in upon this racket like the buccaneer she was. Her influence with the colonel bought her a senior partnership in the graft surrounding him and in a very little time she began to have control of the distribution of raw film—a factor that must have carried weight with the San Miguel Studios—and of new auto tires.

There was boldness in Eva's methods but no originality; unique as she was, she was not original. As she did in all her activities she seized upon and made the utmost use of circumstances already in existence in the structure of Argentine society. In Buenos Aires it had always been necessary in any negotiation, whether it were a matter of renewing a passport or of getting a government contract for a million dollars, to employ a go-between who would at least expedite the matter even if he were not necessary for its actual achievement. Any company of standing had on its staff some knowledgeable little office boy who had a friend in the post office or a cousin in the police department and could get a package through the customs house in a trice or a driving license for his employer without the formality of a test; and among their directors there would be one suave gentleman whose business it was to know the right people in the government and to whom and how the necessary contribution should be made—and this, in the case of large government contracts, was quite frequently to the lady friend of the official rather than to the official himself. Eva created a monopoly in this under-the-counter business; it was to her and her alone to whom the suave gentlemen must bow, and her creatures to whom the knowledgeable little office boys must run.

Eva had now reached a degree of success which must have seemed fantastic to her friends of five years before. She had in fact reached what she considered to be the height of a radio career, for she received a higher salary than any other star, and she had no other standard by which to judge accomplishment. But her ambition was already carrying her further still and what to others would have seemed impossible—just as her present success had seemed impossible—was already half reality to her. But not enough of reality to appease her insecurity.

She had begun to spend money lavishly but still in the manner of one who has not been accustomed to money for long. She was buying her clothes from a young French designer and, although she ordered extravagantly, when the bills came in she insisted that each detail should be itemized—so much for so many yards of silk, so much for a buckle or braid or buttons. She knew to a centavo what each item cost and she was obsessed by the fear of being cheated—to *throw* money away was a gesture of magnificence, to be *cheated* out of it a sign of weakness. Since the whole of her future depended on getting the better of others she dared not admit that anyone might get the better of her.

Eva's position was still very far from secure. From almost the outset of her relationship with Perón the G.O.U. had been her most severe critic and most dangerous rival. It was not that they disapproved of the relationship. Had Eva been content with the extravagances and small social triumphs that satisfied most of the women they knew, they would have dismissed the colonel's indiscretions with a joke or two; another man's infatuation is always a little ridiculous. But here was a young woman who lacked a proper respect not only for their uniforms but for their male superiority, who not only ordered her lover about but had begun to order them —and what made it so confoundedly awkward was that, because of her particular position, they often found it politic to obey—and who called the most pompous among them by the familiar "thou." There seems to have been a little, understandable, malice in the prompt use Eva made of privileges to treat these gentlemen in so cavalier a fashion; that she enjoyed treating them so was evident. But to an Argentine gentleman his personal dignity is his most important possession and to an Argentine officer it is doubly so. They complained stuffily to Perón that his affair with this actress person was becoming altogether too notorious. Perón retorted jauntily that he was, thank God, a man of normal appetites and that it was

64

better for the prestige of the Army for his name to be linked with that of an actress than with those of actors; a retort that no doubt caught some of them on the raw.

It was in fact the intrigue and scheming among the officers themselves that gave Eva the opportunity to meddle in the affairs of state, for many more of these were resolved in secret meetings than on the floors of the Senate and the Chamber of Deputies, and many of these meetings took place in the apartment in Calle Posadas. Her first encounter with statesmanship was not calculated to give her any great respect for the statesmen. Eva, with that lack of decorum which was among her more likable qualities, received them sometimes in the informality of her house pajamas and, while they were talking, lay on the floor to do her physical jerks.

Eva was at heart an adventuress and perhaps the knowledge of her insecurity added zest to her career, for she had, then at least, a tremendous enjoyment of her spreading power. She knew, however, that her future rested not merely on the colonel's whim but on the stability of a government that had had in eighteen months a turnover of three presidents and forty ministers. To establish herself she had to make herself indispensable to Perón and do all she could towards making him indispensable to the country. His cause was indeed hers and she threw herself into it with that wholehearted lack of hesitation or restraint that was, perhaps, the secret of her success. His schemes became hers and she was much more energetic in their execution; his enemies became hers and she was the more bitter and implacable in their pursuit; his friends became hers and she made more self-interested use of them. The enemies of those days have vanished and the friends too have almost all gone. It was not safe to know Eva well. The first to go were those who threatened Perón with immediate rivalry: Colonel Imbert, whom Eva had already discarded and who was out of office before the end of 1945; a General Perlinger, who was Minister of the Interior and threatened Perón's control of the War Ministry; and General Avalos, who was in command of Campo de Mayo and who nearly ousted Perón once and for all. There were those of whom Eva made use for a while before they became dangerous to her vanity and had to be discarded: Juan Atilio Bramuglia, with whom, when he gained too much prestige as Foreign Minister, Eva had so bitter a feud; Cipriano Reyes, who organized labor in defense of Perón and who, when he protested the exploitation of labor unions, found himself in jail; and Miguel Miranda, whose crafty brain was behind Eva's finagling of import permits and who had a pudgy finger in every financial pie in the country before he had to hurry over to Montevideo for his health. And there were the nonentities, Colonel Farrell, who became the most ineffectual of all presidents before he disappeared, and Colonel Mercante, the closest of all friends, whom Eva called "the heart of Perón" until six years later he threatened to rival her for the vice-presidency. It was with these men and against the formidable machinations of the G.O.U. that Eva had to contend.

In her book[2] Eva gives Perón the credit—she gave him credit for almost everything less than creation—for teaching her how to deal with men, but it seems likely that it was rather her previous experience that made it possible for her to hold her own in the intrigue and treachery that surrounded her. It became virtually a duel between herself and the G.O.U., and it was Eva who survived.

But she could not have survived without the indulgence of Perón, and this she cultivated with all her heart. Whether there was ever any sincerity in the adoration she so fulsomely expressed for him probably not Eva herself could have told. Those who knew her best say that she had a phenomenal aptitude for feigning love and passion. Certainly her lover, twenty-four years older than herself, was not ready to detect any hollow ring and, had he done so, it would have been difficult for him to resist the flattery of the adulation she poured over him. That was his weakness, and perhaps all he really loved in her was this rosy reflection of himself. Eva had those qualities of energy and arrogance which are a challenge to the possessive instincts in some men who have

[2]*La Razón de mi Vida.*

66

a certain weakness in their own characters—as if to possess the woman who possesses those qualities were to gain the qualities themselves. The ruthlessness of her character incited desire rather than love, and although at this time and in the first years of her marriage there was a voluptuous quality in her which was later scalded out, there was never any sign in her of that relaxed contentment which comes from loving and being truly loved. But however much she ordered Perón around in public or nagged at him in private, she always spoke of him as if he were a god—and this was a flattery Perón could not resist.

Eva, being the experienced woman she was, could not have expected Perón's infatuation, even if she believed it to be true love, to last. She may have been scheming already to marry him, but she knew how seldom a man in his position married his mistress and she had the enmity of the G.O.U. to reckon with and their persistent efforts to cause a break between herself and Perón. But that she had already dreams of a greater and more lasting influence over him is evident in the roles she allotted to herself in radio—by this time she had full control over her own program; she played in a series of historical romances woven around such figures as that of Lady Hamilton and the Empress Josephine; and, as Eva interpreted history, there would have been no Nelson or Napoleon had it not been for the wit and wisdom of the women in their lives.

There is no doubt that Eva inspired confidence in Perón from the very first and that he hid none of his ambitions from her. She could be an eager and intent listener and he could have had no doubt of her interest; that she profited from the discussion of his plans is evident from the use she made of his methods later. But her fault was in overeagerness, and fast as events moved they were not moving fast enough for her, and her impatience led her into an indiscretion that might have cost Perón his success and her, her influence. She boasted among friends—and who could be sure who was a friend?—of Perón's ambition to become Vice-President. One can imagine the fury of abuse and accusation that followed; each had the language of the dockside at command and she could be as shrill as a parakeet. But there is an uxorious soft-ness in Perón's character that allowed him to accept the domination of a woman when he could have tolerated none from a man, and the matter was smoothed over and his plans only postponed.

But this same year and a half of Eva's blossoming was the most disturbed in the history of Argentina since the days of the tyrant Rosas, a hundred or more years before.

The government, now entirely in the hands of the military, was divided against itself; one faction under General Rawson, a man of courage and integrity, demanded that Argentina should fulfill her promises to the Allies, break with the Axis and put a curb on the Nazi agents who were using Buenos Aires as a base and causing so much loss to South Atlantic shipping. The other and by far the stronger faction in the Army were still under the old spell of German militarism and were convinced that the Axis was unconquerable. Perón was at first the instrument rather than the leader of this pro-Nazi group; they meant to use him only so long as he served their purposes.

A week or so after the San Juan earthquake, Ramirez, the Little Stick—and like a little stick he allowed himself to be buffeted this way and that—found himself forced by public opinion at home and abroad to break off relations with Germany. This brought the disapproval of the G.O.U. down on his head. Perón, for all his Nazi sympathies, must have been secretly delighted, for it served his ends excellently and, where his ends were to be served, he was ready to shout *Viva la Democracia!* with the best or, as he admitted frankly later, turn Communist if the country should be Communist.

Almost immediately it was announced that President Ramirez had to go into retirement for reasons of health. As he had appeared in public a day or two before in very good health indeed, there was some suspicion of foul play, but when reporters questioned Perón—they were already beginning to turn to him for official announcements—he assured them blandly that nothing out of the usual had occurred.

Later it was learned that a group of officers had called on the Little Stick in the middle of the night—and among them were some who only a month before had publicly avowed their personal allegiance to him—and had forced him at pistol point to announce that he would retire. Two weeks later he resigned and Colonel Edelmiro Farrell became president by decree and appointed his friend Perón to take his post as Minister of War. Whether or not Farrell had observed the pattern of events—Ramirez as Minister of War had ousted President Castillo and had in turn been ousted by Farrell, his own Minister of War—the new President had very little choice in the appointment. He was never more than a figure-head, which became clear at once when in a press conference all he had to say was that he endorsed all that Colonel Perón had said.

It was while such drastic changes were occurring in the government that Perón and Eva came to know each other intimately, so that she was with him from the first days of his success and was closely involved, if not immediately in evidence, in all that followed.

The figure of Juan Domingo Perón had begun to emerge from behind the presidential chair but it was impossible as yet for the public to get a clear picture of the man. Nothing was known of his past; he so smilingly disavowed all personal ambition, and promised, with such an ingratiating show of frankness, a return of civil liberties and justice for the workingman. Even the sturdiest among union leaders, the most clear-sighted of liberals and anti-military of Socialists were ready to believe his promises. But in that year and a half, when first he was Minister of War and then Secretary of Labor also and finally added the office of Vice-President to the other two, almost all pretense of civil liberty came to an end; and it had been little more than a pretense since Irigoyen's day. Newspapers were closed, leaders of the opposition arrested, union leaders imprisoned and replaced by henchmen of the Labor Secretariat, strikers were put into jail and tortured, university professors dismissed, students jailed, and one independent little school-girl who refused to write a glowing essay on Farrell was expelled and refused admission to any public school.

69

For all Perón's continued insistence that *Peronismo* is a wholly indigenous doctrine it is in fact no more than Fascism elasticized to suit the circumstances and temperament of South American peoples. And during his stay in Europe he had taken one lesson close to heart: that the working people could be welded into just as effective a weapon as the Army. He had developed the old Department of National Labor into the Secretariat of Labor and Social Welfare, which carried the status of a ministry; now, in imitation of Mussolini, he began to syndicalize the independent labor unions, in pretense of strengthening them, under the *Confederación General de Trabejo*. With the full weight of the C.G.T. behind him he was able to set up special courts to settle disputes between labor and management, as had been done in Italy, and to force the employers to give what wages and conditions he decreed. An alleviation of working conditions and an improvement in salary had been desperately needed and the workmen, who had been exploited for so long and were in the great majority politically naïve, did not see that they were trading their independence for a bonus, and in the enthusiasm of the moment allowed their veteran union leaders to be replaced by leaders of Perón's choosing, who seemed able to procure so much for them. With wages going up thirty and forty and fifty per cent, a month's wages as bonus every year to every workman, paid holidays and sick leave and protection from arbitrary dismissal, it was no wonder that labor was ready to acclaim Perón. He could boast now that he had an army of a hundred thousand trained soldiers and four million workers armed with clubs at his back. But this boast was a threat not only to those who opposed him but also to those who supported him. He was in a position to play one against the other, to threaten the workers with Army discipline if they ceased to obey him and the Army with civil rioting if they withdrew their support. But the public was fed only on his ingratiating smile and his promises; any radio station that ventured criticism would have lost its license—and in this he had Eva's able co-operation—and any newspaper that opposed him was likely to be closed.

70

The Argentines do not take readily to rebellion; those who live in the rich provinces around the capital are in the majority too comfortable and well fed; those who are very poor are also very ignorant and live in places so remote, very often, that what goes on in the government seems to have no relation to their lives. Yet the unrest in the country was increasing. The *porteño*, to whom a loss of dignity can be more important than a loss of liberty, had been disgusted by the government's philandering with the Axis— the civilian sympathies lay more with England and with France with whom Argentina had long held trade and cultural ties; and now the *porteño* was further humiliated to find that Argentina had, as Winston Churchill put it, "chosen to dally with evil and not only with evil but with the losing side." He was not even allowed to rejoice in Allied victory, for when Paris was liberated—and Paris has always been the spiritual home of the cultured Argentine—the crowd of three hundred thousand who gathered to celebrate were dispersed by the police; when Berlin fell all celebrations were forbidden and the groups that dared gather to cheer were attacked by hooligans under the protection of the police. A last-minute declaration of war by the government, who had finally been persuaded that Germany would lose, only served to humiliate the *porteños* more.

When Japan surrendered the crowds burst into the streets to celebrate and in the clash with the police that followed two students were killed and their deaths set off a series of strikes among students and university professors all over the country. In Buenos Aires eight hundred students, boys and girls, barricaded themselves inside the university. The police surrounded the building and opened fire and at last invaded the building with tear gas, the students defending themselves with tables and chairs. The young men were dragged off to the dreaded Special Section of the police and the girls were taken off to San Miguel Prison, which is usually reserved for prostitutes, while libelous stories about them were circulated by the government-controlled press.

There was in command of the Buenos Aires police force at this time a Colonel Filomeno Velazco; he had been given the post by Perón and the two were at the time close friends. Eva eyed this friendship with some mistrust although it was not of Velazco's methods she disapproved—these were not corrected when she finally got him out of office—but of the man himself, for he was not ready enough to follow her lead. He had already become notorious for his arbitrary arrests—his minions, like those of the Gestapo, would arrive in the middle of the night to drag their victims off to jail—and for his sadistic methods of torture.

In September 1945 a great march of protest against the government was staged and General Rawson, who had loudly advocated co-operation with the Allies, harangued the crowd jubilantly as they passed beneath his balcony on the way to Congress. He received only a mild rebuke for this so that he was not deterred from carrying forward a plot he had concerted with a fellow officer who was in command of the garrison in the provincial city of Córdoba. But a week later, when they were ready to march on Buenos Aires, he and his fellow conspirators were abruptly arrested and put in jail.

The Army had not for a moment been hoodwinked by Perón's genial smile and disavowals of personal ambition. When he had taken on the office of Secretary of Labor it had seemed a thankless one, but they had watched with growing uneasiness as he welded labor into a weapon to be used against them; and still more uneasily they watched the machinations of the colonel's lady, who seemed less and less content with her successes in radio and with the fortune she was making on the side—and this they would have been prepared to allow her as a perquisite—and more and more inclined to interfere in government affairs and to advise the Vice-President as to whom this office should be given or who dismissed from that. Moreover it was noted that it was to her friends and to her relatives, rather than Perón's, that these offices were given.

Eva's mother, the perennial Doña Juana, had made a new friend, one Niccolini, a post-office employee. Eva had used her influence on Perón to give Niccolini the directorship of Posts and Telegraph, a position that carried with it considerable influence since under it came the control of radio and film industry and all public means of communication. Eva had had a finger in this pie from the start, for her erstwhile friend Colonel Imbert had occupied that post—it had, indeed, been his chief attraction. But now that her stepfather-by-courtesy had taken over Colonel Imbert's office, Eva moved into an office alongside of his. It was evident who really had control in the offices of Posts and Telegraph.

This flagrant misuse of her privileges was more than the G.O.U. could tolerate. It was evident by now that Perón, for all his assurances that he had no presidential ambition, meant to run in the elections which must, if there were not to be a civil war, be held soon; he was already courting one political party and then another and unblushingly changing from Labor to Conservative overnight. If he were elected there would be no holding Eva at all. And since the people were demanding a reform and would not be satisfied without a political shake-up of some sort, it seemed to the officers under the command of General Avalos in Campo de Mayo a good moment to throw Juan Domingo—and Eva with him, incidentally—to the wolves.

They presented their ultimatum and Perón, always more ready to be prudent than bold, accepted it. He was, since the disturbances of the last month or two, not quite so sure if those four million workers with their clubs were behind or in front of him, and he must have persuaded Eva that a temporary retirement was politic.

On October 10, 1945, it was announced that Colonel Perón had resigned the offices of Vice-President, Minister of War, and Secretary of Labor and Social Welfare.

Eva was out.

Five

I flung myself into the streets looking for friends who might yet be able to do something for him. E. P.

On the morning of October 12, 1945, when the first young green of spring hazed the dark branches of the acacia trees, a crowd began to gather in Plaza San Martín. The Plaza stands at the fashionable end of Calle Florida on the barranca above the port, the site of the old slave market in colonial days. On one side the august edifice of the Plaza Hotel turns a huffy shoulder on a parvenu skyscraper of apartments and on the other stand the massively baroque mansions that until lately had been the *palacios* of the oligarchy. One of these buildings, whose wrought iron and gilded gates are at least two stories high, was

75

now the *Circulo Militar*—the Military Officers' Club. In front of it someone had chalked:

To the gallows with Perón!

The crowds that were gathering below its seignorial windows were not the sort of people that, in any city, would easily be led out into the streets to demonstrate; there were certainly some students among them but the majority were lawyers, businessmen, housewives, writers, doctors, and artisans. But now their temper was aroused and their shouting grew louder and angrier as they demanded free elections, an end to tyranny and the head of Perón. The police, who were mustered in the narrow streets leading to the Plaza, threatened to dismiss the crowd with force, but a young officer, dashing melodramatically out onto the balcony of the club, cried out that he and his fellow officers were ready to lead the crowd against the police if they should interfere.

"Viva! Viva! Down with Perón!" yelled the crowd.

Later, when perhaps as many as fifty thousand *porteños* were gathered there, Admiral Vernengo Lima, the new Minister of Marine, came out on to the balcony to promise in the name of the President—"We have no president!" interrupted the people. "Out with Farrell! Down with Perón!"—that a new cabinet—"A civilian cabinet!" shouted the people—a civilian cabinet should be formed at once and that those to blame for the situation should be punished, Perón first of all.

"Death to Perón! Death to Perón!"

The crowd were still gathered there when dusk had fallen, waiting for news of the new cabinet and of Perón's arrest, when a trumpet call was sounded and a moment later the police opened fire on the people and charged. The men and women who scrambled for shelter in doorways, under the stone benches of the Plaza and behind the acacia trees, and the young doctor shot through the back while kneeling to help a wounded man—they had their answer then, the true answer of an army in power.

But it had not been Perón this time who had given the order to fire. Perón's friend Velazco was no longer head of the police and Perón and Eva were fugitives. His brother officers were only too ready to make a scapegoat out of him and the police had sought him, first in the apartment in Calle Posadas and then in Doña Juana's house in Junín. But neither he nor Eva were to be found.

It was perhaps as much a credit to Eva's daring as it was to her loyalty that she did not waver in her allegiance to Perón in those October days. A less resolute woman might have vacillated until she saw which way the cards would fall, but Eva was a true gambler and had never been one to hesitate. Moreover she had been left in no doubt as to her predicament if Perón did not regain his influence. No sooner had Perón resigned than Jaime Yankelevitch happily cut her off the salary list of Radio Belgrano. He had finished with la Duarte, so he thought.

But in the Posadas apartment, with the young officers who had remained loyal to their leader—or who, at least, thought there was a chance of his regaining power—tramping in and out, and a strong guard set against any possible violence from the mob, Eva and Perón must have gone through harrowing hours of uncertainty before they decided on flight. The thought of leaving behind her all her clothes, her perfumes and her bibelots, which she had earned at such a high price and enjoyed for so short a while, must have been anguish to the acquisitive Eva; and a much more bitter anguish to relinquish her power at that moment when society had been brought to recognize her, and to know that she would leave behind the derision and triumph of her enemies. It was the more cautious colonel who first advised flight and she who protested against it and then at last agreed, knowing, for the first time, fear.

They must have slipped away sometime on the night of October 11, driving out of the dark city, taking a back street so that they would not have to pass the gates of the presidential residence, north towards the river resort of Tigre at the mouth of the delta of the

Río de la Plata. There are a thousand and more islands in the delta separated by a thousand and more narrow waterways that are hidden under weeping willow trees and tangles of honeysuckle. At Tigre they took a launch and set off along one of the wider channels, their wash curling up the muddy banks behind and sucking the reeds and water hyacinths into dipping, swaying curtsies.

Their destination was the small resort of Tres Bocas where they had stayed for week ends in the early happier days of their intimacy. It must have seemed the perfect sanctuary to them now with the wide channel that led on from it to the open waters of the Paraná and the friendly-seeming coast of Uruguay on the horizon beyond. But the river police had had word that they were hiding there—certainly all their old haunts were watched—and set a guard on the channel and sent word of their whereabouts to the capital. On the evening of the twelfth, when the police were firing on the crowd in Plaza San Martín, Perón was arrested and, with Eva, brought back to the apartment in Calle Posadas.

There was evidence then of a fundamental weakness in Perón's character; he trembled when he was arrested and on the trip back into the city complained rather peevishly that he had a touch of pleurisy. It was not, he conveyed, at all good for his health to be under arrest. Later that night he was taken aboard a gunboat and put off on the prison island of Martín García, from whence he wrote letters to his old friend Farrell complaining again of his pleurisy and of the rain that came in through the windows. But he was, in fact, in not any such uncomfortable circumstances as the workers and students whom his friend Velazco had sent to Villa Devoto prison after beating them up in the Special Section of the police.

Law and tradition in Argentina give the political prisoner a choice between exile and imprisonment—there is no death sentence even for the murderer. And even now in Perón's totalitarian state he prefers to ruin his political enemies financially and then allow them to escape into exile, and it is only those who present a real

78

threat to his supremacy or who are too poor to be punished otherwise and too obscure to be avenged who are imprisoned and ill treated. It is significant that now, when Perón was separated from Eva, he wrote asking to be allowed to go into exile. One cannot imagine that he would ever have weakened to such an extent had she been at his side. It was then, in that moment of weakness, that she gained her hold.

It was during those few days when Perón was imprisoned and the Army itself was without any strong leadership—General Avalos who led the faction against Perón was no *Lider*—that the tragic weakness of the democratic opposition was most apparent. They had at that moment a great part of the country behind them and had they been capable of any unified action they could have reestablished a constitutional government. But that great curse of the Argentine character, to which they themselves refer with such pride as their *dignidad de hombre,* their "manly dignity," would not allow one Radical to give way to another Radical, much less to a Socialist, in any detail of policy or choice of minister, so that they were incapable of deciding on a popular and democratic cabinet. When the Supreme Court, which in Argentina takes over the executive power if for any reason both President and Vice-President are out of office, did at last present a list of ministers, it was as unpopular as it was conservative and the people, again disillusioned in their democratic leadership, were ready to make do with Farrell, who was too much of a nonentity to be personally unpopular.

But while Perón sat in his room—he was not put in a cell—on Martín García and grumbled about the weather, and the Opposition quibbled over points of leadership, Eva showed neither weakness nor hesitation. She had wept and stormed with fury when they had taken her lover off but no sooner was he gone than she began to fly around among their erstwhile friends, shrieking at them, bullying them, cajoling them and threatening them, demanding his release.

79

It is one of the few incidents she describes in her book,[1] and there is a note of authenticity in her words.

. . . I flung myself into the streets searching for those friends who might still be of help to him. . . . As I descended from the neighborhoods of the proud and rich to those of the poor and humble, doors were opened to me more generously and with more warmth.

Above I found only cold and calculating hearts, the "prudent" hearts of "ordinary" men incapable of thinking or of doing anything extraordinary, hearts whose contact nauseated, shamed and disgusted one.

Eva was not without financial resources or without friends at this time—there were many who stood to lose all if Perón were lost. It is said that she and Perón took with them fifty thousand dollars in cash when they fled to Tres Bocas; certainly they would not have gone with empty pockets and, if it were so, the money must have been with Eva, for Perón would not have taken it with him to jail. What is certain is that, of the ten million dollars collected for the victims of San Juan a year and a half before, some six million had already disappeared. This was said to have been spent in finding homes for orphans but of the hundreds of children left parentless or homeless only one hundred and thirty-one had been helped. Even with the lavish notions of charity which Eva later proved to have, it is impossible that six million dollars were spent on a hundred-odd small children, and since from that time Eva and Perón seemed to have possession of a magic crock of gold, it is not surprising that they were so often accused of misappropriation of funds.

There is a story, among a thousand others, that Eva, shortly after the fund for the victims had been raised, returned home one evening to find an exquisite ermine cloak spread across her bed. "Oh!" she cried in rapture. "What saint can have brought me this!" Perón popped his head from behind the curtains, where he had

[1] *La Razón de mi Vida.*

concealed himself to watch her surprise, and answered with a smug smile on his face, "San Juan!"[2]

But wherever the money came from, Eva did not stint the spending of it now or the spending of her own amazing energy. One can imagine the promises she made to any who would help her and how scornfully those promises were often received—and how that scorn has been regretted since. But some who listened to her promises had even more reason for regret. Her feud with Juan Bramuglia, almost the only able and honest man in the Perón regime, was born in those days when he lagged in helping her to get Perón out of prison; yet Bramuglia lasted longer in office than Cipriano Reyes who acted for Perón so promptly and energetically and found himself, just three years later, in jail.

It was Cipriano Reyes perhaps more than anyone else who was instrumental in rescuing Perón. Reyes was a leader in the labor movement; he had organized the meat packers' unions in the tough slum districts that lie south of the Riachuelo, a smokestack-banked stream that runs into the city's southern docks. As Secretary of Labor Perón had supported the meat packers' strike and the two men had become close friends, Reyes visiting the apartment in Calle Posadas frequently and informally. Now it was he who helped Eva make preparations for a demonstration of workingmen.

By October 16, groups of workers had begun to drift into the city. The Opposition claimed that these ruffians were no workers; the syndicalized unions—the General Confederation of Labor— had not yet risen in support of Perón; the meat packers were among the roughest and most disorderly of workers; but it is not unreasonable to believe that many sober workmen, who owed their better wages to Perón, were ready to rally with very little encouragement to his support. The rowdies paraded up and down the narrow streets shouting, *"Viva Perón!"* while the police, uncertain now of how the business would turn out, stood around with their thumbs in their belts, and the *porteños* who had gathered in Plaza San Martín only four days before, stayed at home behind shuttered

[2]Saint John.

windows—*they* knew they could expect no protection from the police.

By this time the military themselves had done an about-face which, by the celerity and neatness with which it was executed, said much for the efficiency of their German training. General Avalos, who had been foremost in forcing Perón's resignation and who had taken over the Ministry of War, now announced that Colonel Perón had not been under arrest at all but had been taken to Martín García under protective custody since there were undisciplined elements loose in the city that had threatened his life.

Perón, still complaining about his health—and he did present rather an old-womanish picture at this time—had been moved from Martín García to the Military Hospital in Buenos Aires, where Eva flew to embrace him in her emotional style. But however sincere were her tears of relief on seeing him again, one can fancy that there was a shade of difference in her manner towards him since they had said good-by, a difference that may have been scarcely perceptible but was most profound.

Hard on Eva's heels came General Avalos and a troop of other officers all anxious to butter their bread on both sides.

By October 17, the General Confederation of Labor had declared itself for Perón; a day's stoppage of work throughout the country was announced and great crowds of "shirtless ones,"[3] as Perón's followers were from this day called, began to gather under the balconies of the Casa Rosada. Later the rally was spoken of as a spontaneous demonstration of the "shirtless ones," although they had been brought in in trucks from the shanty towns of the southern suburbs, carrying banners and flags and portraits of Perón which could not have been assembled, much less manufactured, overnight. They streamed over the bridges of the Riachuelo—in her book Eva says they swam, but since there are bridges and it was winter and the stream, which drains the meat packing district, is

[3]The word used is *descamisado*, literally "shirtless one," but it is taken to mean a man in his shirt sleeves, a "coatless one."

peculiarly foul it seems an unlikely gesture on the part of any sober man however carried away by enthusiasm—up along the cobbled dockside avenue and gathered in a great unruly, vociferous, odorous throng under the balconies of the Casa Rosada. All through the day the crowd increased and each moment grew more unquiet, disturbed by rumors that Perón would speak, that there had been a counterplot, that Perón was free and would in a moment appear.

"Perón! We want Perón! Perón!"

Behind the pink walls of the government house Eva Duarte listened and smiled. They had not yet begun to shout Evita—Little Eva—as they soon would, but as yet it was enough that they called for Perón.

Near midnight, when it seemed that the violence of the crowd could be contained no longer, Farrell and Perón stepped out on the balcony. A great roar greeted them. They embraced, clasping each other around the shoulders and kissing first on one cheek and then on the other, and the crowd bellowed itself hoarse.

"Here," said Farrell, "is the man we all love—Juan Perón!"

"Perón! Perón! We want Perón! Where did they put you, Perón?"

It was a dramatic moment, even if much of the drama were synthetic, and Perón was not the man to miss a teardrop of emotional appeal. He embraced his beloved "shirtless ones," he said; he had understood their suffering because they had suffered as his poor little old mother had been suffering. He was resigning from the Army now because he wanted to be part of the sweating, suffering masses. Melodramatically he snatched off his sword belt and gave it to Farrell. The two men embraced. The crowd roared. But now, said Perón with tears in his eyes, his "shirtless ones" must disperse quietly to their homes because there were women in the crowd who might be injured, and he himself was worn out and tired—but before they dispersed let them stand there a moment longer so that he might feast his eyes on them.

Within, Eva must have been listening with that curious little quirk of triumph that appeared sometimes in one corner of her mouth when she was not smiling her official smile, and her dark eyes must have snapped with malice as she looked around at the generals and the colonels and the discomfited gentlemen of the Supreme Court.

A few days later, with an even greater secrecy than they had used when they slipped away to the island in the delta, and with Doña Juana and Colonel Mercante as witnesses, Eva and Perón were married.

campaigning. Political slander in Argentina wore the cloak of the *caballero;* an opponent might be called a robber, a coward, and a liar, but it would have been ungentlemanly to have used as a weapon against him any irregularities in his private life—especially since almost all were equally vulnerable. Even Irigoyen, whose catholic gallantry had been notorious, had not suffered from the fact politically. Indeed, incontinence can hardly make an effective weapon of defamation against a man, for the Argentines have no puritan tradition and a man who is a bit of a libertine is considered more of a man. And it seems unlikely that Eva would have had any need to threaten or to bluff, even if Perón's infatuation were disregarded.

While Perón was imprisoned on Martín García, Eva had proved that she was not only useful to him but indispensable, for it is quite probable that Perón might have gone into exile then if he had not had Eva's enormous energy working for his recall. He needed that boldness of hers to make up for a certain overcautiousness in his own character. He had, until Eva's appearance, always worked from behind the figure of someone else—indeed, he continued to do so afterwards, for it was Eva who took the foremost place in the public eye. There is a certain quibbling, almost lawyerlike quality in his nature which in an emergency will hesitate before the bold decision. He would like to give to his most tyrannical acts a semblance of legality. Perhaps the difference between them was that while Eva wanted only recognition he wanted popularity. She never cared a fig for legality so that he was able to leave to her account the most barbarous actions of the regime and preserve for himself a semblance of dignity. But he was as necessary to her as she was to him; she could get nowhere in that man-dominated culture without the protection of a man and, handsome and successful as he was, her indisputable possession of him was as flattering to her ego as was the possession of all the furs and jewelry she was acquiring with such avidity. Pride in each other's personal appearance must have been mutual, for her looks had improved as rapidly as her fortune and there were times now when she might be taken for a truly beautiful woman—and she had never been mistaken for anything but a desirable one. In Argentina a man's virility rates next in importance to his "manly dignity," and it was very flattering to Perón's virility to have so beautiful and vivacious a young woman utterly devoted, at least outwardly, to himself and his career. Like many men who are more under the influence of their women than they care to admit, he got considerable satisfaction from her tongue-lashing of others, although at times he had to suffer a tongue-lashing himself; and Eva, not at all underestimating her influence over him, got even more satisfaction from making full use of it. Perón was a shrewd politician and even if his infatuation had not been so complete he would have recognized in Eva excellent material for publicity —since it was not to the oligarchs he intended to appeal—and an invaluable assistant in certain rather dubious affairs of finance in which it did not suit him, as president, to mix. Moreover her energy, which drove him into action, could be blamed when that action went askew. There is no doubt that he knew he could make good use of her; but it is doubtful if he knew just quite how large a genie he was about to uncork.

But perhaps the strongest bond between them, and perhaps an unconscious one, was their similarity of origin. This gave them a mutual confidence and a sense of complicity. They did not have to explain or excuse their motives to each other. They could be at ease together; Perón did not even have to mind his manners or curb his language before her as he would have had to do to save his own face in a more conventional relationship, as he probably had done in his first marriage with the nice little schoolmarm. And Eva did not have to feel towards him the resentment she had felt for men friends who were better born and wealthier. She need not resent Perón's success since it ran parallel with her own and was the triumph of one of her own kind over her enemies; indeed, they could share in private their triumphs over society. They both coveted that triumph, although Perón never showed the rancor that motivated Eva's actions; and at times he curbed her spite— he ordered the removal of the fish barrow from under the windows

87

of the offended Jockey Club and scolded her for having had it placed there. They were two of a kind, opportunists and accomplices in adventure, both setting out jubilantly on the same road towards a seemingly limitless wealth and power which they were ready to seize, not only at the expense of the oligarchs who hated them, but of the simple people who trusted them so implicitly.

Perón and Eva had taken a holiday after his triumphant re-instatement, and they returned from it married, although the marriage was not publicly announced and the circumstances of it have been kept secret since. They plunged at once into the presidential campaign; and now there was no pretense of hesitancy on Perón's part, for had not the shirtless ones themselves called for him? The elections had been promised early in 1946 and there was talk of Colonel Domingo Mercante running as Vice-President —indeed, the promise of the vice-presidency has been held out before the little man like a carrot before a donkey ever since. He has been so close to Eva and Perón that they have sometimes been spoken of as a triumvirate, although he has, in fact, never been allowed to assume any position which might by accident or design bring him to the throne. Perón eventually chose as his running mate the handsome and elderly Hortensio Quijano, who until now had been unknown in politics; he was related to Velazco, whom Perón had reinstated as Chief of Police, and he had the advantage of the appearance of an elder statesman with neither the experience nor the resolution to make him an effective one.

Perón had every physical advantage for political campaigning. He is a tall man—six foot is very tall in South America—and has a fine presence. His heaviness of figure had not yet run to flabbiness and was an advantage in a country where corpulence was considered a sign of affluence. He was what Argentines call "a good piece of man." His misleading air of simple bonhomie was perfectly suited to the business; he could with such natural ease become "one of the boys" and eat barbecued beef with his fingers and a hunting knife, grow expansive on the harsh red wine—though, in fact, he much prefers a scotch and soda—and clap his supporters on the

88

shoulder and tell questionable jokes in the argot of the city or the dialect of the provinces. And he was just as ready, with a sweaty shirt hung up beside the Argentine flag above his head, to whip his shirtless ones into frenzies of patriotic fervor or, in a broken voice and with tears streaming down his face, to thank them for their loyalty in his hour of tragedy.

The "manly dignity" of the individual Argentine, which makes him so often ready to receive as insult the friendliest criticism or reproof, becomes, in the collective Argentine, as touchily defensive of national integrity and as wary of foreign interference however disinterested that may be. Perón, no statesman but as clever a politician as ever came out of Tammany, made full use of this. The American Ambassador to Argentina at this time was Spruille Braden, who had unhesitatingly denounced the infiltration in Argentina of Nazi influence and ideology—Perón was and still is advised by Germans trained under the Nazi regime; his private secretary during the campaign was the handsome young Rudolph Freude, son of the Nazi Bund leader in Argentina who had been decorated by Hitler for his services. These denunciations earned the Ambassador Perón's enmity; Perón personally threatened his life. It gained for the Ambassador the friendship of many democratic Argentines but offended others, who themselves criticized the regime but whose pride would not stomach criticism from a foreigner; and those who welcomed Braden's championship were disillusioned later when succeeding ambassadors were not only friendly but effusive towards Perón. Perón made capital out of his countrymen's resentment of Braden's interference; he made the issue of the campaign appear to be between himself and Braden, Perón representing all that was *criollo*, of the country, and Braden representing the sinister forces of *Yanqui* imperialism. *Perón, yes! Braden, no!* the headlines of his propaganda ran, as if Tamborini, the opposing candidate, were only a puppet of the United States.

The opposition had little means of counteracting such inflammatory propaganda. Almost all the press and all radio was under the Peróns' control. With Perón's reinstatement Eva had sailed back into Radio Belgrano, and Jaime Yankelevitch had been only too glad to take her back at double the salary and retain for himself at least a titular position. It was very soon after this that Eva bought up Radio Belgrano, but she kept Yankelevitch on as director; she had him completely under her control. Perón, with lawyerlike observance of appearances, allowed the Opposition a semblance of liberty; they were allowed to hold meetings which were more often than not broken up by the police; they were allowed to publish newspapers which were forever being closed down for some infringement of the rules; they were given a minimum of time on the radio but their broadcasts were censored before they went on the air. In a country where so many hamlets are remote and newspapers the prerogative of the well-to-do or the town dweller, the radio had a virgin field for propaganda. The people it reached had voted before only as their *patrones* told them to vote, often just handing over their voting cards in return for the price of a drink and not having any means of discovering the advantages one candidate or another might offer them. Now they could vote themselves —as the radio told them to vote.

There was one other means by which the poorest and most remote hamlet might be reached and this was through the parish priest. Argentina is almost a hundred per cent Roman Catholic; the Church exercises an influence exceeded only by that of the Army and that of the General Confederation of Labor; it was, moreover, an influence that could neither be fully controlled from within nor denounced to pious Argentines as interference from abroad. The Church was a power that neither Perón nor Eva dared ignore. Eva's attitude to the Church was that of a warily respectful opponent rather than that of a devout daughter, and there were times when she allowed her antagonism to appear, although after each lapse she always found it necessary to make prompt amends. She was never able to flout and outmaneuver the Church as she did the military, nor was she able to cozen and to bribe it as she did with Labor. With Cardinal Copello, the mundane and unsaintly-looking head of the Buenos Aires Archiepiscopate, she found she had to move with a circumspection to which nature had ill-suited her.

The Argentine clergy have been divided in their attitude towards the Peróns. There have been those like the much loved Bishop Miguel de Andreas and the courageous parish priest, Father Dunphy, who regarded the new regime with distrust from the first and, when their distrust proved well-founded, preached so outspokenly on the rights of man that their position could not be misinterpreted. The bishop, accountable only to the Pope, could not be touched. Father Dunphy, less prominent and more vulnerable, was eventually deprived of his parish by the cardinal and, when he was allowed no opportunity to defend himself, he put aside his cassock in protest and went to work as a layman in a factory. But the majority of the clergy, from the worldly Copello down, willingly gave their support to Perón's campaign, many, no doubt, under the sincere conviction that he would better the conditions of their poverty-stricken parishioners. In this they had encouragement, if not actual instructions, from the cardinal, for he had enjoined his congregation not to vote for any party that did not advocate compulsory religious instruction in the schools or that threatened to institute divorce. The Opposition, who were endeavoring to reach concerted action under a coalition known as the Union Democratica, might be said to have sinned on both counts, since the Socialists had advocated divorce and they all opposed the compulsory teaching of religion in the schools; they made the mistake of campaigning against compulsory religion in schools rather than for free lay schools. Loyal followers of the cardinal were left no choice but to vote for Perón, who had made religious teaching in the schools part of his political platform, rightly judging that it would please many a small parochial priest with the promise of greater authority; and those of the less scrupulous clergy who brought politics into the pulpit were not rebuked, at least in public, by their cardinal.

In Belgrano, a comfortably residential suburb just north of Buenos Aires, a Father Filippo made such overt use of his pulpit for electioneering purposes that the good ladies of his congregation, who had attended en masse for the purpose, rose and left the church when he began to speak. While he preached they prayed loudly outside the door that he might be made to see the light, although he dispatched a curate to tell "those women to shut up" and eventually called the police. Some of the ladies were taken off to the police station but one of them was embarrassingly pregnant and, since she refused to leave unless they were all released, the local police, always more amenable where wealth or the Church might be involved, allowed them to go home. They received no worse punishment than abusive and threatening calls over the telephone from loyal Peronistas and scoldings from the more circumspect members of their families. Father Filippo became a member of the Chamber of Deputies—the equivalent of the House of Representatives.

Some fifty miles west of Buenos Aires is the Basilica of Luján where, so the legend runs, a wagon of colonial times became bogged in the mire and could not be released until a promise was made that a chapel should be erected on the spot. A hideously garish cathedral has now taken the place of the little adobe church that had become the mecca of a yearly pilgrimage; on its walls hang thousands of discarded crutches, horridly realistic models of human organs whose cure had been petitioned, and melodramatically composed photographs of children about to be crushed under the wheels of trucks or of houses swept by flame, with, under them, a prayerful verse of gratitude that life had been spared. These lurid mementos were the background for a frenetically enthusiastic ovation for the Peróns. They had stopped at Luján on their election tour and were received and escorted to the Basilica by Monsignor Serafini while the crowds lining the streets shouted, "Perón! Quijano! Perón! Quijano!" The name of Evita had not yet become a battle cry. From the pulpit Monsignor made a rousing political speech and called down the blessing of the Church on the candidate. The ceremony was completed by the crowd singing a campaign song, *I will give you, my pretty, something that begins with P—Perón!*

Eva was in her element during the campaign. She had begun to take over the tutelage of Perón's shirtless ones, as the workers had been called since October 17. At that time she had had a practical demonstration of their usefulness and, since Perón had been instrumental in raising their wages, she rode in on a tide of popularity. But Eva's popularity was by no means all secondhand.

In defiance of those who thought they understood mob psychology she toured the country on Perón's campaign train dressed in the most opulent fashion. She had so lately acquired her fine clothes and jewels that it may not have been so much sound judgment on her part as an unwillingness to forgo the joy of flaunting them. Whatever her original motive she was quick enough to catch on when it worked, and her jewelry, her brassy pompadour, her triumphant grin, shone tirelessly under the hot December sun as she leaned from the window to scatter gift packages and peso notes to the humble folk gathered along the railway track.

To the servant girls and modest housewives of the towns through which they passed, Eva, in her rich and variegated array of dress and with the bevy of uniforms that danced attendance on her and her handsome husband smiling at her side, was the incarnation of their every Cinderella dream. "Evita" they were learning to call her and as "Comrade Evita" she began to refer to herself, reminding them that she was one of them and seeming so to promise a share in her glamour and her wealth.

In the more remote districts—and so much of Argentina is still remote—peasant women trudged leagues along the dusty roads to watch the train go by. To these simple women who had perhaps never seen a movie, seldom heard a radio, never entered a carpeted room or climbed a stairway, and never in their laborious lives seen a young and beautiful woman stylishly dressed, Eva was much more than the Cinderella dream. There was only one image in their barren lives to whom she was remotely comparable and so they believed in the promise of those lavish peso notes as they believed in the life to come and reverenced the golden hair and gleaming smile as they reverenced the little Virgin in the adobe parish church.

The packages handed out held raisin bread and candy and bottles of cider and the picture of two smiling faces on a card that said the gift came from Perón and Evita who wished their beloved shirtless ones a happy Christmas and New Year. These packages of raisin bread and cider and picture cards became a Christmas institution and were distributed, so Eva boasted, to several million homes a year—no small item on a Christmas shopping list, if it is true.

Months after the campaign was over a priest in the forests of the north, too overworked and too conscientious to be concerned with politics, was trying to arrange for an old-age pension for a crone who lived with her dogs, her pig, and a tethered cock in a shelter little better than a lair. He asked her, not with much hope, if she had some document that would prove her age. With delighted and childlike eagerness she produced this card from Perón and Evita. She could not read what was written on it, but she had treasured it against some such emergency and, as she handed it to the priest, the expression in her candid eyes told of her utter faith in its sufficiency.

The tour was a triumphal procession; the crowds that lined the way and filled the station stops were in the majority the very poor and the very young, those to whom Eva and Perón seemed to promise most, not only in realities but in dreams. On the four-hour stretch between Buenos Aires and Rosario teen-age girls ran in relays level with the train. Horsemen of the pampas in their flowing white *bombachas* and with their rawhide bridles jingling with silver, dug in their spurs and, with cowboy whoops, raced with the train, raising a cloud of dust and locusts in their rear. That year the locusts had descended in what is popularly supposed to be a seven-year cycle, and the hoppers crawled inches deep on the roads and clung to boots and clothes so that it was impossible to avoid their

94

nauseating contact and their stench. But heat and dust and locusts had not deterred the crowds that gathered at the station stops; rough country fellows came barging forward to demand a handshake from the candidate almost at pistol point, women fainted, half-broken horses plunged and lashed out, and sometimes Perón and his party were forced to defend themselves and Eva with their fists. A more gently nurtured woman would have swooned in the heat and the crush or at the bawdy language with which they were greeted; but to Eva the dust, the crowds, the heat, the noise, and the rude adulation was so much champagne.

Only one incident warned them of any hostility. It was discovered that an axle of their train had been sawn in half. Fearing an ambush, Perón's bodyguards leaped out with guns in their hands. But, whatever may have been intended, nothing more violent occurred.

Meanwhile Tamborini, the opposition candidate, had had his speeches punctuated with revolver shots. While Perón's headquarters were well guarded, the meetings of the Democratic Union were dispersed by the police who, in what they insisted was self-defense, fired on the crowd or charged them with drawn sabers. When Tamborini and his party went on tour his train was set upon, rocks came hurtling through the windows and a fire broke out in the baggage compartment destroying a quantity of campaign posters and literature. Tamborini complained that it was the police themselves who transported the hoodlums to the scene in trucks and stood by while the damage was done. When Tamborini returned to Buenos Aires the crowd that had gathered in Plaza Once to welcome him were fired on by the police, who asserted later that they had done so to restore order; three young men were killed and many others wounded, all innocent of any crime but that of participation in civilian rights and duties.

A quite extraordinary optimism prevailed among Perón's opponents until the very day of the election; they seemed as incapable of facing reality as they were of presenting a united front. On the formation of the Democratic Union the Radical party had again split, one faction refusing to join forces with Progressive Democrats, Socialists and Communists, although both Tamborini and his running mate Mosca were Radicals themselves and the most conservative choice of Radicals. They would not, in fact, vote for their own candidates if a Socialist or Communist voted for them. Again their unco-operativeness—another facet of their "manly dignity"—made them betray their country's interests. It was surprising that, with such help from the opposition, Perón won with no more than a fifty-five per cent majority.

The Army had promised that the voting should be conducted in an orderly and honest fashion, and honest it was to all appearances. Perón had reversed the tactics of his predecessors, who had allowed a reasonable fairness during the campaign but had intimidated or suborned the voters or juggled with the urns on election day. The city was as peaceful as a cemetery on the day Perón was elected President.

Perón made good use of the time during which he was president-elect by persuading the obliging Farrell to make decrees that gave the Executive Power a much greater authority. A Central Bank was formed which had control of all loan and foreign exchange operations and it was Miguel Miranda, who had tutored Eva in piracy, who was put at the head of it. Scarcely had the hubbub that this aroused died down when Farrell had six universities "intervened" and put under the control of a government-appointed *interventor*. This "intervention" is a too-frequently invoked law by which the federal government can take over the control of a provincial government or any government department which has been accused of corruption. The man appointed to "intervene" in the universities was the flamboyant Dr. Oscar Ivanissevich, one of Eva's favorites, who has since, like so many of her favorites, vanished into oblivion. The universities had been the nursery of much of the opposition to the military regime and to Perón in particular, and Dr. Ivanissevich seemed well chosen to stifle their independence since he announced over the radio, when he became Minister of Education, that he was prepared to fight with all his might against "parasitic intellectualism."

On June 4, 1946, three years to the day after Castillo had been ousted by the intrigues of the G.O.U., Perón swore by Almighty God that he would uphold the Constitution of his country.

For the ceremony in the White Salon of the Casa Rosada the grenadiers in their shakos and their Napoleonic uniforms stood shoulder to shoulder around the wall; Perón was in the uniform of a brigadier general, heavy with gold braid and scarlet epaulets; the room was crowded with red and blue uniforms, the sashes and decorations of diplomats, the crimson and purple of ecclesiastic robes and the shimmer of silks and the glitter of the newly acquired jewelry of the ladies of an incoming aristocracy. With tears streaming down his face the retiring President Farrell handed over his mace of office to Perón and the two men embraced. Eva, the glitter of easily sprung tears in her eyes, a smile of triumph on her face and in her heart heaven knows what jumble of emotions, stood by.

Seven

With blood or without blood the race of oligarchs, exploiters of man, will without doubt die in this century. . . . E. P.

Eva had reached what must have seemed the crest of her ambitions; she had become the First Lady of the Land. But megalomania carries with it a self-inflicted goad and no power achieved can satisfy the victim. Like the sailor adrift who drinks of the sea Eva was racked by a thirst that could never be quenched, that was fed and not slaked by each new draught of power, that must, if death had not reached her first, have driven her insane.

Yet at the time there were signs that have convinced many that had Eva been accepted by the Argentine aristocracy—those same landed oligarchs who were among her bitterest enemies—she would have forgone any further acquisition of power; and the same argue that it was not her dubious past that made her inacceptable but her unscrupulous present.

That she could ever have been accepted on equal terms by the exclusive matrons of *porteño* society is highly improbable. Tradition had set an almost insurmountable barrier between mistress and wife, and the man who was so injudicious as to marry his mistress knew that he could not expect his friends to receive her. Had Eva been sufficiently meek and undistinguished, and had the irregularities of her past been less flamboyant, they might have extended to her, now that she was the wife of the President, their patronage. But not for one moment, not even in their most magnanimous moments, would they have forgotten, or allowed her to forget, their difference in birth.

And Eva gave no definite sign of any desire to be reconciled with society; what overtures she made, if overtures they could be called, were designed to humiliate rather than conciliate. When she first moved into the Residency she held a reception for the wives of the government officials and all the *porteño* drawing rooms were set tittering because she had stood on a dais to receive her guests and; after they had filed past in silence, shouted, so it is said, for her bodyguard to show them out. No doubt her manners lacked a certain polish, as her language certainly did. That she could assume a social charm when she chose was proved a year or two later when the James Bruces were in the American Embassy and she visited Mrs. Bruce frequently, charming her hostess and the other guests by her apparently unaffected simplicity. She had by that time gained in poise; but at no time did she show herself to be really at ease in the society of *porteña* ladies. Recognition was necessary to her but it is doubtful whether she cared if it were accorded from approval or from fear; she had already shown that her ambition far exceeded what society had to offer her. Had the Argentine élite accepted her it is certain that she would have used her position to humiliate them, for her resentment had its roots in the humiliations of her own youth, as the pattern of her revenge has since made clear.

100

There was, however, never any possibility that they would accept her on her own terms or she allow herself to be accepted on theirs. The antagonism between them was too strong and too primitive, the age-old antagonism between the tribe and the interloper, hatred driven by fear. It was a formidable array against her, all those ladies of irreproachable reputation, vast wealth and enormous families. They waited for her to go down on her knees for their favors, and she faced them with a whip in her hand. They used against her the polished weapons of polite society; she fought them with gangster methods. They sniggered and whispered because she appeared at the opera without gloves or sat next to the cardinal at a banquet with one shoulder bare; she expropriated their properties and put their persons in jail with prostitutes; they whispered scandal about her in their drawing rooms; she libeled them on the front pages of her newspapers.

While they swore they disapproved of her only because of her interference in politics and because of the injustices committed in her name, the basis of their resentment against her was revealed in their preoccupation with her sexual life. Their gossip attributed to her a licentiousness the details of which neither their experience nor their imagination could supply, and which no woman's stamina could have withstood.

The last weapon the *porteños* use against a fellow countryman in the public eye is the first that comes to hand when a woman becomes notorious.

As the First Lady Eva had very good reason to believe that the *señoras porteñas* would be forced to accept her whether they liked it or not.

There had been for the last eighty years in Buenos Aires a wealthy and exclusive charitable organization, the Society of the Ladies of Benevolence, administered by the doyennes of Argentine society under the patronage of the Church and with the help of government grants. It had done a great amount of good if in a leisurely and somewhat feudal manner and with rather more con-

101

cern for the souls of the ladies who gave than for the bodies of those who received the charity. It was above scandal and immune to the infiltration of new ideas.

It was customary for the wife of the President to become the honorary president of the Benevolent Society.

When Perón was inaugurated the good ladies were in a dilemma. They could not possibly invite "that woman" to be president of their society. It would mean establishing some sort of social contact with her and, really, she was the sort of person who should have been at the receiving end of charity! It was unthinkable, so they made no move.

But Eva was not the one to allow herself to be passed over so easily. She sent to inquire why they had not come to offer her the presidency of their society. With their unfailing urbanity they replied that she was, alas! too young, that their organization was one which must be headed by a woman of maturity.

Eva at once proposed that they should make her mother, Doña Juana, president—a suggestion that almost makes one credit her with a sense of humor.

This proposal the indignant ladies turned down flatly and not even the bland and rather terrifying Cardinal Copello, to whom Eva appealed, could make them change their minds. It was, perhaps, with the idea of dazzling the cardinal and obtaining his cooperation that Eva had appeared with her beautiful shoulder bare, for it was, it seems, on that occasion that she had enlisted his interest.

This rebuff had consequences which these ladies, who had for so long occupied an impregnable position, could not possibly have foreseen. Eva set out to destroy both them and their Society, and out of this fury of destruction there rose the plan for her own charitable organization, that most piratical and fantastic of social welfare ventures, the Eva Perón Foundation.

The ladies of *porteño* society, helpless when faced by such unscrupulous boldness, vented their frustration in the most bitter vilification; the vindictiveness of some of their gossip is perhaps ac-

102

counted for by the fact that Eva represented the "other woman" in their marriages, who was tolerable only while she remained obscure. Eva was well aware of all the gossip that went on around her name, not only of the gossip in the drawing rooms but of all the slanderous jokes and bawdy limericks scribbled on the walls of cafés and bars—for she had the police make the rounds of them and fine the proprietors where they were found. She knew of all this spite fermenting around her and it must have added to the hate and spite fermenting within herself and to her lust for revenge.

The role that Eva played during the campaign, and which she continued to play before her public for some time to come, was no sign of any willingness on her part to play second fiddle to anyone —even to Perón; it was only a further example of her shrewd understanding of man, of Argentine man in particular. She played the part of a devoted wife dedicated to her husband's cause. She spoke of herself as the "most humble of the shirtless ones" and of her "faith and resignation and absolute prostration before his ideals." Anyone less resigned and prostrate would be hard to find!

"I am," she declaimed, "only the most modest of the collaborators of this idealist who is General Perón; I am no more than a woman who works and tries to collaborate with this great patriot who is shaping the great future of our nation. . . ."

She threw herself into this part with such enthusiastic energy that it is difficult to believe that she did so quite without sincerity. It is probable that there was a very strong element of comradeship in her feeling for Perón; but there is no doubt that had his career been a hindrance rather than a necessity to her, she would have jettisoned him at any point. She had reached the highest position open to a woman in Argentina, but she had reached that position and was able to maintain it only by virtue of her husband's success. What further ambition she already nursed she could not so much as hint without running the risk of having her present powers curbed. Probably not to Perón himself could she speak of any personal ambition. A woman in authority could not be tolerated in that man-made society and she had to work under cover of her husband and to appear to be working only for his ends. But since her success ran parallel with his own it was not difficult for her to express a boundless devotion to his cause.

It is, however, very possible that her ability to dramatize herself convinced her of her own sincerity, for in the ability to delude oneself lies the fine art of deluding others. She flung herself into a part with too great an abandon, with too complete a lack of self-consciousness, for it to be possible that she acted with any degree of objectivity. To a very great extent her success was due to this lack of self-consciousness; she never hesitated for fear that she might appear ridiculous; she was unconscious of any limitation in herself, so that any role she chose could seem real to her. And any role she chose absorbed all of her faculties for the time, and she could be utterly convincing as the girlish hostess who scribbled down the address of the presidential residence so that her guest, the wife of an ambassador, would not forget to write to her, grabbing at the tip of her own nose in an urchin gesture of amusement when she made a gaffe, or running upstairs to fetch a length of silk to give her friend as a parting gift. And equally convincing as the young career woman dashing into a meeting—of bankers, newsmen, or labor representatives—followed by a flock of secretaries and crying, "Come on, boys! Hurry, hurry, hurry!" Or as the solicitous young wife wrapping a shawl around the shoulders of an elderly and famous husband and fussing lest he be sitting in a draft.

The role she undertook depended entirely on her audience but, once undertaken, absorbed her whole personality. Even in those parts she overacted and which seemed to betray her insincerity it is possible that she was not always consciously dishonest. With almost every public speech she made, and in those days she spoke whenever she could seize the opportunity, she gave her enemies occasion to sneer at her melodrama.

"Because I also," she screeched in half hysteria, "like our companion workers, am capable of dying and of ending the last moment of my life with our war cry, our cry of salvation, 'My life for Perón!' "

"Embraced to the *patria*," she cried with a break in her harsh voice, "I will give my all, because there are as yet in this country those who are poor and unhappy, without hope and sick. My soul knows it. My body has felt it. I place my soul together with the soul of my country. I offer all my energies that my body may be stretched out like a bridge towards the common happiness. Cross over it with firm tread and high head towards the supreme destiny of our new *patria*. Not fatigue nor fasting nor sacrifice can be of importance when you are trying to put an end to the fatigue and suffering that dwell in the country's vitals."

To the educated this emotionalism was nauseating and her extravagance as ridiculous as the melodrama of early movie days. But it was not to the educated that her speeches were directed, and it is that very melodrama that appeals to the simple and untaught, who are readier to believe a promise made in impassioned voice and abstract terms than they are one which is made with the restraints of honesty. It is a melodrama that would have appealed to Eva herself, and for this reason she may have used it without conscious insincerity, for if she was cleverer, more ruthless and more energetic, more determined, more experienced than the little shop girls and country women who listened to her, she was not more emotionally mature.

However she may have disguised her real motives to her audience and herself, they become quite clear when her inexorable progress towards her goal is seen in perspective. Her real aim was betrayed by her maneuverings to put her relatives and parasites into key positions in the government and to get the sources of her husband's power into her own hands. It was her own position she was consolidating and not his.

She had already contrived to get her mother's friend Niccolini appointed Director of Posts and Telegraph so that all means of communication were virtually under her control. As soon as Farrell had handed over his staff of office to Perón in the Casa Rosada, Eva persuaded her husband to take on her only brother Juancito as his private secretary—his former secretary, young Freude, was made chief of the Presidential Department of Investigation, Perón's private spy system. Juancito had had no other experience for his new position but that of a soap salesman in Junín and small-town Lothario; she used her influence to have her eldest sister's friend, Major Alfredo Arrieto, elected Senator for the province of Buenos Aires; her second sister, Blanca, had married a lawyer, Dr. Rodriguez—in Argentina all who have doctorates are called by the title, whether the degree is in medicine, law, or philosophy—and Eva saw to it that he was appointed Governor of the province of Buenos Aires and, later, made a member of the Supreme Court. In political matters the province of Buenos Aires, which has about one third of the total population of the country, carries more weight than all the thirteen other provinces together. The husband of her third sister, one Orlando Bertolini, who had been employed as an elevator operator, was made Director of Customs. Thus through her relatives alone she had direct supervision over radio, post and telegraph, the policy of the provincial government, unsubornable allies in the Senate and, later, in the Supreme Court, and a check on the President's daily schedule. In placing her relatives in these positions she was not guided by any ability they might have shown, much less by any family affection, except perhaps in the case of Juancito, but by the fact that, since their fortunes depended entirely on her own, self-interest would ensure their loyalty.

From his entry into politics Perón had used every gangster method possible to gain control of the press. He had said that a strong state should have an ample press of its own and should weaken and deplete the opposition press. By the time he assumed the presidency this was virtually accomplished; by cutting down supplies of newsprint, invoking a series of minor regulations, instigating strikes among the employees, and using out and out violence he had been able to buy up or drive underground or handcuff

106

almost all the opposition papers. In 1945 soldiers, supposedly off duty, created a disturbance outside the offices of the newspaper *La Critica.* The disturbance took on the proportions of a street battle, with some five thousand street fighters, a hundred police and four armored cars taking part and the newspaper's siren, reserved as a rule for the announcement of some world-shaking event, wailing its distress signal. The editor had to flee to Montevideo and the owner, a widow, sold out to Perón. *Vanguardia,* the Socialist paper and perhaps the most democratic of any, after a series of fines, summonses, closures—the last time its plant was closed was on the excuse that the unloading of newsprint obstructed the traffic—had finally been driven underground. The two English-language papers were able to remain in existence only by maintaining a strictly neutral attitude on internal affairs; they seldom voiced any opinion of their own but in writing of the Peróns quoted the eulogies of the Peronista press; their editorials had to be printed in Spanish as well as English. The only two newspapers in Buenos Aires that retained their independence were *La Prensa* and *La Nación,* both unimpeachable organs of the oligarchy, which continued to report the news with dignified objectivity. *La Prensa,* the more openly anti-Peronista, was subjected to a persecution that ended in its expropriation in 1951. *La Nación* continues perilously to exist; its quota of newsprint has been so reduced that those who are not subscribers pay black-market prices for a copy, while the government-sponsored papers were at one time turning over tons of unsold copies to the scrap dealers every day. In 1947 Eva acquired the ownership of *Democracia,* which has been the official government mouthpiece ever since and is now the morning paper most in evidence. She and her friends, Alberto Dodero, Colonel Mercante, José Espejo, and Major Aloé, formed the *Associación Literario Editorial Argentina,* of which Eva was the principal shareholder, with the purpose of gaining a monopoly of the press. They acquired *Noticias Graficas* for about a million and a half dollars and, later, the *Haynes Editorial* which published the best-known of the tabloids, *El Mundo,* and controlled *El Mundo* radio network.

Since by this time Eva owned or had control of the four principal radio stations in Buenos Aires—according to the report of the Inter-American Broadcasters' Congress of 1948, *all* radio stations in the country were under government control—she had in her hands virtually all means of publicity. And again her real aim was betrayed by the far greater publicity accorded to herself than to Perón. Pages of her photographs would appear in *Democracia* and in one short news film her person would appear three or four times. To this weapon of publicity she began now to add that of Labor, whose management she was to take over from Perón, and two new weapons of her own forging—the Peronista Feminine Party, a vast new supply of votes, and the fantastic resources of the Eva Perón Foundation. To Perón she left the Army, which had never been willing, except in individual cases, to fall under her spell, and was far from undivided in its loyalty to him.

It might seem strange that Perón should have been so ready to allow her interference in the country's affairs, if one did not bear in mind the part she had recently played in the October crisis; he owed his position in great part to her and she was not the one to allow such a debt to lapse. Moreover, having worked his way up from the Army to the government by virtue of plot and counterplot, Perón knew better than any how little trust he could place in his former brother officers. She was the only person whom he could trust and even if his infatuation were wearing thin, and there was no sign of this, he knew that he could trust her as long as her career depended on his own which, since their marriage, was until the death of one. Far from discouraging Eva in her activities, Perón often referred to her the Labor delegates who came to him for assistance and he insisted that all the dignitaries that paid their respects to him should be equally attentive to her. Perhaps some obscure feeling of humiliation in their personal relationship made him find satisfaction in forcing senators and deputies and provincial governors and foreign diplomats to kowtow to her. Certainly he was in no way apologetic for his unconventional marriage. He was obviously proud of her; his attitude had sometimes a hint of Vic-

married woman continues to use her maiden name. It was only later that she became simply Eva Perón. In appearance she was the apotheosis of the demimondaine; there was a voluptuousness about her that did not come from the prodigal display of ornament alone but from a lushness of the flesh itself, as if that, in sympathy, had ripened with her material success. There was a tendency to plumpness in her now that was no longer the ungainly heaviness of adolescence; she displayed the smooth curves of maturity and a softness and a womanliness in her face that quite vanished later. To the discriminating her appearance was vulgar; beautiful as her clothes were they might have been chosen for the star of some super-colossal Hollywood production. Perhaps in this showy array she found a needed reassurance, for none could question her ability to wear such clothes to their full advantage. If not at all dismayed by the position in which she found herself, she was very much aware that her enemies were ready to make capital out of her social blunders; she did betray some unsureness—it was almost the only unsureness she ever betrayed and was probably unconscious—in her uneasiness when she was interviewed—she very much preferred to be photographed—and by her endeavors to appear more cultured than she was. All the Western Hemisphere knew the story published in *Time* magazine of her reply to a reporter who asked her who her favorite author was. "Plutarch," she said, adding, "He's an ancient writer, you know." *Time* and *Life* magazines were banned in Buenos Aires for stories such as this, and must still be read surreptitiously. She had not gained enough self-assurance to admit easily to any lack of learning. In her book—and unrelated to factual truth as that is, yet in its invention and its reticences it sometimes unwittingly reveals a grain of truth—she says that while she and Perón were both devoted to the same cause—that of the people—he knew very well what his aims were while she had only a vague idea of hers; he worked with his intelligence and she with her heart; he came prepared for the struggle but she was ignorant, although ready for anything; he was cultured and she was simple; he was enormous and she was tiny; he was the master and she was the

110

pupil. He was the substance and she the shadow. He was sure of himself and she was sure only of him.

When the overlay of adulation which clots so much of her public speech and writing is removed there remains a residue of truth in this. She must at times have felt herself unprepared and ignorant and even small and shadowy placed as she was so suddenly in the limelight and faced by so much disapproval and enmity. And she was sure of only one thing: since their marriage, of Perón.

It is characteristic of Eva that at this point, knowing herself ignorant not only of protocol but of the usual exchanges of polite society, she did not try to bribe her way into society or set up a rival aristocracy of *nouveaux riches;* that such society came into being was the result of the overnight fortune-making the Peronista policy encouraged and it was the careers of these newly rich and not their social life that revolved around Eva. She set out to challenge her rivals on the very grounds of their complacency.

Among the Argentine oligarchs a yearly trip to Europe was almost as much *de rigueur* as the migration of the less exalted to the country and the sea in January. But, perhaps because of some inherited resentment against the mother country which had patronized *porteños* as colonials, they looked upon Paris and not Madrid as their spiritual home. No Argentine could pretend to culture unless he had spent a while in Paris and no Argentine lady could pretend to fashion unless she could bring home a dozen trunkloads of Parisian models every year.

Now Eva, determined not merely to rival her enemies but to outshine them completely, decided on a European trip that would make their junkets seem like a drive around the park. She herself said that she went chiefly to make a study of social aid institutions in the Old World and it is true that when her glamorous progress through Europe allowed her the time, she visited orphanages, schools for artisans, and the like. But since the ladies of the *Beneficencia* had treated her in so cavalier a fashion, her interest in social aid, based as it may have been on some real identification with the downtrodden poor, was also linked with her resentment

111

against *porteño* society. There is no doubt that she went with the hope of receiving a papal marquisate, an honor that she knew would be a smack in the eye to her social enemies. It is a distinction that had been conferred on only one or two of the most pious among Argentine dowagers, and Eva's subsequent treatment of them confirmed her resentment at not receiving the honor for herself. But just as she was to make use of their own weapons to confound the ladies of the *Beneficencia* by inaugurating a social aid program that was not only a thousandfold more lavish but was based on a system that she boasted, with reason, was unique, and made political capital out of it, so she undertook her trip to Europe on a scale with which even they were unable to compete and in such a manner that she was able to make political propaganda out of it. The hundred and fifty thousand shirtless ones who came to see her off watched her set out on a trip to Spain and Italy, the homelands of the parents and grandparents of so many of them. She left until the last her assault upon the Paris of the oligarchs.

Eight

My simple woman's heart . . . E. P.

The Foreign Minister, Juan Atilio Bramuglia, had advised
Eva that her visit to Spain would be undiplomatic at a moment when Argentina was seeking the friendship of the United
States. For the realization of his five-year plan Perón needed American machinery and, later, American credit, and now that Spruille
Braden was gone, Perón and the American Embassy were on the
best of terms. But Eva had no liking for Juan Bramuglia who was
both too honest and too able to be manipulated as she liked to
manipulate her "friends." She chose to ignore his advice and in
April, 1947, he had to announce that she had accepted Franco's
invitation to Spain.

113

The elaborate preparations for her trip, which was scheduled for June—winter in Buenos Aires and summer in Madrid—aroused a storm of protest from the opposition and some more carefully voiced disapproval among Peronistas themselves. There were already signs that the government's wild expenditure was leading the country into difficulties. Eva retorted that her expenses would be paid from her own purse, and gave up the idea of crossing the Atlantic in a naval vessel. Even with this reduction in expense and the fact that Spain alone spent from two to four million dollars on her visit it seems unlikely that the money she had earned as a radio star, fabulous as her salary had been, could have been sufficient to pay for more than the wardrobe she took with her on the trip.

At the last moment she must have been attacked by doubt, knowing, as she must have known, how her enemies would intrigue while she was gone, and perhaps she felt ready to abandon the trip altogether when, during the broadcast of Perón's farewell speech to her, a voice interrupted, ghostlike, on the air with, "Death to Perón!"

Her departure was extravagant and emotional as all her exits and her entrances have been—it is in the South American tradition that there should be much embracing and weeping at any farewell. At the airport a hundred and fifty thousand people had gathered to see her off. "I go," she said, "to the Old World with a message of peace and hope. I go as a representative of the working people, of my beloved shirtless ones, with whom, in going, I leave my heart."

This representative of the working people traveled with as costly a wardrobe as the bride princess of an Indian state, with jewelry that Cleopatra would not have scorned and with three or four exquisite costumes for each day of her two months' trip.

But her opulent appearance was a matter of pride to the shirtless ones gathered to see her off, many of whom must have felt the vicarious satisfaction of returning, fabulously wealthy and successful, to the birthplaces of their emigrant families. "Evita! Perón! Evita! Perón!" they roared as Perón and Eva emotionally embraced and she turned to wave them a last farewell.

114

The plane she traveled in was a Douglas DC-4 belonging to the Spanish Iberian Airways; it had been totally refitted for the journey with bedrooms for herself and the lady who accompanied her, with beds, vanity tables and green velvet curtains, and a dining salon with tables and chairs. Escorting the plane as far as the island of Fernando de Noronha were two military planes. With Eva went the Señora Largomarsino de Guardo, wife of the president of the Chamber of Deputies; Juancito Duarte, Eva's brother; Alberto Dodero, a shipping tycoon who, much to his own financial advantage, had cultivated a close friendship with the Peróns; a couple of aides and a secretary. Father Benitez, her Jesuit confessor, had gone ahead to prepare for her reception in Paris and Rome; her own doctor, maids, hairdresser and dressmaker had all traveled ahead. No oligarch making her summer trek with her family to her *estancia* could have traveled more well accompanied than this!

On the journey the party was a gay one—they had not yet had time to get on each other's nerves as seems to have happened later on. They drank each other's health in champagne and, crossing the equator, "christened" in traditional style those who had not crossed the line before. One can imagine that at that moment Eva did not need champagne to add to the exhilaration she felt.

Meanwhile most extravagant preparations for her reception were going ahead in Madrid—it should be remembered that Spain was much in need of Argentine wheat. The exact moment of her arrival on Spanish soil was recorded; it was on Spanish African soil when the plane made a stop at Villa Cisneros. An escort of forty-one fighting planes were sent out to welcome her, guns boomed an official salute, the Madrilenian newspaper *Arriba* devoted its front page to her fulsome praise; indeed, in one issue they devoted three and a half pages out of a total of eight to the record of her every movement and paeans in her praise, while the touchy question of the Generalissimo's succession was almost banished from the news. Even the pilot and the steward of the uneventful plane trip had their stories of the crossing in print.

At the airport a crowd of some two hundred thousand waited to welcome her; Franco himself and Doña Carmen, his thin elegant wife, were there and a crowd of nobility, high government officials and members of the diplomatic corps, although some of these had thought it discreet to be away on holiday.

One incident relieved the awful formality of her reception. The Argentine Ambassador to Madrid, Dr. Radio, had arrived on the scene in good time, but due to some oversight the authorities had not given orders for him to be admitted within the official enclosure. When at last he made it clear that he of all men must be on hand to welcome the lady, the plane was already down and the crowd were milling around the barriers. Desperate, as one can imagine, the poor man shoved and battered his way through the crowd, arriving at last before the immaculate Eva with his coat torn and his hat lost, and three quarters of an hour late. Eva, never a lenient woman where a slight to her own person may be discovered and always unrestrained in temper, trounced him there and then, not mincing her words nor curbing her language, much to the chagrin of the Ambassador and, no doubt, to the amusement of those near enough to hear.

But the program arranged for her in Madrid did not leave her any time for grievances; it must, indeed, in its ostentation, have satisfied for the time even her insatiable appetite for show, and must have worn poor Doña Carmen, who had to go with her everywhere, to the bone; there were very few who could compete with Eva's driven energy. She was rushed from official reception to banquet to ball; she was whirled off on sight-seeing expeditions, to visit churches and museums, each with an official reception committee waiting her; she received union delegations, visited trade schools and medical dispensaries and, in an open Cadillac, with "by chance" a reporter from *Arriba* following her, toured the workers' districts and visited "the clean homes of the happily smiling working people" to whom she brought, so she said, the presence and the spirit of Perón. More acceptable were the hundred peseta notes she lavishly distributed, more money than some of these poor folk had

116

handled at one time in their lives but not, perhaps, an adequate return for the millions her visit was costing the country.

On the day when she was to be decorated by Franco shops and offices were closed for four hours so that the people could gather before the Palacio Real to listen to the ceremony broadcast from within. In the Throne Room Franco in his resplendent uniform of Captain General of the Army, wearing the collar of the Order of San Martín that Perón had given him, presented Eva with the Great Cross of Isabella the Catholic, the highest decoration Spain could bestow. Standing between the Generalissimo and Doña Carmen, Eva received the officials and diplomats and church dignitaries who filed past—and this the girl who had struggled for a bit part on the radio only half a dozen years before!

When, with the Generalissimo and Doña Carmen, she moved out on to the balcony, the crowd roared its disciplined applause, arms raised in the Falange salute. Standing there in her mink coat in the sweltering summer sun—she was still at the stage when she had to wear her fur coats and jewelry whatever the climate or the occasion—the rouleaux of her golden pompadour almost hiding her osprey hat, her smile as glittering as her jewels, Eva gave the Falange salute in return.

One evening during her stay in Madrid the Plaza Mayor was barricaded off for a folk-dancing festival given in her honor. The dancing went on until three in the morning and Eva was presented with fifty provincial costumes by the women's section of the Falange, each costume, lying in the coffin-shaped basket in which it was separately packed, a museum piece of exquisite embroidery.

At the bullfight arranged for her in the Plaza de Toros only the most skillful of matadors were to perform and only bulls of the Muira stock, famed for their ferocity and the high prices they fetch, were to be used. The entire circle of boxes was draped with multicolored mantillas and the arena itself was spread with colored sand in intricate design, red and yellow for Spain and blue and white for Argentina, and in the center the coats-of-arms of the two countries, a design which must have cost hours of skilled and patient labor

117

and took only a moment to destroy. Eva, seated in the royal box, blond and all in white, stood out in startling contrast against the dark-haired Spanish women, most of whom habitually wear black. First there was a parade of Granada gypsies playing their wild songs and dances on guitar and tambourin; then came a stately procession of the Royal Coaches; and then the Muira bulls. . . .

There were gala banquets at Franco's palace of El Prado and at the Ritz, excursions to the Escorial, bishops and officials to receive her everywhere, titled heads bent over her hand, flowers and fabulous gifts—one was a four-thousand-dollar flask of perfume—her name in great welcoming letters, flags and streamers and bands playing, homage and acclamation from crowds everywhere—oh, she did not have to give a fig for any oligarch!

A tour around Segovia in one exhausting day was filled also with banquets and receptions; a flight north to Galicia, mother province of so many Argentines, and south to Sevilla and Granada; peasant women everywhere thrusting themselves forward to see or touch this glamorous vision who seemed to them the materialization of the dreams of wealth and plenty conjured by the parcels and letters that came to so many of them from South America. Here she paused to make a speech in a gunpowder and explosives factory, there to lay a wreath on the tomb of Catholic kings—one wonders who had the choosing of her itinerary!—then to visit the Church of Nuestra Señora de Buen Aire, for which the city of Buenos Aires was named, then to a tobacco factory and to the Colonization Institute, where she gave a thousand grants of land to prospective Argentines, more museums, fetes, and religious services—and at last she was ready to leave Spain.

"My simple woman's heart," she broadcast to the women of Spain, "has begun to vibrate with the eternal chords of immortal Spain. I feel more Argentine because I find myself in the mother country. The supreme efflux of love can only be experienced by a woman when the vibrations of her heart coincide with the eternal rhythm of divine harmony. For that reason I now feel drunk with love and happiness because my simple woman's heart has begun to vibrate with the eternal chords of immortal Spain."

Drunk with love and happiness and vibrating with eternal chords she flew to Barcelona, where Franco and his wife and daughter, who had not accompanied her on her whirlwind tour of the provinces, were waiting to see her off; after a further spasm of activity, including a visit to the theater to see *A Midsummer Night's Dream* performed in Spanish—and how modest a little fantasy that must have seemed beside her own!—she took her plane to Rome, and Franco and Doña Carmen returned, one imagines wearily and thankfully, to Madrid.

Those few weeks in Spain were, to date, the most spectacular of her by no means drab career. Everywhere she had gone she had been received with enthusiasm not only by officials but by the people—an enthusiasm she was not to encounter again in generous quantities until she reached home. As in all totalitarian states it is difficult to judge how much if any of that enthusiasm was genuine. Certainly she and her hosts had done all they could to predispose the masses in her favor: the authorities by harping in press and radio on her womanly qualities, her charity and piety, and no doubt by strict injunctions that a cheering crowd must be on hand for all her appearances; she, by acts of largesse and grace—she pleaded the release of two prisoners who had placed a bomb in the Argentine Embassy in Madrid just before her arrival, and offered to stand godmother to any child born during her visit. Yet it was more likely her beauty, the almost legendary fame that had begun to surround her person and the fact that she represented—and so adequately!—the land of milk and honey to which so many of these poor people dreamed of escape, that drew the most enthusiastic crowds. The government officials, the clergy, and the nobility welcomed her because she represented a financial loan and so many shiploads of much needed wheat; but to the poor her presence promised more than food. She was the opulent promise of a land

119

of sunshine, of one city where the streets were still paved with gold. Only the rich and highly born took some offense at the somewhat patronizing graciousness with which she bestowed largesse on their poor and accepted their courtesies, and only a few saw the irony of the costly dresses that she cast aside after wearing them only once in a country where many of the poor she professed to love so much were starving.

There is one anecdote of her stay in Spain, quoted by the New York *Times,* which deserves to be remembered if only because it is one of the few anecdotes that show her in a favorable light. When Eva told Franco that she intended to send a shipload of wheat as a gift to the Spanish people, the Generalissimo looked surprised.

"But," he protested, perhaps offended by her condescension, "we don't need wheat. We have so much flour we don't know what to do with it."

Eva, who knew very well the value of such totalitarian boasts, retorted bluntly, "Why not try putting it in the bread!"

She sent the shipload of wheat as a gift to the people of Spain, but they have paid for it, time and again, by the exorbitant price they have had to pay for Argentine wheat since.

Next to the United States it was to Argentina that the peoples of Europe looked for the food they so badly needed and for the loans with which to pay for it; and everywhere that Eva traveled she went not so much as an emissary of peace, as she boasted, but of plenty, and it was as if her ripe golden presence were a promise of good things to come. As one French commentator put it, "Beautiful as Madame Perón is, she would be more welcome dressed as frozen beef." But hungry as were the Italians and the French, they did not look upon her visit with the naïve optimism the Spaniards had shown.

The preparations for her reception in Rome were not on the large official scale of those in Madrid. But the Argentine Embassy turned itself inside out to welcome her; a twelve-room suite was totally refurbished and refurnished to receive her—her bedroom was furnished in her favorite Louis XV style—and provided with a new oil painting of Perón, and one of Christ, the entrance newly tiled and the front of the building floodlit, all at a cost of more than two hundred and fifty thousand dollars. Before her appearance whole truckloads of gifts and flowers began to arrive; there is available no list of the presents she received on her European trip but they must have filled more than one hold of a ship.

But at the airport a crowd of only some fifteen thousand were gathered to meet her and many of these were government officials and members of the Argentine colony. There was none of that apparently spontaneous welcome she had received from the people in Spain, and although the Foreign Minister, Count Sforza, and the Signora de Gasperi, wife of the Premier, were there to receive her, the reception was not on the same high official level. She was not here as the official guest of the government and it was the wives rather than the officials themselves who attended her. Here, as everywhere she went, the Spanish Embassy was foremost in receiving her. And a further disillusionment awaited her. Outside the Argentine Embassy a small crowd had gathered. When she appeared on the balcony the shouts of "Perón! Perón!" in the rhythm of the old cry of "Duce!" were interrupted by shouts of *"Abbiamo fame!* We are hungry!"* There threatened a disturbance and the police had to interfere, arresting those who had so inconsiderately complained. Next day the Chief of Protocol called on Eva to apologize. Like Spain, Italy was hoping for a loan, but it did not do to have their distinguished guest disturbed by so sordid a display of want. The visit had not started well.

In her heart Eva had hoped for more honor from this visit than from her visit to Spain; but she was to be sorely disappointed. As the presentation of the Cross of Isabella had been the peak of her visit to Madrid, so was her audience with the Pope to be the climax of her stay in Rome. She was dressed for the occasion in the required long-sleeved black dress which clung most voluptuously to her figure, and over the elaborate coils of her hair she wore a black lace mantilla and on her bosom gleamed the blue and silver Cross

121

of Isabella; in the hand the costume had no doubt seemed as sober as the occasion demanded but on Eva it was transformed into what was scarcely discreet.

The story has it—and it seems a credible one, for Argentines almost never arrive on time—that Eva, on the arm of the one-eyed Prince Alessandro Ruspoli in elegant court knee breeches, arrived twenty minutes late, and that His Holiness, in dignified rebuke, kept her waiting exactly as long again. The Church did not go out of its way to honor her—certainly there was no suggestion of a marquisate; the audience, given in the papal library, lasted the half hour usually allotted to the wives of foreign potentates. The Pope thanked her for her generosity to the Italian poor but spoke with warmth of the ladies of the *Beneficencia,* many of whom he had met when as cardinal he visited Buenos Aires for the Eucharistic Congress. Eva must have had some difficulty in maintaining her reverent attitude at that moment, for there was no mention of any recognition for herself. Never totally disconcerted, she hinted that she would be happy to take some token of the Pope's favor to Perón; to which he replied with imperturbable graciousness that he would indeed be glad to honor the Argentine President but that the decoration would, of course, have to go through the usual channels. Indeed, next day the Cross of the Order of Pope Pius IX, not quite the highest decoration at the Pope's disposal, was dispatched to the Argentine Ambassador for delivery to Perón. To Eva His Holiness gave a rosary, the usual gift on such occasions, and after she had presented the members of her suite, the party retired. Perhaps it was that Eva visited the Sistine Chapel and the Borgia Palace and the Basilica of St. Peter's where she prayed—one supposes for patience—and that such tours are notoriously trying on the temper and the feet, but it is said that when she got back to her fine rooms in the Embassy she took off her shoes and threw them at Alberto Dodero's head.

Although the Italian government did as much as was its official duty in entertaining her—the Premier escorted her to a performance of *Aïda* given at the Baths of Caracalla under the stars when Eva, with more congruity, was able to wear her fox cape although, heaven knows, it was hot enough in Rome, and he entertained her at lunch and presented her with white orchids—it all fell a little flat after the fanfare in Madrid; and there was a certain note of aggressiveness in the speech she broadcast to the Italian women, "I have a name that has become a battle cry for women the world over—Evita!" This does not seem to have the same vibrations as "the simple woman's heart" of which she spoke so movingly in Spain. Her trip was cut short; the official reason given was that her doctor ordered her to rest, which, considering her schedule, may well have been true, but rumor had it that outbreaks of hostility were feared; the extremist leaders, right and left, wore mourning during her stay. Whatever the real reason, she went, accompanied by Count Sforza and her retinue, to recuperate for a day or two on the Italian lakes. Before the beauties of Lake Como she made the inevitable Argentine exclamation, *"Que maravilla!"*

Eva's visit to Paris seems to have marked the point at which she conquered the lack of social assurance that had troubled her. It must have presented something of an ordeal to her, for however scornfully she derided the "degenerate" oligarchs and their culture she was not without fear of them; she would not have set out to destroy them with such implacability if she had not feared them. And now it was into the very stronghold of their culture she must go; Paris was the home of so many wealthy Argentines and so full of their friends. Moreover, Paris had been for so long the arbiter of fashion, had had even more influence on the fashions of Buenos Aires perhaps than on those of any other city in the world, that she must have felt some qualms, unconscious perhaps, in the one area in which she had hitherto felt secure; at least, it was not in Madrid where her reception had been so magnificent that Eva displayed her finest clothes; these she had reserved for Paris of whose reception she was unsure.

She need not have been so uneasy. If the French were not quite so reverent as she could have wished, at least they gave her beauty

123

all the admiration she craved. In Spain she had been a symbol; in France she was a woman—even if it was not forgotten that she was the woman who could grant them bread. In Spain she had distributed largesse in the "clean homes of the happily smiling people"; in Italy the poor cried, *"Abbiamo fame!"* under her balcony and were put in jail; but in France her hosts at an official banquet served her with bread not very palatably made of corn to remind her of their people's need. The French could not quite be made to believe that her presence was indispensable at the Quai d'Orsay for the signing of the agreement granting them a six-billion-peso loan —the Argentine Ambassador was there and capable of signing— but if a beautiful woman chose to believe herself necessary to the affairs of state, they were the last people to refuse to humor her. But there was no spreading of her picture and her story all over the front pages of the newspaper. In their own country no woman could have gained quite the arbitrary power that Eva was to hold and it was difficult for so mature a people to take her seriously. But if she did not command all their serious respect, from the moment of her landing she had their full attention. Foreign Minister Bidault, who had gone to Orly airport to meet her, gave her radiant, white-clad presence one startled, appraising look and then bent discreetly to kiss her hand.

Only at the reception at the *Cercle d'Amérique Latine* was she treated with the deference to which she had become accustomed and there it was the diplomats of South America who were presented to her. They, at least, had begun to learn that the deference she demanded was no pretty woman's whim. She wore for this occasion the most sumptuous costume of them all; she was clad in gold from head to foot, a cloth of gold gown that clung to her body like a mermaid's skin, a gold lamé veil draped over the ripe rolls of glossy hair and hanging to her train, heavy jewels at her throat and her ears and her wrists and her hands—everywhere that a jewel could be worn—and gold sandals studded with sparkling stones. No wonder the Latin-American diplomats who were presented to her behaved as if she were royalty, the ladies retreating three steps and

124

curtsying. But later, after midnight, when she went to have supper at the Pré Catalan in the Bois de Boulogne, the undisciplined Parisian crowd clambered on the tables to catch a glimpse of this wonderful dame in the golden gown and gave voice to their admiration in the most appreciative and disrespectful way. Moreover, those who set out to entertain her unofficially seemed to have no notion of the seriousness of her mission and expected her to enjoy herself just like any other women in the night clubs and the salons of the couturiers. The couturiers hung about the lobby of the Hotel Ritz where she was staying, ready to lay the whole of their collections at her feet, if she would favor them; but to them she said that her mission in Paris was too important and she had no time to waste on dress. It might have been that even her acquisitiveness was satiated at last, but it seems that here in Paris was the beginning of a new and stranger obsession.

For a woman who had begun to take herself so seriously there were many petty annoyances in Paris. At a night club she visited with friends a "camel" in the floor show presented her with a bouquet; since it was the rear end of the "camel" that made the presentation the affronted Eva got up and walked out. The food in the Ritz was not prepared to her liking—and for the sake of her figure she had to watch her diet carefully; it was much too rich, and she had to send one of her maids down to the kitchen to tell the chef just how she wished her food prepared. One can imagine how amiably such instruction was received by Monsieur le Chef! The heat in Paris was excessive and the Parisians had not the South American custom of keeping the rooms shuttered against the sun. But perhaps most tiresome of all was the fact that some wealthy Argentines living in Paris, some staying in the very hotel, had refused to pay their respects to her. Heat and fatigue and pique were too much for her, the fatigue alone would have been too much for women of stronger constitutions, and one night she fainted when she returned to the hotel. Her program had to be cut short again; a visit to the Louvre was canceled and Father Benitez had to deputize for her over the air. She left Paris and went for a few days of rest to Alberto Dodero's chalet in Biarritz. But she was incapable of rest; to relax, to pause for a moment in her spiral climb was to feel herself slipping back into oblivion again. She set off on a lightning tour of the French Riviera and from there went on to Switzerland.

There she was to receive the most disrespectful reception of all; Switzerland was not as hungry as Spain and Italy and France. When the President drove with her from the station at Berne, stones smashed the windshield of their car. Later, less dangerous but perhaps more insulting, tomatoes were thrown at her, splattering her dress. Through both incidents Eva sat, pale and composed and furious. Official apologies were tendered to her; the miscreants were a couple of fanatics—Communists, no doubt—and were already in jail. She did not ask for their release. In a pet she cut her visit short and went to spend a day or two in St. Moritz.

Eva had not been able to enjoy even the most pride-satisfying part of the fanfaronade without preoccupation with affairs at home. She and Perón had long midnight conversations by trans-Atlantic telephone. Some say they used a high frequency ultrashort-wave radio telephone so that it could not be tapped, but the Opposition claim to have tapped their conversations regularly. It is said that he implored her to return—and he did show signs of nervousness while she was away—and that she berated him for the attentions he was showing to a certain lovely young woman whom Eva herself had recently crowned queen of a grape festival in the north. Whether she had such a cause for preoccupation or not—and a serious preoccupation it could not have been, for Eva always showed herself capable of demolishing any rival in less time than it takes to squash a roach—there certainly was cause for anxiety in the pressure the Army were bringing to bear on Perón to make his wife retire from public life. Perón himself seems to have been the one most disturbed, for although Eva gave, as one of her reasons for not visiting England, the need for her to hurry home to attend to urgent affairs she did not, in fact, show herself in any particular hurry to return. Her trip to Europe seemed to have supplied her with what little arrogance and assurance she lacked.

More trivial than the difficulties at home but no less annoying was the moot question of her visit to London. When her trip to Europe was first discussed it was suggested to Whitehall that she would be graciously willing to accept an invitation to Buckingham Palace; after all, the British were in need of Argentine beef. The suggestion was not received with any great enthusiasm by the British authorities, while some of the London Press said bluntly that she would not be welcome there since she had been so very welcome in Fascist Spain. British businessmen, anxious, and with good reason, over their investments in Argentina, tried to smooth matters over. Unofficially she would be very welcome indeed, they intimated, and the Queen would be graciously pleased to invite her to tea at the Palace. One could wish that she had visited London if only that so gloriously an ill-sorted tea-party might have taken place! But an invitation to tea was not enough. She wanted, it was rumored, to stay in the Palace itself. British Royalty replied with not too strong an accent of regret that, alas! they would be out of town. Eva, tired of being treated as if she were practically a no-body, refused to go to England at all. It has been said that in later bargaining between Britain and Argentina this rebuff added considerably to the price of beef, but there was no sign that Eva was ready to treat the more appreciative Spaniards with greater generosity when it came to haggling over the price of wheat.

Eva was now in the unusual position of having time on her hands, for she wanted her return to coincide with the Inter-American Defense Conference that was to be held in Rio and which George Marshall was to attend. Juan Bramuglia was to represent Argentina at the conference and Eva had already begun to look with suspicion at the reputation he was making for himself. To time her return to coincide with the conference she took the plane to Dakar, stopping briefly at Lisbon en route, and from there took the S.S. *Buenos Aires,* one of Dodero's ships.

Rio de Janiero had been well prepared for her reception; the

Argentine Embassy there had mailed thousands of postcards urging Brazilians to unite in preparing for her arrival and to acclaim her as the Leader of Women. Yet the propaganda seems to have had no very great effect, for beyond a dinner given in her honor by the Brazilian Foreign Minister at the Palacio de Itamaraty, at which she was decorated with the *Orden Nacional do Cruziero do Sul,* her reception was staged chiefly by the Argentine Colony. The Argentine Embassy gave a magnificent ball for her to which all the local grandees and diplomats attending the conference were invited. George Marshall excused himself on the grounds that he had his speech to prepare. But Eva herself went to listen to his speech at Quintandinha next day, accompanied by Juan Bramuglia, with whom she seemed to be on the friendliest terms, and listened to it with her air of intense concentration. Later she drank champagne with Marshall and Bramuglia with an equally intense amiability before she took off on the last lap of her journey.

The manner of her reception at home had been under some discussion; posters announcing her return were plastered all over the city for days before. It was not easy to assemble a large enough crowd at the military or civil airports which lay outside the city; a bigger and noisier reception could be arranged if she arrived in the port which is the entrance to the city itself. And to make sure that the crowd would be large enough the enrollment cards of the workers—as necessary to them as a social security card is to the American worker—were taken from them to be returned at the port, while trainloads of shirtless ones were brought in from the provinces.

This change in program entailed the breaking of her journey in Montevideo. She had been in Uruguay in her early and impecunious days when she had sometimes crossed over to spend a week end with a friend at the seaside there, as so many more conventional Argentines did. But now she must have contemplated her visit with some qualms. The small republic of Uruguay, which lies just across the river—certainly, it is the widest river in the world—from Buenos Aires has throughout the Perón regime remained more in-

128

dependent than any other Latin American country of Argentine influence, and has given harbor to those of the Argentine opposition who have had to flee their country, dozens of whom in times of mass arrests slip across in small boats and private planes to be made welcome by the friendly Uruguayans. Eva's route from the airport to the city was lined, almost shoulder to shoulder, with a police and military guard.

Next morning she saw Buenos Aires, dazzling white in the bright sun and floating, as it seems to float, on the muddy waters of the Río de la Plata. As her ship pulled into harbor, past the old yacht club of the oligarchs, the sirens of all the ships in port began to wail, tugs boomed their welcome, flags and pennants fluttered out from masts and shrouds, and on the dockside and in the wide streets leading to the docks a mass of shirtless ones chanted her name. The crowd may have been bullied into attendance by the confiscation of their *libretas* and bribed by free travel, food and entertainment, but neither bribery nor threat accounted for all the fervor with which they chanted the names of Eva and Perón. She has exercised, and still does exercise to an extent the opposition do not like to recognize, an extraordinary sway over the more simple of her fellow countrymen, the same mystic and romantic sway that Royalty have exercised over the simple peoples of Europe in the past, that stars from Hollywood and baseball players exercise over some Americans. The educated man can escape from the anxieties of living through books or music or art; the less cultured, whose existence is often both more full of anxieties and more drab, must see his dream in flesh and blood. Eva has been the symbol of this dream to many thousands, perhaps millions, of simple people who have no understanding of politics at all; and she will continue to personify their dreams after death, until a newer and better dream is offered them.

Perón, of course, was on the dockside to welcome her. There had been talk of his setting forth in the presidential yacht to meet her but neither could forgo so dramatic a piece of publicity as their embrace on the dockside occasioned. Eva stood on the bridge of the ship waving and wiping the tears from her eyes; and there were tears in Perón's eyes—in Argentina it is quite natural for a man to weep.

She must have felt a vast sense of relief to be home again, not only because here she could be sure of her reception, but also because to the uneducated girl she had been only a few years before the world beyond Argentina was unknown and unimaginable, the map of the world was meaningless. A young girl who came not so very far from Junín at about the same time that Eva came and with much the same background, to work as a domestic help in Buenos Aires, was utterly amazed at her first sight of the ships and docks and the river beyond. She took the river for the same one as some Russian emigrants had told her they had lived beside at home; when it was explained that that river was on the other side of the world and that the world was round, she burst into the most spontaneous and infectious laughter and cried, "Oh, I may be only a poor country girl but you can't fool me like that!"

No doubt Eva had been taught at school that the world was round but by all standards she had returned from an amazing and wearing expedition and she could not entirely have outgrown a country-bred fear of foreign travel.

But now she was home again and the church bells were ringing out. A mass of thanksgiving was held in the Cathedral, colored pigeons—they dye them pink and blue—were freed to whirl and settle and whirl up again into the glittering sky; from airplanes olive twigs, tied with ribbons of the flags of all nations, were scattered over the city. *Democracia,* her own newspaper, printed four pages of her photographs, and four pages even in the most favored press was, with the newsprint shortage, almost half the issue. No statesman or general having negotiated the peace of the Western World could have been received with more acclaim. And it was evident that thus they thought of her, or she thought of herself, for *Clarin,* a Peronista newspaper, announced rather sententiously, "Evita has done for her country what has never been done before by any other ambassador. All countries are now waiting for her message of love and peace, and clamoring for her solution to end the misery and hunger in the world."

But in the more fashionable movie houses the pictures of her arrival were greeted with boos and whistles that caused the theater to be closed, or with a dead silence followed by wild cheering for whatever picture followed hers, whether it were a football match or a champion bull. And in the north the independent newspaper *Intransigente* was closed for publishing a cartoon which showed Eva being told that it was with rotten tomatoes the Swiss always welcomed their guests.

On the dockside Eva and Perón embraced emotionally in full view of the crowd. "After several months' absence," she said—she had been away just over two months—"it is with profound emotion that I return to this my country where I left my three great loves, my homeland, my shirtless ones, and my beloved General Perón!"

greater illusionary success. That her role as reformer or evangelist was not based on realities made the power she derived from it no less real and dangerous, nor her belief in her fantasy necessarily less sincere.

The change in her was not at once evident; she was still the luscious and disturbing blonde who had brought whistles from Parisian boulevardiers and languishing glances from young Spanish officers; more than ever she seemed to be the Doña María Eva Duarte de Perón of the tightly swathed and low-cut satin gowns and massed jewelry; there was little evidence of the new, thin, brittle, infinitely more destructive and more tragic Eva Perón of the scraped-back hair and trim tailor-mades that she was to become.

On her return she ordered the Señora de Sosa Molina, wife of the pudgy Minister of Defense, to hold a reception for her which the wives and daughters of the Army officers were requested to attend—and the invitation was something more than a request. The reception was to be held in the *Circulo Militar,* the officers' club before whose imposing gates the words, *To the gallows with Perón!* had once been chalked. The élite of Argentine society saw this reception as but another futile attempt on Eva's part to enter their esoteric ranks and could afford to be amused by it since, but for a few exceptions, the military were not of their kin. Possibly some desire for social recognition did motivate Eva's demand for the reception, but since in her absence it had been the military authorities who had tried to bring about her retirement into private life, it is more probable that such a reception in such a place was a gesture of imperiousness, a flourish of the whip to bring the military lions slinking into place. Not all the ladies were willing to attend; some pleaded a convenient indisposition but there were about a thousand, concerned for their husbands' careers, who milled around an Eva resplendent in a velvet picture hat with bird of paradise plumes.

One might have supposed that Eva's appetite for rich clothing, furs, and jewelry would have been slaked to saturation point after her return from Europe. Certainly from that time on, avid for possession as she continued to be, she began to flaunt her rich clothing less and less; even her hair was turned a less brassy blond. The change in her appearance coincided with her new role but that she was not changed fundamentally was proved by the wealth she continued to accumulate, which was the subject of bitter disputes in the Chamber of Deputies. Generous as her salary had become while she was still an employee and not yet the director of Radio Belgrano, it could in no way account for her fabulous expenditure. Neither she nor Perón had been in possession of any personal fortune when they met; neither his Army salary nor his salary as President, which was then under two thousand dollars a month, could have supplied the forty thousand dollars she had begun to spend annually on clothes from Paris alone—she sent her own "couturier envoy" to buy models from Dior, Balmain, Fath, and Rochas. Perón's salary—and she had no salary now—could not have filled the three large rooms in the Residency lined with roomy closets packed with hats and shoes and dresses, or bought the fur coats she owned by the dozen; she had an ermine bedjacket as well as an ermine coat, an ostrich feather cloak and an azure mink she boasted had only one duplicate. The story runs that in her early and still impecunious days she visited her tailor, intent on persuading him to make her something new while her bill was still unpaid. While she was waiting—those were still the days when she could be kept waiting—she picked up a swatch of a dozen or so sample furs, mink, sables, ermine and all the luscious lot. When the tailor turned to her at last, demanding payment for his overdue bill, she flourished the furs in his face, crying furiously, "You fool! You pester me for that miserable bill. Don't you know that one day I shall own a coat of each one of these furs!" The tailor, impressed, agreed to make her new cloth coat before she settled her bill. Whether the story is true or not, she acquired the furs. Argentines, who, like others in this hemisphere, are fond of bragging that they have the biggest and the best of everything, boasted that her collection of jewelry was the most valuable in the world, since Cleopatra's day by one account. Much of it was given to her by officials of the government who wished to curry favor or by labor unions

135

who collected the price of the gift peso by peso from their members; some she got by more piratical methods. Among her closest friends in those days were Alberto Dodero, an enormously wealthy shipping magnate, and his young American wife. Dodero had had a monopoly of the river shipping and he planned to start a commercial airline to Europe and had already spent hundreds of thousands of pesos trying to get the necessary permit for his enterprise. One day Eva rather pointedly admired a diamond ring on his wife's finger, worth a trifle of some twenty thousand dollars. Dodero immediately whipped it off his wife's finger and presented it to Eva. There was no more difficulty over his permit. Alberto Dodero has since died and his shipping lines and his air service belong to the government, and, in 1951, Eva was fighting with his heirs for possession of his chalet in Biarritz where she stayed on her European trip and which, she claimed, he promised her.

When Eva first became *la señora Presidenta* her methods of acquiring a wardrobe were equally arbitrary. Before her trip to Europe she had ordered some twenty dresses from a shop in Calle Florida. The dresses were sent with a bill, but the check that was eventually returned was for only half the amount. When the couturiere pointed out the discrepancy she was told that she should consider herself honored enough by the First Lady's patronage. The foolish woman continued to protest that she could not afford to give away her models, even to the wife of the President. An inspector arrived at her establishment, found some minor infringement of regulations and the police closed her business down for a week. When Eva used similar tactics with a fashionable furrier—again she paid only half the amount on the bill—he, very wisely, did not protest.

The presidents of Argentina have two official residences; one is the old Palacio Unzué which stands on the barranca, the old riverbank, and the only "hill" in the city, and looks out across the wide Avenida Alvear and the trees of Palermo Park towards the river. It was bought for the presidential residency in Castillo's day and is still furnished in the old somber and ornate style. The lawns of the palace run down the slope and are planted with magnolias and the lovely blue-flowered jacaranda. This is where the Peróns usually resided and it was guarded by a special squad whose wailing sirens warned the traffic police in Avenida Alvear to clear the way for the señora's car. The second residence is in Olivos, a suburb a few miles north of the city whose park runs down the slope of the same barranca. Part of the park has been turned into a children's playground and on the grounds Perón gave barbecue parties to entertain provincial governors or party leaders, all in their shirt sleeves, with Eva playing at being the simple hostess who had herself seen to the baking of the meat patties that follow the dishes of cold meats, of soup, of pickled partridge and a dozen others that are no more than the side dishes of a good Argentine barbecue.

Besides these official residences the Peróns acquired a number of private estates. With the first big money Eva made on the movies in 1945 she bought an old property in the not very fashionable suburb of Colegiales, ten minutes from the city. She must have bought it before her ambitions went higher than the stage since the site is so much more convenient than fashionable. She pulled down the old house and built herself a new one which could not have been paid for out of her earnings; by the time the house was built the property was worth a quarter of a million dollars; it had a cold storage vault where her furs could be kept, and an art dealer was sent to Europe in search of paintings and objets d'art with which to decorate it. It was here that Eva and Perón entertained most intimately, here they had birthday parties and sometimes family reunions.

In San Vicente, another of the suburbs along the barranca to the north and a much more fashionable one, Perón bought himself a property of some forty-five acres and built himself a house which has been the subject of bitter governmental debate and the cause of the expulsion of at least one opposition deputy from the Chamber. The house has a salon for the private showing of American movies, which are not always shown to the public—there is another movie salon in the Palacio Unzué—and two swimming pools, one indoors and one out, with machinery to make artificial waves. Architects, landscape gardeners and experts of all kinds were called from Uruguay, from Ecuador and from the United States to further the design of the house and the park through which flamingoes, storks, *ñandus*—the swift little ostriches of the Pampas—guanacos and llamas roam. But what has caused most discussion, besides the three quarters of a mile of paved road to the house constructed at public expense, is the impressive wall by which the house and gardens are surrounded, twelve feet high and nearly one and a half miles long. It is protected by an electric alarm system and, alone, must have cost more than eight hundred thousand pesos, which, in those days before the devaluation of the peso, was nearly two hundred thousand dollars. It is significant that it was Perón's property and not Eva's that was thus fortified—within the house there is an armory—and made into what might be used as the base for a last stand.

The Peróns had a further property in the hills of Córdoba bought, so Dr. Ernesto Sammartino tells us in his book,[1] from money raised among the employees of the Secretariat of Posts and Telegraph as a mark of homage and appreciation towards the general and his wife. Later they acquired an *estancia* near Canuelos, south of Buenos Aires; it was the shooting lodge of some young millionaire, but the laguna where duck and snipe once rested has been filled in and another pleasure park designed

These are but the better known among their properties; a full list of what each owned was perhaps not even known to the other. That both Perón and Eva were prudent enough to hoard money away in other countries is to be understood, but how much they deposited was naturally a matter of the greatest secrecy. It was said that they had fortunes accumulating in Switzerland, Uruguay, and the United States and large properties in Brazil.

Over and above the expenses of their various estates and the funds salted away in foreign countries, it is difficult to account for

[1] *La Verdad sobre la Situación Argentina.*

138

the money the Peróns spent in buying up newspapers and radio stations, or that spent on publicity and political campaigning, on the charity which Eva distributed before the Eva Perón Foundation was established, to say nothing of her personal expenses and the expense of her European trip.

When Perón assumed the presidency he made, as was the custom, a formal declaration of his property which was sealed and put away in the custody of the Attorney General. Eva made a like declaration of her own property. Perón declared that he owned the house in San Vicente, a Cadillac and some small property he had inherited from his father, probably his share of the land in the south. What Eva declared has not been discovered but there is a story that Perón, seeing that she declared no more than a million pesos, exclaimed in disgust, "Is that all you've got!" Eva is supposed to have retorted grimly, "I spent the rest in making you a president."

When a member of the Opposition demanded in the Chamber of Deputies that an investigation should be made into the sources of the Peróns' wealth, a ceremony was made of having Perón's sealed declaration opened in the presence of ministers, officials and newsmen. He would prove, he declared indignantly, that he was not a thief as the Opposition claimed, and that he had owned the San Vicente property, which was the base of their accusations, before he came into office and had mortgaged it to pay for the improvements on it. Eva's declaration was not opened and the ceremony failed to convince the Opposition since it did not explain how a property worth three million pesos—since the devaluation of the peso it must be worth ten times as much—came into the possession of a man who had had to live on his colonel's pay. A short while later, in a speech he made before the railroad workers' union, Perón pooh-poohed the idea that the San Vicente property could be worth so much and said he would be glad to sell it to anyone who would offer fifty thousand pesos for it. Radical Deputy Cattaneo, who had demanded the investigation, promptly offered to buy it at that price, adding courteously that he would be glad to allow the President to continue to make use of it during his term in office.

Perón was extricated from this predicament shortly afterwards when Colonel Cattaneo, whose inquiries had become persistent, was expelled from the Chamber and had to escape across the river to Uruguay.

Probably the sources of Eva's and Perón's fortunes will never be fully unraveled—unless Miguel Miranda is writing his memoirs over in Uruguay. But it is necessary to know only a little about the country's finances for a surmise to be made as to the origins of their wealth. Graft and fraud among Argentine officialdom is unfortunately no novelty. Hipólito Irigoyen stands out as one of the few who come to the forefront of politics and remained a poor man. But at no other time in Argentine history has it reached the proportions of this last decade; with Perón's policy of industrializing a fundamentally rural country, it is bringing to ruin a nation that was potentially one of the richest in the world, and bringing within sight of want a city where, ten years ago, if bread and butter was given to a beggar he threw it to the dogs and the dogs sniffed at it and let it lie because they were full fed on meat. Now milk is bought by the cupful—and some days cannot be bought at all—and *coima* must be paid to the butcher before he will produce a good piece of steak in a city where, ten years ago, tenderloin could be bought for fifteen cents a pound and pasteurized milk was four and a half cents a quart.

Perón had, while he was still president-elect, formed the Central Bank with powers that reduced other banks virtually to subsidiaries; it was necessary to obtain a permit from the Central Bank for any loan or foreign exchange. He made Miguel Miranda, an obese, shrewd businessman who owned a dozen or so factories, head of the Central Bank. In the same year, 1946, Miranda formed a colossal state trading agency, known as I.A.P.I.[2]—*Instituto Argentino de Promoción del Intercambio*—which was to control all foreign trade. Through I.A.P.I. and the Central Bank the Peróns—for Eva was not left out of this—and Miranda had a stranglehold on all business in the country. On the pretext that a government agency

[2]Pronounced "Yappy."

140

could much better bargain abroad for good prices for Argentine meat and grain I.A.P.I. bought up all the farmers' produce. Indeed they did obtain much higher prices—though in some cases, as in that of the linseed oil and tanning extract they would have sold to the United States, they held out for so much that they lost the market—but the farmers got no advantage from it; the wheat that I.A.P.I. bought from the Argentine farmer at $1.35 a bushel was sold in Europe at prices that went as high as $5.75 a bushel and the Argentine farmer was almost as much a loser in the deal as the hungry European. Perón has claimed that with the profits I.A.P.I. has made the price of food in Argentina has been kept down, the country has been enormously developed, and the necessary machinery has been imported.

It is true that the price of food has remained relatively low, especially when judged by standards of exchange; milk that cost four and a half cents a liter—that is, just over a quart—ten years ago could still be bought for five cents in 1951; but in 1941 four and a half cents was twenty centavos and in 1951 four cents was eighty centavos. The cost of living rose a hundred and fifty-five per cent between 1946 and 1950 and continued to rise three per cent per month in 1951. To the American tourist visiting Buenos Aires food seems both astonishingly cheap and plentiful, for his dollar is now worth over twenty pesos—it went over twenty-six in 1951—when it was once worth only just over four, and the hotel where he stays will be well supplied. But the Argentine housewife, whose husband's salary has perhaps not risen quite so fast as the cost of living, has to stand in line to buy half a pound—she is not allowed more—of coffee; has to buy sugar and rice by the cupful and quite often cannot buy milk or butter at all; and Buenos Aires has over a hundred square miles of dairy farm land in its backyard! Early in 1952 Perón declared that there would be one meatless day a week,[3] explaining in his persuasive way that this was to accustom the people to a more balanced diet—the average Argentine consumes about double the amount of meat most Americans

[3] Later a second meatless day a week was announced.

141

do and is the biggest meat-eater in the world. Only a severe shortage could have forced Perón into an economy that must be so unpopular with the meat-eating *criollo* workman who cannot, in any case, afford the substitutes, for fish, chicken and eggs are comparatively dear.

The Peronista press lately boasted that Perón has completed 76,230 public works and with characteristic lack of data says no more than that 70,000 of these are in the interior. The Opposition have accused him of confining these works to the cities and of neglecting the interior of the country which stands in so much need of development. In and around Buenos Aires evidence of such construction is on every hand; new avenues, parks, public buildings, roads, bridges—many of which, however, had been initiated or planned before Perón's appearance—and all the well-advertised buildings of the Eva Perón Foundation are there to dazzle the beholder's eye. But take a train for a few hours' run out of the city and you will see that the small farmer lives with no more convenience than he did ten or twenty years ago and that the pueblo is almost as little changed. The only farmers in Argentina whose methods had been up-to-date were some of the landed aristocracy and the large foreign-financed land companies; they bred their cattle scientifically even if they exploited their men. The Peronista policy was to harass, tax and sometimes expropriate the large landowners and, as Perón promised, "give the land back to those who worked it." Unfortunately he offered very little incentive for anyone to work it. The increase in price for grain, meat and dairy produce was microscopic in comparison to the increase in wages, taxation, and the cost of living; the tenant farmer could afford neither to hire labor nor buy the machinery that might make help unnecessary; even his sons and daughters, upon whom, as a sharecropper in the past, he had been so dependent, were lured to the city by promise of a higher wage and gayer life. It became more economical to graze cattle than to plant grain and, presently, more economical to fatten steers than to milk cows. But many of the

142

farmers themselves, among them numbers of emigrants that had been brought over from Italy and Spain and settled on the land, began to drift into the city. Two years of drought and the greater consumption of a crowded city did nothing to make food more plentiful. Perón boasted that there were nearly two million more head of cattle in 1949 than in 1946, but the Opposition claimed there had been a decrease of ten million head—and the "meatless day" seemed to bear the Opposition out.

It is true that during the first years of his term I.A.P.I. had imported a vast amount of machinery, but whether it most benefited the farmer or the officials who doled out permits for its import is a matter for speculation. In 1947 and 1948 the docksides of Buenos Aires were cluttered with imported machinery which lay there for months to rust and rot either because it was inappropriate to Argentine conditions or the price was beyond the would-be purchaser. There were endless scandals attached to I.A.P.I.'s purchase of foreign machinery. In 1947 I.A.P.I. bought five thousand Empire tractors in which deal some twenty million pesos were said to have stuck to fingers on the way; the tractors were unsuitable to Argentina and only a few were sold. More than four thousand jeeps which I.A.P.I. had paid for as new cost as much to be reconditioned; twenty were turned over for the use of the staff on *Democracia,* Eva's paper, and the rest sold as scrap. Three thousand railway cars were bought and then discovered to be the wrong gauge and left overseas. Plans were made to transport an entire aluminum factory from Italy to Argentina, an enterprise that involved some eleven million pesos, until it was discovered that there was no such factory—and involved in this scandal were Perón's co-ordinator for his five-year plan and the chief of the presidential bodyguard. The most notorious scandals have surrounded Juancito Duarte, Eva's brother, whose finaglings on the black market brought the peso tumbling from twenty-two to twenty-six to the dollar in a few days; he had been granted the license to import some three thousand Fiats and American cars, but not having been granted the exchange with which to pay for them he bought dollars over in Uruguay. It is such speculations that have created a parvenu aristocracy who are in no way preferable to the old. Juancito himself, who became a millionaire overnight, plays the role of the *niño-bien* of the old oligarchy, with new cars, smart parties, expensive gifts to little actresses and the inevitable night club brawls.

From the start Miguel Miranda had been Eva's mentor in affairs of finance. How fully I.A.P.I. financed the establishment of the Perón regime will perhaps never be known; it was through I.A.P.I. that they had gained control of press and radio and with Miranda's help that Eva had purchased her own press. With Miranda she had formed a company for the import of medical supplies and equipment which eventually gave her the monopoly of imported drugs. No doubt he advised her, when the Eva Perón Foundation was first mooted, on the most painless way of extracting money from unwilling pockets; certainly the deals in which they co-operated gave her the experience necessary for the development of the Foundation which was to make her one of the wealthiest women in the world. They had one thing in common; the army officials disapproved heartily of both of them and did their best to get them out. In one case they brought pressure to bear on Perón to revoke a deal in tinplate which Miranda had signed and which the Army authorities felt was, with its perquisites, within their domain. Miranda is no longer in office. He is over in Uruguay with, if not of, the exiles. But it was Eva and not the Army who got him out.

It seems that Miranda had come to believe that the Peróns could not manage without him. He might have learnt caution from the high-handed way in which Eva had dealt with Maroglio. Maroglio, who pictured himself as Miranda's rival, was briefly the president of the Central Bank; neither Eva nor Miranda liked him but for a while they made use of him. On a trip to Washington, Maroglio was given the reception usually accorded to visiting officials, but when the American Ambassador mentioned this to

144

Miranda, Miranda laughed and said that it was not at all necessary as Maroglio was to be dismissed immediately on his return. The Ambassador pointed out that this would not do at all since it would affect the standing of any further officials sent to Washington. Miranda was insisting that Maroglio was not on official business but was traveling on dubious business of his own, when Eva came into the room. She wanted to know at once, as she always does, what the discussion was about and Miranda explained that the Ambassador thought it unwise to dismiss Maroglio immediately on his return.

"Oh, that son of a beech!" cried Eva, using for the benefit of the Ambassador the only English expression she knew. "Well, *amigo,* how long do you think we should wait before we fire him?"

"Well, sixty days, at least . . ."

"Right! We fire him at the end of sixty days."

Perhaps Miranda regarded Eva's airy dismissal of Maroglio as a sign of his own firm establishment in her grace, although there had already been signs of his eclipse. There was a scandal over a big textile deal with Brazil which had to be called off, although a twenty-million-peso bonus had already disappeared. Radical Deputy Araya, who had demanded an inquiry into the dealings of I.A.P.I., had been shot at and dangerously wounded by plain-clothes police and had had, like Colonel Cattaneo, to flee to Uruguay.

Miranda had the temerity to describe Perón as a politician only out for his own ends; he did this at a dinner party among foreigners, but one of the foreigners, a visiting Mexican senator who admired Perón, reported the conversation. This in itself—and Miranda must have known it—was enough to make the bitterest enemy of Eva, for she could allow no more criticism of Perón than she could of herself.

A few days later—it was at the end of December 1948—Miranda rashly told visiting wool merchants that it was Eva and not he who was responsible for the unfavorable terms of their contracts. This they reported to Eva, and only a few days after this it was

145

offended their conservatism. Whether she exercised more power than Perón may perhaps never be decided; she used her power more flamboyantly and more vindictively; and when she wanted to be rid of a minister or a deputy that man went, whether Perón wanted to protest or not, even though her action were undiplomatic to an awkward degree.

In December 1949, Spain's Ambassador to Argentina, the Count of Motrico, resigned. He had wanted to do so before, but Franco had refused to accept his resignation; now Franco threatened to break off economic relations with Argentina in spite of the need they had for Argentine wheat, and the hard bargain that I.A.P.I. had driven with them was not Franco's only reason for anger. It appeared that the Count had spoken too freely, boasting that he had paid for much of the wheat by conferring honors on the Peróns. Eva, never too friendly towards any diplomat with a title, called him to her office. When he was announced she cried, loud enough for him to hear, "Let the old pimp cool his heels! Show someone else in first." It was after this incident that shipments of wheat to Spain were held up, the Ambassador resigned and the relations between the two countries became strained.

It was due to Eva's influence that the only man in the Peronista government to have gained a reputation abroad for ability and integrity is out of office now. Eva's resentment against Juan Atilio Bramuglia had dated from the earliest days. Before Perón's time Bramuglia had been legal adviser for the Railway Unions, the most strongly organized in the country, so that he was well suited to become Perón's chief assistant in the Secretariat of Labor. In those days the rumor was that he and Eva had seen Perón's possibilities as a demogogic leader and, together, had groomed him for the role, but from a longer perspective this does not seem likely. Certainly he helped Perón gain his control of the Railway Unions; perhaps, like Reyes who organized the Meat Packers' Unions, he believed in Perón's promises. But when Perón was taken off to the island of Martín García, Bramuglia was not one of the first to rally around Eva. It is said that he refused to issue a writ of habeas corpus to

148

have Perón returned, as Eva demanded of him, and that she never forgave him for this. How ever this was, when Perón became President he named Bramuglia his Foreign Minister, and an excellent choice it proved to be, for Bramuglia gained not only the respect of diplomats in Europe and the United States but of anti-Peronistas at home. Bramuglia, who had recently increased Eva's displeasure by advising against her trip to Spain, increased it further by the fame he gained for himself as chairman of the Security Council of the United Nations; he had been made welcome both in London and Washington, neither of which had shown themselves eager to entertain Eva—she hinted more than once that she would be pleased to accept an invitation to the United States. Moreover, there had been talk of conferring on Bramuglia the Nobel Peace Prize, for which Eva had tried, and failed, to get Perón proposed. On Eva's return from Europe she had met Bramuglia at the Inter-American Defense Conference in Rio, had listened to Marshall's speech at his side, drunk champagne with him later and seemed altogether to be on the best of good terms with him. But no sooner was she back in Argentina than it became evident that she was out to remove him from office. The Peronista press, led by *Democracia,* which had devoted pages to Eva's trip and continued to publish an average of five pictures a day of her, dropped Bramuglia's name from the news. *Democracia* omitted his name even when they reported the signing of a new trade agreement with Italy in 1948, which he had negotiated and at the signing of which he was his country's representative. Nor did they mention the fact that he had been received by the Pope and by President Truman. It seems that Eva and Perón did not agree over this matter, for the President met Bramuglia on his return and embraced him warmly and refused to accept his resignation. But Eva's maneuvers were only temporarily thwarted. Eight months later Bramuglia resigned and this time his resignation was accepted. Ambassador Remorino—it is said that he had been one of Eva's friends in her theatrical days and was one of the few to retain her friendship—returning from Washington, accused the Foreign Minister before Perón of having had in a country where doctors have been so distrusted that the whole family very often gather in the room when one of their women is in the throes of labor. Eva, dressed all in white, is said to have remained on her knees in prayer throughout the operation. Later she made an emotional speech over the radio.

"Companion railway workers," she said, after explaining that she could not be with them because she could not leave Perón's side, "I leave you my woman's heart and I tell you once again that your companion Evita prefers to be Evita rather than the wife of the President, if that Evita serves to ease some sorrow in any humble home in my *patria*."

After these emotional heights it is not surprising that Ivanissevich's successful performance of the operation was greeted by *Democracia* as a miracle and that it was announced that a new hospital in San Juan would be named after him.

Nearly two years later, in January 1950, Ivanissevich seemed as firmly established as ever, for Eva was herself seized with an acute attack of appendicitis when she was opening a school for taxi drivers' children, and Ivanissevich was called in in a hurry to operate on her after she had whispered, in her last moments of consciousness, "Viva Perón!"

But Ivanissevich was not there to be consulted when Eva became so gravely ill in 1951. Two incidents seem to have led to his disappearance into that limbo into which all good Peronistas eventually vanish. Eva had demanded a higher salary for her widowed sister Blanca who had been made Inspector of Schools; her demand was no doubt outrageous and Ivanissevich, as Minister of Education, protested. Without a doubt Blanca got her raise. The second incident was over Miel Asquia, a newer protégé of Eva's, who had, in 1949, become leader of the Peronista bloc in the Chamber of Deputies and thus of extreme usefulness to her. He had enrolled in the University of Buenos Aires but failed to pass an examination in law in 1950—it is curious that one so high in the Peronista hierarchy should have thought a higher education necessary, but

151

doubtless Eva had plans for him which necessitated a degree in law. Eva told Ivanissevich bluntly that Miel Asquia must be passed. Ivanissevich offered to hold another examination for Miel Asquia. A year later certain professors of the university protested that Miel Asquia had been given a private examination and passed without the knowledge of any of them. But Eva had not been satisfied with the part her poet laureate had played and Ivanissevich had resigned and departed abruptly for Chile.

There is left in Argentina only one place where a semblance of free speech endures—the floor of the Chamber of Deputies; elsewhere he who criticizes the regime does so at his own risk. Indeed, the Deputies themselves have not been immune from reprisals. The Senate, by 1948, was Peronista to a man, Perón having procured that happy result by declaring fraudulent those elections that had returned a member of the Opposition to the Upper House and dispatching a Peronista *interventor* to see that they were held again with results more satisfactory to himself. The Senate has been reduced to a mere tool in the hands of the Peróns, and Eva on occasion burst in upon a closed session and told them exactly what she wanted them to do. The Chamber of Deputies may be said to have been divided into three factions, the barely tolerated Opposition, the Peronistas who were for Perón but were not altogether approving of Eva's interference, and the Peronistas who belonged to Eva body and soul. Of these last were both Hector Campora, President of the Chamber, and Miel Asquia, leader of the Peronista bloc.

The rift between the Peronista deputies became evident when Eva returned from her European trip and, having quarreled with the Señora Largomarsino de Guardo, objected to her husband's presidency of the Chamber. Hector Campora was elected to take his place, both sides satisfied that he would add nothing to the advantages of the other, for he was an insignificant and amenable personality. Until Perón's election he had been a small-town dentist, but he had flung himself enthusiastically into the Peronista campaign and had, as a reward, been elected to the Chamber. But now that he became President of the Chamber he showed himself to be as ardently for Eva as he was for Perón. He boasted, "They say that I'm Perón's and Evita's servant. I declare I'm honored to be called their servant because I serve them loyally." His wife became as close a companion to Eva as the wife of the former President of the Chamber had been, and Campora himself visited Eva daily and telephoned her when any debate of interest took place in the Chamber. Had Eva presided over the house in person she could hardly have exercised a more direct control.

In the Chamber Campora used every means to hector the Opposition, striking the bell and declaring out of order any protest they launched. The sessions became so disorderly that it became the custom of many of the Deputies to go to the Chamber armed and a matter for comment when a meeting passed without accusations, threats and insults; criticisms of Eva were followed by violence and the dismissal of Radical deputies.

Her enmity with Radical Deputy Ernesto Sammartino had dated from early days, for he had known her and shown her some kindness when she was stranded with a theatrical company in the provinces, a familiarity Eva found difficult to forgive. His hotheaded and vigorous opposition to the regime kept her rancor alive. He persistently denounced corruption among Peronista officials, proof of whose complicity in fraud, robbery, and extortion he offered to produce. But it was his temerity in denouncing in the most caustic language Eva's interference in affairs of state that cost him his position and nearly cost him his life.

"We have not come here," he declared in the Chamber, "to do obeisance to the lash nor to dance to Madame Pompadour's tune. This is not a fashionable night club or the anteroom of a palace. It is the parliament of a free people and it should be made plain to the people, here and now, that this Chamber will not obey the commands of meddling old colonels nor heed orders given in perfumed notes from the boudoir of any ruler."

Amid the furious indignation of the Peronista deputies Radical

153

Deputy Mercader jeered, "Now let's see who runs to telephone the señora!"

Sammartino tells us that he was attacked in his office by a thug named Raul Costas, the same who threatened members of the American Labor Delegation in that year, 1947; but for the misfiring of the assailant's gun Sammartino would have been killed; one may imagine that the Deputy's quick eye and foot and explosive courage may have helped, for he is an expert duelist. When Sammartino got his would-be assailant to the local police precinct it was a car from Eva's office, the Ministry of Labor, that came with orders that Costas was to be released. Later Sammartino was expelled from the Chamber without being given the opportunity to defend himself and had to escape across the river to Uruguay, from whence he has not ceased to denounce the regime.

In 1949 Radical Deputy Colonel Atilio Cattaneo was expelled from the Chamber for questioning the sources of the fortune with which Eva and Perón were able to purchase their estates and for referring to Eva's relatives "who were so poor in 1943 and now are multimillionaires." He had to join Sammartino and his other friends in exile across the river.

The servility that the majority of the Peronista bloc showed towards Eva and the fulsomeness of their praise would have been ludicrous if it had not involved a nation's tragedy. In August, 1950, when Eva was to present to certain Peronista deputies the titles which, according to the requirements of the reformed Constitution, were to prolong their terms of office, these gentlemen decided that it would be fitting to mark the occasion by a gift to the señora. What the gift was to be was a matter for prolonged debate and only after grave deliberation was it decided to present her with a charm bracelet—one of rubies, sapphires and diamonds, to be sure —hung with an incongruous assortment of jeweled miniatures, the Argentine flag, the figure of a shirtless one, the Senate building, the Peronista arms, her favorite black poodle and nearly a dozen more. In August, 1951, when Perón and Eva received the Peronista delegation that came to inform them they had been nominated as candidates for the presidency and vice-presidency, a photograph was taken of the official group, Campora nursing one of her toy poodles and Espejo, Secretary of the General Confederation of Labor, nursing the other.

Sammartino tells in his book[1] of one uncouth deputy, by name Astorgano, known to have once been a chucker-out in a cabaret, who, when elected to the Chamber, was told by Eva that he need not open his mouth there but if anyone spoke against her or the President he was to break their heads.

The Opposition in Argentina must suffer from a frustration greater than that of the minorities in totalitarian states in Europe. Perón has allowed them a travesty of freedom; even in these last elections *La Nación* continued to print notices of their meetings but, because of the small ration of newsprint allowed, in editions so limited and in print so small as to make it, if you were not a subscriber, a matter of contrivance to get hold of a copy of the paper, and to make a magnifying glass necessary when you did. They were allowed to hold meetings but their programs were as subject to police interference and their leaders as likely to end in jail as if they had been working underground, and Perón had further handicapped them by such laws as the one that prohibited coalitions. They could not join forces against him.

Neither the Argentine character nor the Argentine landscape lend themselves to underground or guerrilla warfare. The utterly flat and almost treeless plains that lie behind Buenos Aires leave all movement disclosed. The gentlemen of the Opposition are only too ready to defend their country or their honor with their sword or with equally sharpened repartee; but the dueling sword is a useless weapon against that of mass psychology. Their most admirable qualities—their chivalry, their individuality, their touchy honor and spontaneous courage—are their worst enemies, useless in a struggle that requires dissemblance and patient self-effacement; they have not the experience or the resources to fight the enormous mass of propaganda and the more Hitlerian methods used against them.

[1] *La Verdad sobre la Situación Argentina.*

155

The Radicals, who form the largest opposition party, have in the past too often proceeded as if politics were a matter to be settled between gentlemen and have lost the confidence of the working people; the Socialists—it is a gentle, Fabian socialism—attracted only the more mature among working people and lacked the vigor to draw in the masses. What strength the Communists may have is a matter for speculation; there are some who believe that it has grown considerably during Perón's regime. He has, time and again, used communism as a cry of *Wolf!,* linking it often with sinister powers in Wall Street, to discredit the Opposition; but in suppressing the Opposition he is opening the way to communism which may, in the future, be the only alternative left to the dissatisfied workingman. The longer Perón remains in power the more likely he is to be followed by communism.

Eva's political career was the story of a running duel fought between the Army officers and herself. It is said that one of her ambitions was to be made commander of a regiment so that, like the new Queen Elizabeth, she might review the troops on horseback and in uniform. This honor—one which South Americans like to confer on the Virgin—she did not achieve; nor did the Army officers, who so persistently intrigued against her, manage to budge her an inch.

The Army officers have been the pampered children of the government since Uriburu's time; in many cases they receive more pay than their ranking equals in the United States Army, and very many more privileges; they are subject to almost no taxation, the houses built for lower-ranking and noncommissioned officers are the envy of the well-to-do civilian who drives by the boundaries of Campo de Mayo, and now, when it is almost impossible for the man in the street to buy a new car, they have their Cadillacs, their Jaguars, their Chevrolets, and Citroëns. But the most favored rank of officers has gradually declined from the generals whom Uriburu preferred, to the colonels who held the reins in Castillo's day, to the junior officers who now hold the rank and file at their command

and are the courted ones. At any moment any one of them may find himself picked out and pushed forward over the heads of his superiors and it is this sort of lottery in careers that holds many of them loyal to Perón. It is said that Major Carlos Aloé, who became director of half the Buenos Aires newspapers and radio stations and who, in 1952, ousted Eva's old friend Mercante from the governorship of the province of Buenos Aires, was no more than a sergeant in 1946 when Perón first recognized his adaptability and made him a major from one day to the next. With such rewards offered to the junior officers it is not to be wondered that the generals were uncertain of their loyalty if the argument they perennially kept alive with Perón over Eva's activity should come out into the open. Perón's Minister of Defense, General Sosa Molina, a martinet at home and in the Army, was, before her last illness, seen close to Eva's elbow on all big public occasions; and in the intervals of ceremonies she could be seen laying down the law to him with forcefully gesticulating forefinger. Had she been less slight and he less solidly rotund one might have expected her to pop him in her pocket at any moment. But he was not securely in her pocket at all. Early in 1949 Sosa Molina and a group of officers visited Perón in his house at San Vicente and demanded Eva's retirement from public life. It seems that Eva had decided to pay a surprise visit of inspection at Campo de Mayo and had found herself stopped at the gate by the sentry; she had furiously protested, but the general had refused to make an exception in her case; visitors were not allowed except on invitation. It is evident that more than a mere visit was involved in this, that Eva had attempted to gain further privileges for herself. There was a news strike on at the time and rumors ran wild in the city when a speech she was to have made was canceled. But with a loyalty that has never faltered towards his wife Perón told the Army officers that if they forced Eva to retire he would himself resign. Far from being in a position to force a presidential resignation the Army were now afraid of the consequences should he resign on his own initiative.

157

Eleven

*And when I say that justice must be done inexorably, cost
what it may cost and fall who must fall, I am certain that God
will forgive me for having insulted them* [the oligarchs]
*because I have insulted them for love—for love of my people!
But I will make them pay for all the suffering they caused the
poor—to the last drop of blood left to them!* E. P.

Like all dictators Eva and Perón had a deathly fear of
criticism and ridicule. Perón's fear was perhaps more within
rational bounds than Eva's, based more on the necessities of a dictatorial machine than on the needs of his own ego, for it did not
lead him into exhibitions of personal spite as it led his wife. He
did once give, as his reason for persecuting *La Prensa,* that the Paz
family, who had owned the paper for eighty years, had in private
spoken ill of Eva and himself, but, since this was said to an American diplomat, it seems that it was merely an excuse and he did not
wish to admit his real reason, which was that *La Prensa* was the
staunchest remaining critic of his regime. Eva herself had urged

159

the persecution of *La Prensa* with the greatest vindictiveness; the paper had seldom referred to her and when it was obliged to mention her it was as "the wife of the President" and not by name. Both in her pursuit of revenge and her thirst for adulation Eva showed the greater imbalance of the two. A reserve in flattery among her followers was the proof of faltering loyalty. In *Democracia,* her own newspaper, she has been called a summons to brotherhood, an invocation to justice, and has been compared to the sun. Ministers, senators, deputies grew flatulent in their efforts to outdo each other in flowery praise.

"Our Argentine lily," the Minister of Public Works once called her, "whom our loyalty and our love will never let be smirched."

"She seems to be," Hector Campora said in the Chamber of Deputies, "the reincarnation of one of those heroines who followed in the dust of their countries' armies"—the slight ambiguity here was surely unintended!—"and in the rearguard selflessly performed the Christian task of staunching wounds, slaking thirst and easing hunger. Eva Perón continues her revolutionary work, opening her arms to the humble and scattering with generous hand her love and goodness in all the corners of the country."

Democracia ran a story, to which half the paper was devoted, on an Argentine airliner that crashed and the passengers who, enveloped in flames, cried upon Eva and Perón for help. "It seems impossible," the paper adds, "that Fate should deal harshly with us with those two names on our lips."

In her own speeches and writing Eva frequently referred to her humility, she called herself "the most humble of the shirtless ones" and Perón's "most humble collaborator," but those who surrounded her knew better than to restrain their panegyrics; her flaunted humility was part of the role she was acting for which she sought constant applause, some of which came close to sacrilege, for she has been called "Lady of Hope" and "Lady of Compassion," titles which have a familiar ring to the pious ear.

Such eulogies were the only comment she could tolerate; any criticism might have destroyed the enormous image of herself which she created not only to humbug others, not only for the wealth and power it facilitated, but to sustain herself, an image which must surely have had at its core the most ghastly vacuum of fear. Physically Eva was a small and courageous woman; mentally she was as inflated, as vulnerable and as heady as one of those ballooned figures toted in a New Orleans Mardi Gras. The venom with which she pursued her enemies was the result of this inner insecurity, for they were not always those enemies who offered any real danger to her or the regime, nor had their offenses always been committed after she became First Lady, nor, indeed, had some of them committed any offense other than that of having been at one time in a position superior to her own.

Few first-class actresses of her own acting days escaped her wrath; some, who had treated her with kindness in those days and whose only indiscretion was to have acted more capably than she was able, are now earning their livings as best they can or have left the country, Argentine stage and movie and radio barred to them for the rest of their lives, or of the Perón regime. To employ such actresses would mean fines, loss of publicity, cancelation of licenses, and ruin. Such well-loved actresses as Libertad Lamarque, who certainly did commit the error of reproving Eva for unpunctuality in early days, and it is said that the two ladies had something of a scuffle at the time, have had to leave the country and continue their careers elsewhere. Lucky were they who, like Lamarque, were already known in South America. Lamarque injudiciously returned to Buenos Aires; she was not forgotten and a great crowd had gathered at the airport to welcome her. But the officials, who had been given orders to inconvenience her in every way possible, took half the night to examine her and her luggage so that the crowd, seeing all the other passengers leaving, supposed her not to have come and, disappointed, dwindled off. There was only one woman in Argentina for whom crowds may gather to applaud.

In the earliest days of the regime some had the courage to ridicule her in public. Nini Marshall, whose little working-girl act was a favorite among radio audiences, mimicked Eva and had to find another home and another job in Montevideo. Sofía Bozán was, for a time at least, luckier; after Eva committed the social enormity of appearing at a banquet, at which she was to sit next to Cardinal Copello, with a bare shoulder, Sofía Bozán appeared on the stage with a cardinal bird perched on her bare shoulder. She escaped with no more than a reprimand and a reasonable fine, but the next evening she appeared with a padlock on her lips. Again she got no more than a reprimand and a fine, a leniency that would be inexplicable if it were not known that the chief of police, the notorious Colonel Velazco, was a friend of hers and no friend of Eva's, who shortly after this contrived his dismissal. But Eva's vengefulness was marked with neurotic inconsistency; on one occasion, perceiving an acquaintance of her actress days among the crowd, she chose suddenly to behave with the utmost graciousness, expressing delight at meeting an old friend and pressing on her a scribbled card to some theatrical manager that would in a trice put her name at the top of the bill and send her salary soaring. But these acts of graciousness were not extended to actresses who had at any time distinguished themselves, and her generosity was but another exhibition of her power.

In 1951 she returned to visit the studio of Radio El Mundo, where she once worked in minor roles and of which she now had complete control. The whole staff from director down to doorman were lined up to welcome her; but she ignored directors, sponsors, actors, writers, and used the whole battery of her charms on an undistinguished young man who had been the office boy in the days of her apprenticeship and with whom she used to drink coffee and gossip in the milk bar opposite. But in the light of her attentions to her other old acquaintances this appears rather as a snub to the directors than as friendliness towards an office boy.

Most evident in her vengefulness was her spiteful desire to humiliate any woman who, because of wealth or birth, might at any time have been in a position to patronize her. Her fine hand could be seen behind the imprisonment of a group of girls and boys of wealthy families, whose only crime was an irreverent mirth. The

162

crowded as Broadway on a Saturday, six of the ladies were arrested as well as two strangers, a Uruguayan mother and daughter over in Buenos Aires for a shopping expedition and quite ignorant, yet, of Argentine politics. The ladies were taken off, charged with disturbing the peace, booked for the night and released next morning with a scolding from the judge. But that, unpleasant as it was, was not the end of the affair. Eva had been out of town. No sooner did she return than they were all ordered to appear at the courts again, a matter of mere formality, they were told. When they reached the courts they were bundled into the Black Maria, which then did the rounds of the police stations to gather up the women picked up on the streets the night before. These, seeing these well-dressed dames already crowding the police van, assumed them to be of the same profession but having the monopoly of a more lucrative beat, and began to abuse them in language no lady should use. In the prison —again the one reserved for prostitutes, San Miguel—the nuns in charge received orders that these ladies must not in any way be segregated but must be made to eat and sleep with those charged with prostitution; and crowded and unhygienic as the prison was it could not have been comfortable shared with the most congenial companions. But when the ladies of the street discovered why the others had been jailed they treated them with consideration and respect. It was not within the prison that they met with cruelty; all were as kind to them as they dared be and when these ladies' lawyers and doctors were at last allowed to visit them, messages of sympathy and gifts came pouring in, while out in the street friends and quite frantic members of the Uruguayan ministry kept watch to see they were not spirited away to some unknown prison camp or the dreaded Special Section. On the first day of their imprisonment the women were questioned and quite unfounded charges laid against them. The Uruguayan women were accused of bringing bombs over on the river boat, a charge as ridiculous as if it were laid against any shopper picked at random in Wanamaker's or Lord & Taylor's; their only offense was that they insisted stoutly that they would have been proud to sing the Argentine anthem had they recognized it because "only in a country of barbarians was it a crime to sing the national hymn." This cost them a month in jail. Among these women was an old lady of seventy-two, as defiant as the rest of them, but to her alone some leniency was shown; she was allowed to spend her prison term under house arrest. Some of the others, whose names were among the most illustrious in Argentine history, were offered their freedom if they would write to Eva personally and plead for it. They refused.

Imprisonment and repeated bullying threats and questionings were not the worst these ladies had to suffer. It is the rule of the prison doctor to take blood specimens from the women who are brought in to discover which are suffering from venereal disease. When the doctor approached these ladies for this purpose, their suspicions were aroused and they refused hysterically to allow him near until their own doctor, secretly advised, arrived on the scene. And it seems that their suspicions were well founded, for when their own doctor, pretending both to humor the ladies and help the prison doctor, offered to take two specimens from each and examine one himself, the project was at once dropped.

Meanwhile *Democracia* conducted a campaign of calumny against the prisoners, saying in print about them what had been whispered in their drawing rooms about Eva Perón and inciting the more irresponsible of the working people to such indignation that the good nuns expected the prison to be stormed and their prisoners murdered any night. Once again they were bundled into the Black Maria and rushed off, banging their fists against the sides of the van and screaming to their watching friends to follow. To elude pursuit the police van went hurtling down the narrow one-way streets against the traffic but the car from the Uruguayan ministry, with its diplomatic number plate, was immune from traffic control and could follow. They were taken to the Courts again for more questioning—they tried to make them confess to some sinister plot—and bullying. In retrospect it has the absurdity of a police chase in an old silent film; but there was no absurdity about it for the women, tired, unwashed, bewildered, enclosed in a small dark

165

space, carried off they knew not whither while the sound of their friends' voices fell behind. At the end of the month they were released as unceremoniously as they had been arrested, and the photographers from *Democracia* were there to catch the poor ladies as they emerged, disheveled and weeping, into the street.

It is significant that the names of some of the ladies imprisoned were those that had headed the *Sociedad de Beneficencia*.

Eva's "supercritics"—the word is hers and it seems that even her enemies were no ordinary enemies in her eyes!—have often called her a *resentido social* which, roughly translated, means someone with a chip against society; in her book[1] she admits freely to resentment but insists that it is prompted not by hatred for the wealthy but by love for the poor they have oppressed. She writes:

I fight against all the privileges of power and wealth. That is to say, against all the oligarchy, not because the oligarchy has ill-treated me at any time.

On the contrary! Until I arrived in the position I now occupy in the Peronista movement I owed them nothing but "attentions," including one group representing the ladies of the oligarchy who offered to introduce me to their highest circles.

My "social resentment" does not come from hatred at all. But from love of the people whose sufferings have for always opened the gateway to my heart.

There is something childishly naïve in her boast that she might, had she wished, been introduced to the highest circles, although no doubt there were some who would gladly have sponsored her in exchange for their own immunity. Her declaration that she fought the privileges of wealth and power only for the sake of the suffering people would have rung more true if she had not become so very wealthy and powerful herself. It is curious that her book, scheduled for publication at a time when she might easily have been at the height of her political success, should be very much in the

[1] *La Razón de mi Vida.*

166

nature of an explanation or an apology in defense of herself. Under the propaganda that is the purpose of the book there is a note that recalls an unhappy child crying, *I'm a good girl! Really I'm a good girl!* But the unhappy child often grows up into the criminal.

Sometimes her actions have revealed quite clearly the personal animosity that directs them. Successful as her European trip had been it had left her dissatisfied on one count: she had not acquired the title she coveted. And in Buenos Aires there were two pious old ladies who had received papal marquisates. One of them was the fabulously wealthy doyenne of Argentine society, the Señora Harilaos de Olmos; among her good works she had built and endowed a church and it was the old lady's wish to be buried within its walls. To be buried in a church, even one you have built yourself, necessitates permission from the Pope and the President; the first the old lady had obtained without difficulty. Now, near her end, she applied for permission from Perón. The reply came back that the permission would be granted if she would receive Eva in her house and accept it from her. The mere thought of it must have horrified the elders of the oligarchy. But the old lady, like so many on the point of leaving their bodies, was most concerned with the disposal of it and consented to receive the wife of the President; her friends excused her by saying that her wits were already wandering. There was no report made public of the interview but the eye of the imagination is entranced by the picture conjured by such a meeting, the querulous, meandering old woman in the somberly magnificent room surrounded by relatives as somber and unrelenting as the furniture, and the young woman who came only to humiliate them, pale, lovely, glittering with triumph and with jewelry, slender and tough as a whiplash. One can only hope that someone present who had retained a remnant of objectivity, perhaps some young and rebellious member of the illustrious family, has described the meeting in a diary which may be revealed in a more liberal day.

In a similar dilemma the Señora de Pueyrredon refused to receive Eva. The señora was dying and wished to be buried in a chapel at her husband's side. Permission from the Pope had been granted but Perón withheld his consent and when the family decided to ignore it and the cortège set out, it was stopped by the police and turned back.

This pursuit of vengeance into the grave can be motivated only by the bitterest hatred, a hatred with which one might have some sympathy if it had not driven its possessor to such cruel extremes. It was not necessary to have known Eva in her youth, to have excelled her on the stage, to have been born into a wealthier family than she, to merit her revenge; it was enough that someone's mere existence frustrated her aim. When her eldest sister Elisa was widowed it transpired that she had not been legally married to the Senator at all, that he had, in fact, left a legal widow who was the rightful recipient of the pension due to his dependents. Since Eva had been instrumental in having him elected Senator presumably she felt she should have some rights over his pension, for, rather than allow it to go to other than her sister, she had an exception made and no pension was granted in this case. Eva's sister did not, of course, stand in the slightest danger of any want.

No one in Argentina now can be sure that they escape supervision, that they run no risk of blackmail, intimidation, beating or arrest. Perón has his presidential intelligence service, his own body of police and his *matones*—the word means "killers" and they are professional thugs used to start disturbances at opposition political meetings, intimidate and sometimes beat up anyone who criticizes the government too boldly; a group of them were at one time lodged in the Emigrants Hotel down on the dockside and were paid what was then six dollars a day. It was probably these who were responsible for the crosses daubed in red paint on the houses of the Opposition before the 1951 elections; under the crosses was the letter G and a number, 1 or 2 or 3, which was said to stand for the group number of the *matones* whose duty it was to "take care" of the inmates of that house if there should be any "trouble." One house so distinguished was that of the great old

Socialist, Dr. Alfredo Palacios, one of the most honored men in South America and a true liberal; he is over seventy and he lives with his old housekeeper and a young boy; but his old age cannot be passed without periodical arrests and threat of assassination. The Special Section of police, of which more will be said later and the very mention of which is enough to nauseate *porteños* with fear or rage, was under the direct control of Eva and Perón. And Eva had her *oyentes;* the word means "listeners" and they were everywhere; the waiter, the woman in the next seat in the movies, the taxi driver, the housemaid, the manicurist—anyone might be an *oyente*. They were to be found in offices and homes, not only of those actively engaged in politics but in the homes of writers, teachers, foreigners, anywhere where a word against Eva might be spoken, and no doubt they were in the offices and homes of her ministers, of those who appeared to be closest in her confidence. Many a simple woman was approached with the suggestion that she might double her salary by reporting on conversations she overheard, and few of them dared refuse. A little sewing woman who had an invalid mother to support applied to Eva's office for a better job and was offered eight hundred pesos a month and a car if she would go around to restaurants and movies and report on what she heard; she refused and she lost the job she had. A teacher who had the same offer made to her and also refused was exiled to a small pueblo in the interior where her career would stagnate. There have been rumors that others who refused to co-operate have disappeared for weeks on end, returned with their heads shaven, refusing fearfully to speak of their experiences; but many of these rumors have in themselves the stamp of terrorism as if they had been invented or at least exaggerated to intimidate others. A nurse who had for years been with the same family and who was devoted to the children whom she attended—and so many Argentines will go to work only in a house where there are children—was watching her charges in the plaza one day when she was approached by another children's nurse with whom she was acquainted, who suggested she might be glad to make some extra money.

169

"You have only to get yourself a position in a house that is on the suspected list," she was told.

"What do you mean—the suspected list?"

"Oh, we have a list of the families who are under suspicion. We put someone in each house to report," said her acquaintance.

Pretending to be interested in the proposition the nurse asked to be shown the list. On it was the name of her own mistress' sister.

"Oh," she said, "I think I could get a job in that house."

"We've got a woman there already. She went in last week."

The nurse reported the conversation to her mistress who, at once and in great agitation, rushed round to warn her sister and found that it was indeed true that she had taken on a new maid the week before. By setting little traps for the girl they discovered that her job was to spy on any correspondence that left the house. Since she was an efficient servant and anyone else they employed was just as likely to be an *oyente* they kept her on.

The young proprietress of a suburban beauty shop was less fortunate. She gossiped too loudly with one of her customers, mentioning Eva's name with scorn. A head, decorated with the paraphernalia of a permanent wave, poked out of the opposite booth. "I'll report you for this!" shouted the lady with the embossed head. Next week the beauty shop was closed.

In 1949 a law was passed which made any disrespectful statement about the President or the government punishable by imprisonment, whether the statement were true or not. They had not been able to quell the continued criticism of the regime. The word used was *desacato* which is best translated by "irreverence," so that the law may be applied to almost any reference to the regime that is not eulogistic; indeed, even silence can be interpreted as *desacato* —one modest governmental employee swearing in to the new Constitution was dismissed for "lack of enthusiasm." Not only is any word of disrespect toward Perón and his wife and anything that is his punishable by three years' imprisonment but this law has been stretched to such ridiculous lengths that it covers any word spoken against the other great tyrant of Argentine history, Manuel Rosas of bloody memory, whose character Perón has chosen to revive and whitewash. In 1951 two lawyers were sentenced to jail for speaking disrespectfully of this man who is pictured by most South American historians as one of the most brutal tyrants since Nero's time and who has in any case been dead for a hundred years!

This law of *desacato* has been applied with such pomposity that it has provoked the most ludicrous situations—although never ludicrous to the victims of the discipline. The year 1950 was consecrated to the Argentine liberator, General San Martín; fifty newspapers were closed in one week for not carrying at their mastheads the proper inscription recording this. In that year every public building had to install a bust of San Martín, along with the pictures of Eva and Perón which were obligatory in all but private homes. In the suburbs of Buenos Aires there is an English boarding school for boys which has for the last fifty years kept up the most dignified traditions of the English Public School system for the benefit of those Anglo-Argentines who could not afford to send their sons "home" to school. Since the permanent bust ordered by the school was not ready in time a plaster bust of San Martín was set up temporarily in the school grounds. One evening one of the young masters, too lately out from England to have learnt the respect due to a plaster bust, returning from a gay party in the city and, seeing the bust left out in the rain, gathered it up to carry it into shelter— at least, that is how the tale is told. Unfortunately he stumbled on the threshold of his room and dropped the bust, which broke into a hundred pieces. Then he must have realized the enormity of his crime, for he went at once to the headmaster to confess the accident. The school authorities were not for a moment in doubt as to the gravity of his offense, for they got him on to a ship that was sailing for England next day. This flagrant case of *desacato* was at once reported by someone to the police; certainly so dangerous an institution as an English Public School would not be without *oyentes* planted there to report. The school was then "intervened" by the government—that is, its management was usurped by gov-

171

brought up in the Chamber of Deputies. She was, with the help of Mercante, Dodero, Aloé and others, directing a propaganda campaign that made use of all the radio networks in the country and almost all the newspapers; she herself gave a weekly talk on the radio, had a daily column in *Democracia,* made speeches almost daily and gave "lectures" in a Peronista school. She participated with Miranda, Maroglio, Dodero and others in financial transactions as involved as those of a giant cartel; she was organizing the Peronista Feminine Party and campaigning for votes for women; she intrigued to remove those who, like Bramuglia, limited her sphere of influence; she received all foreign diplomats who came to her country and persistently endeavored to sway their policy; and added to all this she ran the most colossal private welfare organization in the world—the Eva Perón Foundation.

She was in her office in the Labor Secretariat both in the mornings and late afternoons, fitting in her hours of concentrated activity there between conferences and banquets she attended, speeches she delivered, schools and factories she visited elsewhere. Not only were her hours excessively long—she worked from eight in the morning until after midnight very often—but she worked at extraordinary pressure. At the Residency, in the morning, one or two secretaries were with her taking notes while one maid finished the arrangement of her hair and another saw that her hands were manicured to perfection, and in the office beyond, from eight o'clock or earlier, privileged callers waited to gain her ear. Sometimes before her make-up was completed she would rush out in a negligee to talk to them, maids and secretaries running after her. She gave interviews, discussed business and labor problems or political questions while she drank her coffee, not failing to impress her foreign visitors with the unaffected way in which she offered to pour a cup for them. At ten or perhaps later—for like all South Americans and with much more excuse than most, she was invariably behind her schedule—she was rushed off to her office in the Labor Secretariat where more callers, and three or four more secretaries, awaited her, and there she would receive, one after the

174

other, a bakers' union, a taxi-drivers' delegation from the provinces, a union of printers from Córdoba, a delegation of maté[1] growers from the north, a group of students, a Jewish organization, the president and directors of an auto import firm—all these in one morning —talking to them in her rapid, almost frenetic manner, listening with the sudden intense stillness of a bird. Later in the afternoon she would be at her desk again, three or four secretaries hovering near with pen and case history cards and order forms, while past her there filed with the stoop of immemorial servitude, the peasant women with their nutshell faces and timid eyes peering anxiously from under the dingy fringe of shawls, their wondering brown-eyed babies clinging with limpet paws to their skirts, and the *paisanos* shuffling forward on their rope-soled *alpargatas,* turning their black hats round and round in their knotted hands, all with tales of want and hunger, sickness and injustice, and with implicit faith in Evita's power to cure. No sooner had the day's quota of mendicants passed her desk than Eva would dart out into the further office where a couple of foreign ambassadors, the governor of a province, the wife of a deputy, a banker, a priest and a dozen or so more waited for a word with her. She would hasten from one group to the next, a word or two here and a word or two there, even a glance from those all-observant, unrevealing brown eyes of hers was to be coveted.

She did not confine her activities to the city; when the need arose she would campaign up and down the country for the election of senators or deputies. The New York *Times* gives her schedule for three days in 1950: on one day she drove to Rosario, a hundred and ninety miles away, made three speeches, opened a railway workers' housing project, and drove back; on the next day she flew to San Juan, seven hundred and fifty miles away, to attend the funeral of the governor, and on the third day was at her office as usual and attended the meetings of railway workers and brewery

[1] Yerba maté is an infusion, sometimes known as Paraguayan tea, and drunk by country folk in Argentina as coffee is drunk in the United States or tea in England.

175

workers, and in the evening left for Tucumán, seven hundred miles away.

It is obvious that had Eva had the experience and the training in dealing with labor problems, welfare cases, and foreign diplomats, she did not have the time to give serious consideration to their affairs. Her meetings with Labor and business organizations were very often perfunctory, no more than a few compliments and time for a photographer's flash. Probably in her dealings with them she was guided by Perón's greater experience—one wonders when they found the time for discussion—but she brought to the business her own peculiar genius, a lightning mind for the superficial grasp of detail, an alert memory that at the click of a shutter recalled to her all relevant references; she never lost her power to subdue and manipulate men and added to it the art of entrancing and subjugating women. That she had no profound understanding of the problems brought before her did not in any way limit her influence on labor, finance and diplomacy; she saw these problems only in relation to her own campaign—she would have called it the Peronista cause—and when she interfered it was in as arbitrary a fashion as if she were ordering the management of her own house.

In the case of a small utility firm whose directors came to plead that their business could not stand the increase in wages demanded by their employees—and this was at a time when Eva was seeing to it that almost all the demands of labor were granted—Eva intervened in a manner that was almost as flippant as it was highhanded. "Give the boys what they ask for," she told the harried businessmen.

"But we can't do that, señora," one of them protested.

"Nonsense! Give them what they want."

"But we shall go bankrupt if we do, señora," and he explained that the profits of the business could not possibly cover such a raise.

Frowningly Eva asked what the deficit would be.

176

"Leave it to me," she said confidently, when she was told the sum. "You see they get the raise. I'll arrange everything."

The company raised the wages of their employees—they dared do no less—but when nothing was done to offset their loss they returned to Eva's office to complain.

"But don't you know I never forget my promises?" she cried indignantly. "What did you say the deficit would be—a hundred thousand pesos a month? Here's an order on the Central Bank. They'll make it up to you."

From that day the deficit was paid by the Central Bank, probably from the funds of I.A.P.I.—an unorthodox way, to say the least of it, of granting federal aid.

There is no doubt that Eva gave a great proportion of her time and energy to the poor, but her treatment of them was as highhanded as her treatment of the businessmen and labor representatives who also came to her for favors. She did not grudge her person or her time to the poor; she bent her beautifully immaculate head close to theirs when she listened to their troubles and allowed her hand to be seized and covered with their kisses and their tears. Her propagandists used this as evidence of her compassion; her enemies attributed it to Machiavellian design. But perhaps it was that the hunger in her for recognition and applause could never be appeased; from the poor at least she had more reason to expect sincerity.

The recipients of Eva's charity were chosen at random from among the tens of thousands who applied for help by letter. There was no system of social aid centers where they might apply locally; they had to write to her personally and, while they might have received all and more than they asked for, there was no guarantee they would be helped at all. The donations they were forced to make did not assure them attention and her "social justice" had no more system than a lottery. Those who reached her office were treated with a lavish generosity which seemed to be dictated by her needs rather than their necessities; she kept a stack of fifty or hundred peso notes under her blotter and handed them out as freely as if they had been tickets to a soup kitchen; she gave orders for new clothing, new bedding, new furniture, for a new house on some occasions, and, with sublime assurance in her own infallibility, doled out streptomycin and other drugs without medical advice at all.

To the pregnant woman who came to her with the sorry tale of a drunken husband and four small children to be fed, she gave a hundred-peso note and told her secretary to call a hospital and arrange for the woman to be accommodated at once. The hospital authorities replied that their beds were all filled and that they would have no vacancy until the next day at noon.

"Tell them not to be such fools," cried Eva. "The baby will not wait. Tell them to send an ambulance at once."

The ambulance was sent, but whether the woman needed to be hospitalized at once or what patient may have been prematurely dismissed to make way for her Eva did not pause to discover.

She was ready to force anyone and everyone into collaboration in what she insisted was not charity but social justice. One of the directors of a movie company was unfortunate enough to pass her office at a moment when she was considering the case of a widower with six children and no work.

"Come in here," she cried to him. "You're just the man I want to see. You've got to give this man a job."

Dubiously the discomfited director read the card with the man's case history on it. "But, señora," he said, "this man wouldn't be of any use in the film business. I don't know what I could give him to do."

"You have an *estancia,* haven't you? Give him work on the *estancia.*"

"Well," he agreed, "I suppose I could do that."

"Then write an order now to your major-domo to take him on," she said with her usual energy. "And he'll need a house since he has six children. Tell your major-domo to give him a house."

"Whatever you say, señora," said the unhappy man whose own

178

living depended so largely on her favor. "A house it shall be."

One can only wonder that she did not order a wife to be provided for the widower as well!

There is no evidence that Eva followed any of her cases through, beyond the accomplishment of her immediate orders, to see whether they were re-established once they were out of the hospital, or that the work they were given was work to which they were suited, or the house adequate to their needs.

She brought a hundred children down to Buenos Aires from Santiago del Estero in the north, from homes that were hovels, from conditions that bred incest and brutality, she dressed them in new clothes, lodged them in luxurious hotels, fed them on ice cream and steak, took them to the movies and round the city in chara-bancs, and then, after a week or two, sent them home to their hovels. On another occasion she invited six hundred children from Tucumán, among whom probably not one had slept between sheets before or was to do so again, lodged them in a fashionable hotel in Mar del Plata, the Monte Carlo of Argentina, for a month's vaca-tion and then sent them home again. The social justice of which she boasted was as autocratic as any oligarch's charity.

The metamorphosis of the gold-digging Eva Duarte into the charity-dispensing Eva Perón was perhaps the strangest facet of her strange career. Writing in 1951 of her welfare program Eva ex-plained that it grew haphazardly from her desire to maintain a close contact between the presidency and the people, that since Perón was too busy to give time to the million and one small problems that presented themselves, she had dedicated herself to act as a bridge between the people and her husband and for that purpose had established herself in an office in the Secretariat of Labor and Public Welfare. She was, she says, nothing but a humble inter-mediary. The pitiful cases brought to her notice there—and, indeed, there was and there still is in that rich land poverty to wring the closest heart!—determined her that a prompt solution to their misery must be found, and she undertook the journey to Europe with the object of discovering how such problems were treated there. As has been said before she did take the time to visit housing projects, schools and so forth in Spain, and in Paris she planted a ripe kiss or two on the foreheads of small orphans marshaled outside the Ritz Hotel to welcome her. In her book she sweepingly dismisses European social welfare as being institutionalized, niggardly and without heart. The Eva Perón Foundation, she claimed, was a labor of love, its policy governed by the heart and guided by the principle that the poor are deserving only of the best. She maintained that the poor of this generation should be compensated for the sufferings of their parents and grandparents—a theory of justice which, if carried to its logical conclusion, might land a good many of us in jail. According to Eva's Robin Hood doctrine the rich, so be it they were not the Peronista rich, deserved only to have their wealth wrested from them and the poor deserved not only comfort but luxury. Since even she could not put luxury, or even the modest comforts, into every *ranchito* in the country, she filled her hostels and homes with furniture the like of which was only to be found in a *palacio*. What effect a glimpse of all these luxuries has upon a simple woman who is lodged there for a while and then must return to her earthen-floored *ranchito,* and whether this glimpse is in any way more satisfying than the peek that a kitchen girl gets into an oligarch's salon, Eva did not seem to have considered. Nor, in fact, did she consider whether her untutored guests might not have preferred a comfortable old rocker to the beautifully damasked Louis XV chairs she provided for them. In many, many cases Eva supplied the needy with clothes and food and medical care, in many cases she made their dreams—of a little home, toys, a holiday—come true; but she spent fortunes, fortunes which wisely spent might have brought a measure of decency to every hovel, in a huge fantasy that served mostly to satisfy her own lust for aggrandizement.

It has been said that Eva's interest in welfare work arose only out of her desire to humiliate the ladies of the *Beneficencia* and that the Eva Perón Foundation was nothing but a vast scheme of self-advertisement, both of which are partly true. But distorted as her actions were they did, perhaps much more than is usually understood, arise out of identification with the poor. The indignation against social injustices of which she spoke so much did exist, for she never recovered from the bitterness of her own childhood. An incident of her theatrical days reveals the anger she could feel at a humiliation that might easily have been her own. When she was working for Radio El Mundo some of the better-paid performers made fun of one of the poorer employees whose dress was shabby and out of date. Eva, overhearing them, at once burst out furiously, telling them that the woman they mocked was far more elegant than they could ever hope to be. There must have been very many times when she had felt herself ridiculed because her clothes were worn and out of date. Eva boasted that her social aid was administered "from the heart"; it would be more exact to say that it was governed by the emotions.

Before long the line waiting for attention in Eva's bureau of relief had grown beyond all manageable proportions—she was receiving petitions by mail at the rate of eight, ten and even fifteen thousand a day—and it was necessary to form an organization capable of dealing with them. It was thus that the Eva Perón Foundation was conceived and initiated and its funds used in part to build schools, hostels and hospitals, all on the most extravagant scale. Perhaps the most pretentious of these institutions is the *Ciudad Infantile,* the Children's City, in Belgrano, a northern suburb of the city, pretentious not in size but in bizarre design.

Here, as in all branches of the Foundation, the would-be visitor had first to apply for a permit, then a date was set for the visit, the staff of the institution was informed and the visitor set out with an official sponsor. At the gate there was further formality while the permit was inspected, the directress informed by telephone, and whispered consultation took place between the sponsor and the guard. The white-painted gate and garden wall might have enclosed a prison rather than a children's playground so well were they guarded. But, once inside, the visitor was received with every cour-

181

tesy and encouraged to pry into closets and peek into laundry bins, while the directress, a comely, brisk young woman, kept up an informative chant. "The señora will have nothing but the best for children. Children should learn how beautiful life can be. In the new Argentina of Perón the children are the only privileged. We have some three hundred children boarding here now. Others come by the day. We take children from two to seven years old. They come from the poorest families. Only one from each family so that the good the señora does may spread over the widest area." *And her propaganda too?* wondered the visitor, dutifully smiling and exclaiming as she was taken from one charmingly decorated room to the next. Yet in spite of gay murals on brightly painted walls and spotless cleanliness everywhere there grew upon the visitor a sense of something very much amiss. Certainly in the first room a dozen or so tots, all remarkably sturdy and pretty and healthy-looking for children from the "poorest homes," were playing with a few toys under the watchful eye of a teacher and a uniformed nurse; but in the second room, where a group of older children, five years old at most, rose as one from their pigmy chairs and tables and, with their teacher and their nurse, curtsied to the guest and sang a shrill little chorus about Evita and happiness, there were dolls and toys, expensive enough to tempt any little oligarch, set out on the tops of cupboards, but on the tables around which these little children sang there was not one brick or book, not a pencil or a scrap of paper or a toy of any sort. The blackboard behind the smartly dressed teacher and starched nurse was bare of drawing or writing, the table in front of them bare of book or pencil. What had those mites been doing before the door opened—sitting around those charming little tables in their white pinafores, waiting to spring up like automatons to curtsy and shrill their little song?

Out in the tiled patio, where the waters of the swimming pool glistened green in the bright sun, another small flock walked primly hand in hand in double file, while yet another lot stood in a subdued little row against a wall waiting for some order from their teachers. One little boy burst suddenly into an indignant roar, and quick as a whiplash the directress turned. "See what's the matter with him," she said to one of the teachers, and then, smiling apologetically to the visitor, she added, "Some of them cry when they come here at first."

The curious discomfort in the breast of the visitor persisted as she was shown the auditorium where there were small chairs ranged round small tables for perhaps a thousand small spectators, and a stage that the visitor suspected was meant for one adult alone. On each table, round which eight or ten chairs were ranged, an exquisitely dressed doll was set, more suitable to boudoir than to nursery and which never, it was evident, had been in the hands of a child. The dining room was delightfully decorated with nursery rhymes; the bedrooms had matching window curtains, bedspreads and rugs, and bedside tables and lamps and closets full of beautiful little dresses of organdy, Swiss muslin and English viyella. Surfeited by the sight of so much elegance the visitor longed for the sight of a scuffed sandal, a broken doll or patched denims lying on the floor. But the señora must have everything in perfect order, she was told.

The kitchens—and everything here was open to the stranger's gaze —were so immaculate that it seemed unlikely that a meal, presumably soon to be served to three hundred or more children and their keepers, was in the process of preparation. There was not in that kitchen, the visitor observed, food enough for the eighty or a hundred children who had been in evidence, much less for more than two hundred others that were supposed to be about the place; and it was almost with relief that she began to consider possible the truth of the rumor she had heard, that no children lived here at all nor came into the place except on occasion to impress a guest.

The most extravagant of the Children's City was yet to be seen. In the grounds there had been built a miniature village, eight or ten stucco chalets with red tiled roofs, a school, a chapel, a municipal building, a market, a gas station, streets, lamps, a stream, a bridge, a plaza, all to size. The chalets, solidly built and large enough for an adult, stooping, to enter, were fully furnished, with small tiled bathrooms, frilled curtains, bedspreads, polished furniture, lamps, ornaments, rugs and all. Shops in the little market were stocked with small packets of groceries and dolls' clothes, in the bank there were deposit forms, in the post office telegram blanks—almost everything was there. Certainly there were no cars at the gas station but those, the directress explained, had to be put away because the children would play with them. In the municipal building there were two barred cells.

The main building and the miniature buildings had all two things in common. Nowhere, in large bedrooms or in small, in classroom or in miniature school, in the patio or the lawns around the small chalets, was there any sign of wear or tear; no polished furniture was scratched; no rungs of chairs or legs of tables marked by children's scuffling feet; no pretty ornament chipped; no toy broken and mended; no grass edge worn; no coverlet out of place —nowhere did the visitor see any sign of children's use. But everywhere, in every bedroom large and small, in the classrooms real or play, in dining room and passage and in hall, on almost every wall of every room, were pictures of Eva and Perón. It was almost a matter of surprise that they were not to be discovered above the altar of the little chapel, for above the beds they had taken the place of the Virgin and the Cross.

Besides the lack of wear and tear there were other signs that seemed to substantiate the rumor that the Children's City was not in full daily use. The directress seemed to know none of the children by name and certainly did not know that of the little boy who bawled, and when asked how much milk had to be provided daily answered airily, "Oh, a great deal. The children drink liters and liters of milk a day!" although, if she had forgotten such a detail, the cook was standing by and should have been able to give an exact reply.

The bright sun of Argentina shone from a dazzling sky, the white walls of the little stucco houses glistened and the green lawns were untrodden and smooth, and small, well-groomed children walked docilely, two by two, hand in hand, a nurse at the head of the file, a teacher at the tail—but outside, in the ill-drained street, children played grubbily and intently in the mud, apparently unenvious of the little houses and the pretty stream and lake within.

The Children's City is only one of the fairy-tale establishments —and Eva was right in insisting that the workaday word "institution" could not be applied to them—that have sprung up in and around Buenos Aires at incalculable cost and with enormous publicity during the last four years. Had some little girl out of Walt Disney's imagination been given a wand with which to conjure the results could hardly have been more bizarre or less related to reality than the mushrooming fantasies created by the Eva Perón Foundation.

The Home for Women Transients was in its day what is called in Argentina a *petit hôtel,* a not so very *petit* and most luxurious private residence. The salons—one can hardly give the rooms a less formal name—are ornately and richly furnished in the somber Spanish style. The nun who accompanied the visitor ran on breathlessly about the señora, her great humanity towards the poor, the blessings of her charity which spread to the furthest corners of the land, the generosity of her heart which allowed admittance to hospitals and homes to persons of whatever race and creed—even to anti-Peronistas, the nun added with a little giggle. The visitor was restrained by prudence rather than by tact from remarking that even in the United States Republicans had not been denied social aid during the term of the Democrats.

"The señora is an angel of mercy. She sheds her benevolence on all," the nun continued rapturously, so that the visitor, standing on the threshold of the chapel whose comparative austerity came as a relief to the eye, began to wonder if the good creature was not perhaps mistaking the identity of the Lady in the Blue Mink with that of the Lady in the Blue Cloak. "The señora is very particular," she went on and now there was no doubt as to whom she meant. "Everything must be in perfect order. If she paid us an unexpected visit and found anything out of place she would be very upset." And proudly she showed off the bedroom, shuttered tight lest the

185

bright fall sunshine fade the rich carpeting. The beds were as comfortably mattressed and as finely spread as those in any first-class hotel and the nun threw open the doors of the massive mahogany wardrobe to show, not the belongings of any women occupying the room, but neat stacks of seemingly unused wool blankets.

"Most of the women are out at this time of day," she explained, for the rooms were all empty, "looking for work or visiting relatives or at the hospital. A great many of them come here from the interior to receive medical treatment. Ah, if it were not for the goodness of the señora. . . ."

The loudspeaker system called imperiously through the empty rooms for the Señora Lopez or Mendez or Rodriguez to report at once to the office.

The nun took the visitor on—always accompanied by the official who had sponsored the visit and who never for an instant let his charge out of his sight—to the storerooms where unopened packets of groceries were arranged in exactly the same fanciful pyramids as they would have been in the windows of the expensive store in Calle Florida from where they came. In the room where clothes were stored each drawer was pulled out a little further than the one above so that at a glance the visitor could see the sweaters, skirts, shawls, shoes, toys and medicaments with which they were stuffed; and if any had been distributed the stock must at once have been replenished. In the kitchens half a dozen men, employees, one supposed, in this world of women, were heartily enjoying a meal which two stout cooks were cheerfully serving. The scene was reminiscent of oligarchian days when in almost any comfortably supplied kitchen a relative or two of cooks and maids could be found unabashedly living off the house.

But there were inmates to be found if not in the salons and dining room—tables for four with a vase of flowers on each—in a pleasant sunny patio at the back where children, presumably belonging to women who were having treatment at the hospital, played on bright-painted swings and seesaws under the watchful eyes of nuns, and half a dozen women sat round idly and rather glumly watching. In

186

the back and upper reaches of the building, which in earlier days would have been the laundry maid's domain, four or five women were washing and ironing their clothes; and the shabby little garments on the line could well have been replaced from the overstuffed drawers downstairs. In one small, windowless room, doubtless a sewing room or maid's bedroom in other days and now the sick bay, four small children sat listlessly in their unrumpled beds with never a toy or a book or a flash of healthy rebellion between the lot.

In the Hostel for Working Girls there was, in the gayer and more modern bedrooms, the same utter lack of any sign of the occupant's personality. It was difficult, in fact, to decide if these rooms were or ever had been occupied and, if they were occupied, one imagined that, as is the rule in the more formal English boarding schools, it was strictly forbidden to go to the bedrooms between getting up and going to bed.

In the Hostel, as in the Home for Transients, there were the inevitable two portraits in every room; but nowhere to be seen were those snapshots of family and school friends and pets with which lonely girls like to decorate their rooms. There was in each bedroom of the Hostel a radio; but never a sign of a sewing basket, a movie magazine, a cuddly wool animal or an ornament from the dime store; and, if above the beds of children and the old the two portraits had taken the place of the Virgin and the Cross, here they had to take the place of pin-up pictures of movie stars.

It was perhaps here in this hostel, built ostensibly for girls who came to the city to make their living much as Eva did—if in a more conventional way—that one could see how much of all that Eva provided was the distorted fruit of her early dreams and how little it had to do with the practical necessities of life. The salon —again the word seems the only one applicable for a "drawing room" might be chintzy and comfortable—in which these young working girls were supposed to congregate for festivities might well have been a reception room in the Casa Rosada itself. It was lit by eight or nine chandeliers of crystal pear-drops; thrown across the grand piano in Edwardian style was a most exquisitely embroidered mantilla, a museum piece, given to Eva in Spain; the Louis XV chairs were covered with the palest silk brocade on which there was not the slightest mark; on the mantelpiece and on tables stood Dresden figurines and in the corners huge Sèvres urns. At each end of the salon were oil paintings, large as the wall space will allow, one of Eva and one of Péron; she has been much etherealized in her portrait and seems to float, larger than life, against a vague but romantic background, rather as in the lordly period of Gainsborough portraiture.

More extravagant than this salon was the wing of the hostel that had been turned into a miniature replica of Calle Florida with sidewalks and street lamps and half a dozen or so shops where, the visitor was told, the girls might do their shopping. It was not explained how working girls could afford to buy clothes and cosmetics and have their permanents in these shops which were branches of the most expensive in town; but it was quite possible that Eva had persuaded the shops to sell here at a loss or, for that matter, to give their goods away. But since the hostel lies right in the center of the shopping district where until very lately reasonably priced goods were to be found in abundance and Calle Florida itself lies only three minutes' walk away, it is difficult to see what useful purpose this extravaganza could have served, unless it were to placate the unhappy spirit of an Eva who walked the real Calle Florida fifteen years ago.

Attached to this hostel is a restaurant for working people and this at least is put to full and useful purpose; it is primarily for the benefit of white-collar workers, for the *porteño* bricklayer and his kin will still as a rule take a slab of beef, an onion, a hunk of bread and some wine, and cook their meals over a fire built, perilously it always seems, among the rubble of their work; the onion, of course, is eaten raw. But in the restaurant of the hostel a shopgirl or a clerk can buy a four-course meal for about twenty cents, and since this includes a steak of sorts one should perhaps not cavil at the utter lack of fruit or vegetables, although a few years ago

188

tangerines were sold in the streets at five cents a dozen and soup vegetables at just over one cent a bunch. The restaurant is noisy, crowded, and cheerful, but adjoining it and also connected with the hostel is another restaurant which is not crowded at all; the food here is for epicures and the prices for millionaires—it is here that Eva sometimes entertained parties of Peronista officials—and the explanation that it serves to subsidize its more popular neighbor does not quite remove the incongruity.

The pride of the Foundation is the large new hospital built in Avellaneda, a shockingly poor southern suburb of the city, the Policlinico Presidente Perón. The Policlinico is built to accommodate some six hundred patients; it was inaugurated in February, 1951, but by the middle of the year there were only three or four women patients in its empty wards, a few cases in the emergency hall and a group of out-patients waiting for attention from the dentists who, because it was their afternoon tea hour, were smoking and making coffee in an old enamel pot which looked odd and homely among so much gleaming stainless steel. The matron and nurse—so introduced—who showed the visitors around were not in uniform, were, in fact, neither neat nor clean, and the heavy, wall-like face of the matron and the obsessive determination with which she marched the visitors up every last stairway and into every last hall was irresistibly reminiscent of Dickensian wardresses. And the Kafka-like discomfort of the atmosphere was further increased by a strange young woman clad entirely in black, who hovered around the matron like a familiar spirit and who darted off at intervals through a side door to reappear seconds later ahead, flinging wide doors so that the party might inspect yet another wing where a few nurses, breathless from some hurried exertion, stood sentinel at the doors of empty wards. Only once were the doors flung open too soon and the nurses caught kicking rolled carpets into place.

Here again was luxury without practical use; pretty coverlets, bedside lamps, and rugs, but the beds were not adjustable for support and there was nary a bedpan anywhere in sight. There were

189

cots for the newly-born with frilled muslin curtains, satin bows and feather pillows, and no rubber sheeting underneath. In the operating theater with its dome for watching students was the most complicated of operating tables designed by the Argentine surgeon Dr. Finochietto, brother of him who directs the Policlinico, and who seems, from the little tags attached to each article, to have also designed the rubber gloves, masks and every small piece of equipment provided. Marble and glass and stainless steel everywhere in the operating theater, and, besides the two inevitable portraits, hanging at precise intervals along the walls and the only equipment to show signs of use, were ordinary wire fly swatters.

Here the eyes of a patient would never be able to escape the portraits on the walls; they are on each wall of every ward and they look down upon the delivery table; and on the marble walls of the passages—seven kinds of marble have been used—the sayings of Perón have been inlaid: "Better the deed than the word!" and "For one Peronista there can be nothing better than another Peronista."

Here, along with offices for the medical staff that would put to shame many a specialist's office on Park Avenue, is a reception room that was kept for Eva's use. The great desk with Perón's portrait on it could not turn the room into an office, for the walls were lined with draped pale gray velvet and the bookshelves held de luxe editions of books on art. It had the appearance of a small boudoir created for some Hollywood set, and it seemed to give the clue to the formal salons in the Home for Transients and the Hostel for Working Girls and the auditorium in the Children's City where boudoir dolls decorated the tables. These were designed not for the children or the women or the girls, but as a background for Eva's appearances; and it was not for the children and the girls the little houses and the miniature street had been created but for the child and girl Eva never had a chance to be. These were her toys to comfort her for toys she never had, and, like other selfish little girls, she did not like others to play with them. She liked to find them always in the perfect order in which they had been left.

190

accountants to have kept pace with her capricious spending and no official inquiry could have cleared up the misappropriations that certainly abounded here as much as in the federal government. What is certain is that the income was hugely disproportionate to the resources of the subscribers and to the program that was accomplished, however grandiose that may have seemed, and that, under the absolute control of Eva Perón, it made her the richest and most powerful woman in the Americas, perhaps in the world.

There was no mystery as to where that income came from, for there was no person, except the destitute, in all Argentina who did not contribute. Businessmen, housewives, artists, stenographers, children, foreign diplomats, government employees, peons, from the oligarch whose million-dollar estate was expropriated to the servantgirl who gave half a dollar at her social club, all paid their dues to Eva Perón. Nor did any institution, firm, union, or society escape; from theaters and movies, horse-racing and roulette and houses of assignation, Eva collected.

Whether the primary motive for Eva's interest in social welfare were revenge or identification with the plight of poverty, she certainly saw the opportunities such an organization offered for the acquisition of wealth and power and used them to their full advantage. In a private capacity there was some limit to her highway robbery; she could not in her own name order large business firms to stand and deliver in broad daylight; but with the Eva Perón Foundation to justify her demands there was no curb set on her acquisitiveness. All in the name of Social Justice she could make what demands she chose and only on occasion did she have to make an example of some firm, such as the Mu-Mu Candy manufacturers who were rash enough to protest her demands.

The name Mu-Mu was as familiar to the children of Buenos Aires as Hershey is to the children of New York; as infants they had cut their teeth on Mu-Mu rusks and as schoolchildren they had surreptitiously sucked Mu-Mu caramels in class. The proprietors of the Mu-Mu candy business received a suggestion that they should contribute a hundred thousand packages of candy to the Foundation. They replied that they would be glad to supply them at cost price. That, Eva intimated, was not enough. Since they continued to refuse, a government inspector appeared at the factory; he pronounced the plant unhygienic and reported that he had found rat hairs in the caramel mixture. Eva's papers carried the scandal. The factory was closed, the proprietors ruined, and the fine imposed on them went to the Eva Perón Foundation. It is understandable that other firms have proved more co-operative. Alpargatas, the well-known Argentine firm that makes the rope-soled canvas-topped slipper of that name which most of the countryfolk wear, was asked for a contribution. They sent ten thousand pesos—then about two thousand five hundred dollars. In Eva's opinion this was ridiculous and she refused it. They sent a hundred thousand pesos and she replied sweetly that she would prefer a blank check. The directors begged to be allowed to give a fixed amount. She replied that she would be satisfied with a million pesos, to which they had, perforce, to agree.

It was not only for refusing to contribute to the Foundation that businesses were ruined, but the fines imposed, justifiable or not, almost invariably went to the Foundation. Litigation over the death-dues of the Bemberg estate had been dragging on since 1932 when old Bemberg, who owned multiple businesses over half the world, died. The Bemberg family, not willing to pay the more reasonable duties imposed under the Ortiz and Castillo regimes, now found themselves faced by a fine of seven hundred and fifty million pesos. Such fines resulting from unpaid or misrepresented death-dues are legally the perquisites of the Ministry of Education, but in this case the Eva Perón Foundation was decreed the payee.

The demands of the Foundation gave Eva ample opportunity to revenge herself on the oligarchy whose properties she had the power to expropriate for the use of her organization. The twenty-five-thousand-acre estate of the Pereyra Iraolas, lying on the road from Buenos Aires to the fashionable beach resort of Mar del Plata and therefore as valuable a piece of real estate as any to be found outside the city, was expropriated by the Foundation to be used as a home for the aged. The Pereyra Iraolas were offered nineteen million pesos, with the devaluation of the peso worth at the time about two million dollars, less than the value of the great buildings on the estate, and only about a tenth of what the rolling park land was worth. And it was useless for the old lady whose home it had been for over half a century to beg to be allowed to keep at least the house until her death; Eva would allow no such delay in her program for the old and poor—and perhaps no one but the evicted would have criticized her callousness in one case where so many others were in desperate need, if it were certain that the many would be housed where the one was left homeless. But it is claimed that it is Eva's brother, Juancito Duarte, who lives on this estate.

From the employees of the Argentine Stock Exchange who donated half a million dollars, the foreign ambassador who gave a thousand, the taxi drivers' union from a provincial town who gave fifty, Eva collected. And it was through the unions and from the working people themselves that the greater part of her income was derived. At Christmas, 1950, the Railway workers gave over one and a quarter million dollars to the Foundation. When with a gesture of munificence Eva ordered that a raise in salaries should be made retroactive over three months, two thirds of the retroactive raise went to the Foundation. In 1950 it was decreed that two days' wages of every worker's annual pay should go to the Foundation; when the first of these collections was made, however, it caused so much protest from the workers that it was announced that the Treasury Minister, Cereijo, would return the money. By magic the protests were turned to assurances that no refund would be acceptable and a ceremony was staged in the Secretariat of Labor and Public Welfare at which José Espejo, secretary of the General Confederation of Labor, announced to Eva that the working people had unanimously refused the refund. Eva graciously accepted this "magnificent gesture." "Frankly," she said, "I expected no less of you. I accept your contribution with profound emotion. But I ask that next year you will not make this contribution, so that it may be seen what the Foundation may do on its own." No mention was made of the demand for two days' wages and the protest it had aroused. Thankful to have been let off with the loss of one day's pay the workers applauded her. Such contributions were over and above the usual deductions made for old-age insurance and a percentage deducted annually from wages for the Foundation, a deduction which might be considered as medical insurance if it were not that it did not automatically entitle the worker to free medical care, his right to which depended entirely on the whims of Eva and her satellites.

In the pages of Eva's *Democracia* one could see how much of her income came from donations from working people. On one day in 1951 a syndicate of bakers donated 7,793.50 pesos, a taxi drivers' union from Santa Fe gave 12,256 pesos, the personnel of the State Department gave 52,380.20 pesos, and the syndicate of employees in the Mineral Water Industry gave 200,000 pesos. How many of these donations were voluntary it is impossible to say; the five- and ten-peso notes, although more laboriously earned, were certainly more freely given than the checks; but one thing was sure: any union that failed to contribute would gain no concessions for its members. Nor was it only by regular deduction from their wages and by contribution solicited through their unions that the workingman and -woman supported Eva Perón; at any small festivity at their sports or social clubs, even if it were a Saturday night hop for teenagers in a suburban tennis club, each had to pay a few pennies more; and they were lucky if they were not asked to contribute as well towards some gift to be sent to Eva as a mark of appreciation.

In a stormy session in the Chamber of Deputies in 1948 the Eva Perón Foundation was granted corporate rights. One Radical member declared that the charter should be marked, as unexplored territory is sometimes marked on old maps, *Dangerous! Here there are lions!* for, contrary to the laws of the country, the charter granted the Foundation the rights of a public corporation in the collection of funds and the freedom of a private individual in their expenditure. Taxes were levied for it, land expropriated or endowed —a block in the center of the city belonging to the Buenos Aires University was there and then transferred to the Foundation. It had the right to appropriate for its own uses any state social welfare organization in existence or projected, and public funds were allocated to it as if it were itself a government-controlled service—in 1949 Congress voted the Foundation fourteen million dollars; and Eva was as free to spend the money as if it were her own pocket money. No accounting whatsoever was required of her; she could spend, invest, donate or will the funds of the Eva Perón Foundation where she chose.

However much of all that was claimed by Eva had, in fact, been accomplished by the Foundation, yet there remained the indisputable fact that she used it as an instrument in a vast scheme for her personal aggrandizement. And her dreams of grandeur were not confined to her own country or to Latin America, but embraced all the Western world. She nursed the hope of becoming more world-renowned than Mrs. Roosevelt or Madame Chiang Kai-shek; in her own country she exercised more positive control than either of these ladies ever attempted, perhaps more direct and overt control than any woman in modern history. But it was not enough that she should be celebrated at home; she demanded recognition elsewhere and used the funds of the Foundation in her efforts to attain it. After her visit to Europe a flood of parcels of food and clothing, all marked very clearly as gifts from Eva and Perón, went overseas; wherever in South America disaster occurred, where crops failed or earthquake destroyed, there were planes from the Eva Perón Foundation with doctors, nurses, drugs and food.

In Latin America, where small countries teeter between Argentina and the United States, Eva's charity was received gratefully enough, schools and hospitals were named after her, groups of social workers and teachers were sent to Argentina to study her methods, usually as the guests of the Foundation. It is significant

196

that from Brazil, Argentina's only serious rival in South America, hundreds of young men and women, teachers and social workers, have visited Buenos Aires during the last year or two and have been entertained royally by the Foundation. In Europe her gifts were not always enthusiastically accepted. When Eva sent a check for two hundred thousand francs to the widow of a Frenchman killed in an auto race, the widow returned the money, suggesting that Eva should spend it on the Argentine poor. But when the Pope sent a letter of thanks for gifts of food sent to the Italian poor, *Democracia* made as much a story of it as if Eva had been granted the coveted marquisate. In Washington her unsolicited charity came as an embarrassment to the Children's Aid Society, who had made the routine round of embassies for contributions. They expected no more than a five- or ten-dollar note from each and were startled when they were informed that the Eva Perón Foundation had dispatched six crates of clothing for the needy children of Washington. They were a little indignant and ready to refuse, committee members threatening to resign and local contributors to withhold their support if they did not, when the State Department suggested it would be more diplomatic to accept, which, with all the fanfare that accompanies such presentations, they did.

But Eva made no donation without expecting some return. When she pledged ten million dollars to the United Nations for the hungry children of the world there were indications that she sought to head the South American fund-raising committee herself; and when this was not forthcoming the ten million dollars did not materialize. Her decalogue of the rights of old age, which was admirable insofar as the document went and which was included in the new Constitution, was broadcast the length and breadth of South America and used as a vehicle for the spread of her name and the doctrine of *Peronismo*. When the Inter-American Conference of Social Security met in Buenos Aires in 1951, Eva insisted that the report should include the word *Justicialismo,* an amorphous slogan of Peronista coinage purported to embrace Social Justice, Economic Independence and Political Sovereignty, a national football league match and at the opening in the huge River Plate Stadium the Peróns were present, supported by cabinet ministers and provincial governors, who flocked to her affairs as enthusiastically as spinsters to a bazaar to be opened by a princess.

But it was in the storehouse of the Eva Perón Foundation, built by the Medical Center as a hospital before it was annexed by Eva, that the implications of the organization were brought home to the observer. While in the shops of Buenos Aires food became scarce and the price of clothing had risen so that a shirt now cost what a custom-made suit cost five years ago, in Eva's storehouse there were six floors crammed with tens of thousands of jackets, dresses, shoes, sweaters, toys, aluminum ware, and, above all, books. The goods were stacked as flatly as possible in piles that reached the ceiling, leaving passages between where two people could have squeezed past. In the middle of 1951 there were a hundred and fifty thousand pairs of good leather shoes in stock. These were not the rope-soled *alpargatas* so commonly used in Argentina but were smart leather shoes of a kind the working people would wear, if they were fortunate enough to possess them, only on a Sunday. There were fifty-five thousand boys' shirts and a proportionate number of suits, windbreakers, overalls, vests, and pants. There were straw hats for men and print dresses for women, pretty ones and in great variety. There were overcoats of various designs and colors and of excellent material; there were layettes and First Communion dresses costing four hundred pesos each—nearly twenty dollars even in these days of disastrous exchange. There were tricycles and bicycles and pedal motor cars of the best quality; there were dolls of a variety not to be found in any store in the city; in one pile alone there were twenty-odd thousand dolls and there were three or four such piles. There were, incidentally, several hundred pictures of Eva on each floor, cut-outs of her head arranged heart-shape on the panels of the doors, larger portraits at intervals along the walls and on the six sides of Japanese lanterns that hung from the ceiling. It was explained that parcels were made up here to be sent to poor homes all over the country and that a parcel of clothing for a family of four was usually valued at two thousand pesos, unless, of course, some large item such as a set of heavy aluminum kitchenware or a sewing machine or a bicycle were added. Here and there there was a pile of clothing ready to be dispatched, but there was nothing to substantiate the claim that twenty-five thousand pairs of shoes were distributed every month.

One floor of the deposit was stacked with books, and it was not so difficult to believe the claim that there were five million in stock and that they are dispatched at the rate of a hundred thousand a month. They were school textbooks and storybooks and a great proportion of them were for very young children. There were a few children's classics among the hundreds of thousands of storybooks that thinly veiled their Peronista message. In these storybooks we find that Papa sings at his work in the new Argentina of Perón, that Grandmama no longer needs to take in washing as she did in the days of the wicked oligarchs and it is all, the little heroine is told, because of Eva and Perón. It is interesting to note that while a very great majority of Argentine children, especially among the working people, are brunettes, most of these little heroines are blond. In these stories Eva is pictured as the good fairy arriving at Christmas time with her arms full of toys; sometimes in the illustrations she is shown hovering in the background with a nimbus around her head which might well confuse a small child used to pictures of the Virgin and the saints. One of the favorite stories is that of Eva rallying the shirtless ones to Perón's rescue in October 1945.

But it is not only here that Eva hoarded goods to dole out like the prizes in a quiz program to all Argentines who know the right answer—and the right answer was always a shout of *Evita! Perón!* Throughout the city she opened grocery stores which undersold bona-fide groceries, which well they might as much of their stock had been requisitioned or donated in the same manner as were the funds of the Foundation. These were opened with a great clamor in the Peronista press, Eva herself presiding for an hour or two, like a little girl playing shop, behind the counter of one. They

200

were easily recognizable all over the city by the splash of blue and white paint, the Peronista coat of arms, the huge portrait of Evita and the line of humble housewives waiting for the doors to open.

Clothes and toys and books and groceries do not end the list of goods that Eva was cornering; the Eva Perón Foundation had a monopoly of imported drugs and medical equipment. Penicillin, streptomycin, anti-diphtheria and tetanus serums, sulfa drugs, X-ray plates and a hundred other vital medical necessities were in her hands and hers alone to dispense. The medical practitioner who was not a Peronista could not always buy the drugs he needed. The wife of one patient who was suffering painfully for want of aureo-mycin, which neither his doctor nor his family could procure, went to Eva's office and complained in no hushed voice that her husband was dying for want of a drug of which the Foundation had the monopoly. It was a dangerous thing to do, for it did not suit Eva to have her simple disciples, whose interest like that of many simple people is at once aroused by talk of illness, hear that she might allow even an oligarchian patient to go in need. The wife, persisting in her complaint, was at last allowed to buy the necessary drug from the Foundation at a price considerably higher than she would have had to pay had it been obtainable in a pharmacy.

The Opposition have claimed that the hospitals, schools, and hostels of which Eva boasted have been built not where they are most needed but where they are most visible and that often, when used, like the housing projects for working people inaugurated with so much fanfare around the city, they were not reserved for the needy for whom they were ostensibly built but were occupied by favored Peronistas who were by no means necessarily poor; and that schools and homes and hospitals already in use were left without funds and in some cases abandoned. In Buenos Aires the *Bene-ficencia,* deprived of government support, had to be dissolved, and the hospitals whose free wards had depended largely on its help were left in desperate need of drugs and even adequate food. The home-schools, a program initiated by Dr. Palacios, which were modestly constructed of local materials in the poorest districts of the interior and where children from neighboring shacks were taught to follow their fathers' trades with more scientific and profitable methods and to contrive some decency and cleanliness in their lives, were abandoned. One of the few institutions to survive the encroachment of the Foundation has been Bishop de Andreas' Hostel for Working Women, situated very close to Eva's own and which runs a restaurant not as well-appointed perhaps but just as cheerfully crowded. In the charter the Foundation was granted the power to annex any government-run social welfare institution; later its powers were extended and it could annex any private or public-owned welfare organization in the country.

The ostentation of the furnishings of those buildings that the Foundation built in and around the city, the claims that Eva made and failed to substantiate with details, the contradictions and absurdities of her claims, all tended to bear out the accusations of the Opposition. In 1948 Eva claimed to have established a hundred hospitals in that year alone. In a ceremony in 1951 when Eva symbolically handed over the works of the Foundation to Perón— not, of course, relinquishing an iota of her control—the list given was 12 hospitals, 4 old-age homes, 9 schools, and, in the federal capital, 150 schools and 200 food stores; she did not explain if these included all the Foundation had built or if they were those built in 1951, but there seems to be a great discrepancy between this list and her boast of 1948 and her promises for 1952 when, she said, the Foundation was to build "two huge university cities," 852 schools and 6,000 food stores. In the *Policlinico* the director, the matron, and another official variously informed the visitor that thirty-five, sixty, or eighty other such hospitals were projected and that three, seven, or more were in construction.

A curious and perhaps revealing incident occurred to the visitor here. In the past there has been a great lack of trained nurses in Buenos Aires—except in the British, American and German hospitals—and none in the interior; their place was taken to some extent by nuns and it was usual to supply the patient in a private ward with an extra bed so that mother or wife or sister could be on hand to bear the brunt of the nursing and to keep an eye on the never wholly trusted hospital staff; in free wards the family did their best to encamp around the patient's bed and supply him with all the delicacies forbidden by the doctor. Knowing this, the visitor asked the matron at the *Policlinico* where all the trained nurses were to be found at such short notice to supply eighty or seven or even three other such hospitals; there was obviously only a skeleton staff on hand. The matron replied glibly that the Foundation had already set up a school in the city where a thousand nurses were in training. A few days later the visitor was taken to inspect the nurses' school of which the matron had spoken, but unfortunately the necessary warning had not been given in advance and a flustered directress insisted that no visit could be allowed, adding that anyhow alterations were in progress and no nurses were in training there. "Then where," asked the visitor, "are all the nurses who are being trained for the new hospitals?"

"Oh, they're all in training at the Policlinico Presidente Perón," was the reply.

Indeed, in official parades, hundreds of smartly turned-out nurses, all with lipstick and nail polish to match, marched briskly by; but where they received their medical training is as yet a mystery.

Eva asserted that any person in need, whatever his race or creed, was eligible for help from the Foundation. It is difficult to believe that this included members of an opposing political belief, since criticism of Eva, which could be interpreted as criticism of Perón, was punishable by imprisonment. However sick and needy a workingman might be, if he cried, *Down with Perón!* he would certainly have found himself in Devoto Jail and not in the Policlinico Presidente Perón. And however good a Peronista a needy man might be, it was not necessarily he who found himself luxuriously lodged. It is not difficult to believe that the children on exhibition in the Children's City came from well-to-do Peronista homes—with never a runny nose among the lot! The Hostel for Working Girls has on

203

one occasion at least been used to lodge favored foreign guests, and they could not have been more comfortably lodged in the best hotel. And lately one floor of the Policlinico Presidente Perón was turned over for the sole use of Eva Perón, who was, perhaps, the first patient to have made use of it.

In spite of the Peronista boast that all working people in the new Argentina of Perón are content, there are shanty towns in the suburbs of Buenos Aires that would be shocking in the most backward districts in the world. One is in Avellaneda, not far from the *Policlinico*. The hovels, made of battered tin and corrugated iron, are huddled together on a piece of undrained waste land; no water, light, or plumbing is laid on and only narrow mud alley ways separate one row of hovels from the next. They are inhabited by destitute families from the north drawn to the city by tales of easy prosperity; the women support their families by prostitution and the men have been reduced to crime. It is not a place to pass by after dusk.

It was, however, the attainments of the Eva Perón Foundation rather than its omissions that were the more sinister. Through the Foundation Eva gained control of a further two government departments: the Department of Public Health and Sanitation and the Ministry of Education. Already in control of all public hospitals, with all private social welfare organizations—under which it would have been simple to include all private hospitals and sanatoriums—hers for the taking, with her hospital train and emergency planes to tour the country, with her monopoly of imported drugs, it was not difficult to imagine a day when every pharmacy in Argentina—and there they are pharmacies rather than drugstores—would be owned by Eva Perón. The flourishing pharmaceutical business belonging to the Massone family had already been pushed out of her way; as in the Mu-Mu case, inspectors arrived on the plant and announced that poisonous substances were to be found in the drugs; the business was closed, the Massone family fled to penurious exile in Montevideo and Peronista malevolence went so far as to advise

204

Argentine embassies and consulates all over the world to warn drugstores against the products of the Massones.

The usurpation of the Ministry of Education was the most sinister of all the activities of the Foundation. From the first the universities had shown the stoutest opposition to the regime and Perón had had six universities "intervened" in 1946. His slogan was then, *Alpargatas, yes! Books, no!* Later, when the Peronista publishing houses were established, it was changed to, *Books for the Working Man!* Dr. Oscar Ivanissevich, Eva's close friend and lyric admirer, had been made *interventor* of the universities. Students who went on strike for the liberty of their universities were imprisoned by the hundreds; over a thousand professors were dismissed or pensioned off as too old, to be replaced by others older than themselves or by men without degrees or by those who had so recently graduated that the ink on their theses was not dry. Among those who were dismissed were such renowned teachers as Dr. Palacios, Dr. Ricardo Rojas, the historian, and Dr. Hernando Alberto Houssay, winner of the Nobel Prize.

Dr. Houssay had incurred Eva's personal hostility, for, in 1947, when he received the Nobel Prize for his work on the pituitary gland, Eva had tried to get her husband's name suggested for the Nobel Peace Prize. When the list appeared and it was seen that the Peace Prize had gone to the Quakers, the Peronista press attacked Dr. Houssay viciously, demanding to be told why he had neglected the problems of tuberculosis and syphilis, and adding rhetorically and with astonishing inconsequence of reasoning, "Must we suppose that a theory embalmed in a textbook selling at sixty pesos has more medical importance than saving the life of a single Argentine worker?" It is said that Perón decided that, since Houssay was after all an Argentine even if not a Peronista, a telegram of congratulations should be sent to him, but that Eva, coming in at the moment when he was composing the telegram and seeing to whom it was addressed, tore it up.

But although the universities were now under the control of the government it was not to the students of higher education that the bulk of the Peronista propaganda was directed, but to the children of first- and second-grade age. Perhaps it was Eva's Jesuit confessor, Father Benitez, who taught her the importance of conditioning the mind while it was yet tender. The teachers of grade school were subjected to strict control and periodic inspection and could not hope to retain their positions if they did not sprinkle their teaching liberally with Peronista propaganda; in the textbooks they had to use, the primers from which the children learnt to read, references to the new Argentina of Perón and the blessed Evita were intermixed. Primers and the storybooks for home consumption were littered with good little Peronistas wanting to know why life had suddenly become so beautiful, and even the back pages of magazines, once reserved for innocuous little fairy stories or comic strips, now carried propaganda for the infant mind. In a magazine called *Mundo Peronista,* which has evidently usurped the place of the once popular *Mundo Argentino,* in the issue for November 1, 1951 —an issue reserved in its entirety for Peronista propaganda—the children's page is dedicated to the *"Peronista Kid,"* who is urged to reflect upon the life of General Perón and reminded that a good little Peronista kid is always loyal and brave, and warned, lest he go astray, always to do as General Perón and the Señora Eva Perón do.

It was Eva's friend, Dr. Ivanissevich, who was the Minister of Education until 1950; his creed was that young minds should not be burdened with too many ideas. When he suddenly and discreetly disappeared, Dr. Armando Mendez San Martín, National Director of the Eva Perón Foundation, took his place.

The Foundation is erecting a huge new building on the site that was annexed from the University of Buenos Aires. In 1951 work on this massive building was not advancing as fast as had been planned—the bricklayers were on strike because their wages were in arrears. And there was a curious uncertainty among Peronista officials as to what exact use the building was to be dedicated, although it was generally understood that it was to be the headquarters of the Foundation. There was talk, alternating with rumors of Eva's vice-presidency, of some big new ministry being formed of which she was to be the head, which may have been the reason why Peronistas were not ready to give a title to the building yet.

Eva chose to pose as a leader in social reform and was given the official title of First Samaritan; she had at her tongue tip all the expressions of modern humanitarianism; she spoke glibly of the dignity of the individual, of the humiliating effects of institutionalized charity and dormitories and uniforms. But the words and the gestures were meaningless, for it was not the poverty and unhappiness around she would relieve but the poverty and unhappiness of her own youth she would avenge. Her identification with the needy did not open her heart to compassion and sympathy. If she showed kindness to the poor it was because she was avid for their recognition and while they strewed her path with roses, kneeled at her approach and implored her blessing, she would continue to bestow her largesse; but if they showed the smallest recalcitrance she was capable of the greatest brutality. Hers was the triumphal progress and it must on no account be deflected or interrupted. In the most flamboyant of her early days, before her European trip and before she had assumed the role of Good Samaritan, she made a trip to the city of Tucumán in the north; there had been disturbances among the sugar workers, who have been among the most exploited of Argentine laborers, and Eva's trip, lavishly prepared, was by way of a diversion from their discontent. A fleet of army lorries carried pamphlets and banners up from Buenos Aires, the streets were beflagged, triumphal arches and an open-air stage erected and loudspeakers were set up to chant, *Evita! Evita!* and it was published abroad that she would distribute parcels of food and clothing to the poor. She did, in fact, give out some thirty thousand packages of groceries and clothing, each with the two inevitable photographs —and it is said that one Tucumán firm made three hundred thousand pesos in supplying them, and that the trip cost over a million and a quarter pesos in all. The advance publicity was so successful that the plane in which Eva traveled was unable to land for a while because of the crowds that broke through the barriers and swarmed the field. When it did land seven persons were killed and a hundred injured in the crush. But this did not interrupt the ceremonies, and that evening in the White Salon of the provincial government house Eva was crowned, with a golden, not a paper, crown, Queen of the Sugar Crop.

It was, perhaps, psychologically not strange that Eva, who had ranted so bitterly against the oligarchs, whom she called degenerate, venal, and cruel, had in her charitable works, which she insisted on calling social justice, outdone the oligarchs in patronage and had herself become their monstrous copyist. The matriarch of the Argentine oligarchy looked upon the people who worked on her estates as, at best, her children and, at worst, her slaves. She saw to it that they had a roof and food when they were old, prescribed for them when they were sick, scolded them into church marriages, provided layettes for their babies and Communion dresses for their little girls, brought sweets and toys at Christmas time, and saw herself as their generous benefactress, ignoring the fact that they were ill-paid, ill-housed and uneducated. Eva offered them better pay, in some cases better housing, and education of a Peronista sort. But she still kept them in a state of infantile dependency and indeed was reducing the whole country to economical servitude—and how could people uneducated in the great mass and trained in servility have offered her resistance? She gave them less opportunity than did the oligarchs to reach maturity and just as the oligarchs did she, too, spoke of "my people," stood godparent to countless infants, and sent out parcels at Christmas time as if indeed they were children dependent on her. She might provide overcoats of varied color and design or a variety of print dresses of the prettiest; but the receiver of an overcoat or dress had no choice in color or design but must rest content with what he was given, as the child in one house must rest content with a book when the child in the next house might receive a bicycle. What the people were to wear, what they were to learn, what they were to read, was chosen by Eva Perón.

208

The workingmen had no such pride as the Army officers' that would not allow them to accept a woman's rule, nor did they resent Eva as an upstart as the oligarchy did. She came from their own humble ranks—a fact she never attempted to conceal—and the more flamboyantly wealthy and powerful she became, the readier were they to applaud. And to the workingwomen she gave double satisfaction, for through her they saw themselves vicariously vindicated not only for years of subjection to poverty but for years of subjection to man. It has been this great mass of humble people who have supported Eva and Perón, and to many of them Eva has come first. That union members did not see the danger into which they were being led was not surprising since Perón with his camaraderie and his promises was able to beguile so experienced a labor leader as Cipriano Reyes. The Argentine worker is naïve and friendly, socially irresponsible, often ready to become devoted to any master who will show him a decent kindliness and almost as ready to stick a knife between someone's ribs for any small offense. The country has not lent itself to the growth of independence among the working people; in the interior vast, empty spaces, poor roads, few means of communication, encouraged a system of small communities ruled by a benevolent or tyrannical patriarch, *estancias* ruled by the *patrón,* pueblos ruled by a local *candillo;* in the cities there were, until twenty years ago, almost no big industries and almost no organized community life among the poor. From the middle of the nineteenth century there had been attempts to organize unions among the workers but only in Irigoyen's day did some of these emerge as organizations with negotiable power, the Union of Railway Workers and the Brotherhood of Engine Drivers were the first and strongest of these. In some industries, such as the meat packing, the employers, culpable as any in placing the Peróns where they now are, used all means, including violence, to break the embryo unions. When Perón became Secretary of Labor he gave every encouragement to unions already in existence and lent his aid to the formation of new ones in industries where none had yet managed to survive. It was thus that there began his friendship with Cipriano Reyes who was at this time organizing the meat packers' union. Perón, while still Secretary of Labor, had pushed through the laws that gave the workingman adequate wages, reasonable hours, holidays, sick leave with pay, the decencies of life he so urgently needed. Since neither Conservatives nor Radicals had promised them anything but a return to their former miserable condition, it is not surprising that in 1946 Perón got in on the labor vote. It was then that Eva moved into the Secretariat of Labor and became Perón's unofficial but most active Minister of Labor.[1] Just how much responsibility for the events that followed lie with her and how much with him it is as yet impossible to judge; but if he were sometimes ignorant until after the event of her decisions in the Labor Ministry—and sometimes he reversed them—she, at least, was not in ignorance for a moment of anything that went on there. She was his steward, but it is not unusual for the steward to have more direct power than the master over the estate.

At first it was all, or almost all, sugar and spice between labor and the Peróns; wages were boosted fifty and sixty per cent, a bonus of one month's pay was given to every worker at the year's end; farm workers had half an hour off for breakfast and, besides their luncheon hour, three hours for a siesta in summer. Office workers and farm workers alike were given half an hour off for tea—an odd remnant of British influence. Most of the new labor laws were in theory just, a few verged on the ridiculous, but in practice almost all were used as an excuse for the bludgeoning of the employer. Labor courts had been set up in the Fascist pattern to decide the rights of any problem arising between master and man but, unless the employer was an active Peronista, the decision was sure to be given in favor of the worker. The new laws, even when administered equitably, sometimes caused unreasonable losses to the businessman. One hotel owner, whose business was then running at a loss, was unable to liquidate it because he would have had to pay each employee a month's wage for every year he had been in his service,

[1]The Secretariat of Labor and Public Welfare became a ministry in 1948.

and many of his waiters had been with him over twenty years. However, he must, now that lodging is at a premium in Buenos Aires, have recuperated his losses a hundredfold. These suddenly granted benefits produced a good deal of ill-feeling between employer and employee; the workers understandably took advantage of their new security, and their employers complained that the men spent their extra wages in wine and their extra leisure in abusing their betters. The Peróns were not at all displeased by this ill-feeling, indeed they did their utmost in their speeches to foster it, since they were determined there was to be only one master and mistress in Argentina.

Just as Eva seems to have received some intense satisfaction from doling out fifty- and hundred-peso notes to the poor so did she seem to get satisfaction from granting the workers what they asked and more; when the railway workers asked for a forty per cent raise Eva cried gaily, "Give the boys fifty per cent!" The price that was to be paid for such liberality did not affect the average workingman, indeed, has not affected many of them to this day; he cared very little whether his union was syndicalized or by whom it was run so long as he got his raise; and it soon became evident that no raises were forthcoming for those workers whose unions remained outside the General Confederation of Labor, the C.G.T., and whose officers had not been replaced by men of the Peróns' choosing. Some of those unions—Reyes' Meat Packers' Union and the Sugar Workers of Tucumán—at whose birth Perón had officiated had not yet joined the C.G.T. Now the Peróns began to use every means in their power to force these independent unions into the fold. Perhaps the most reasonable persuasion they used was that of bribery; they had at first bribed the workers themselves with higher wages; now they offered government posts to leaders of independent unions. Angel Borlenghi was made Minister of the Interior after he had handed the Confederation of Commercial Workers over to the C.G.T.; others were made senators or deputies or merely put on the payroll of the Labor Ministry. Those who did not respond to bribery were intimidated or put in prison. If these

212

methods did not work the headquarters of the union were surrounded by police, the union officers arrested, and the union "intervened" by the C.G.T., a procedure that had no legality in the case of independent unions. The *interventor* remained in control of the union until the members saw the light of Peronista day and accepted the leaders that were foisted on them. In 1945 Perón had implemented a decree making it necessary for all unions to be registered in order to have legal standing and allowing only one union to be registered for each branch of industry. It was a simple matter for the Peróns to form rival unions to those that refused to join the C.G.T., to register them and leave the independent union without legal bargaining power. When the *Associación Argentina de Actores,* the Actors' Union, refused to replace its officers with those of Eva's choosing and refused to have Eva herself at their head, she formed the rival *Associación Gremial de Actores Argentinos,* had it granted legal status and made it impossible for those who did not join it to get work on the stage or in the studio; those who had opposed her attempt to appropriate their old union had to find other means of earning their livings, and at least one not-so-young actress had to start life anew as a stenographer. In 1950, on October 17—which, since 1945, has been celebrated with impassioned speeches as Loyalty Day—officers of Eva's *Associación Gremial de Actores Argentinos* made the rounds of the theaters requesting all actors to sign a loyalty pledge to Eva and Perón. In the Teatro Astral six refused to sign. The theater was closed down by the police. The manager and one of the stars went to Eva's office in the Ministry of Labor and begged her to allow them to reopen before they were ruined. She replied quite amiably that they could reopen as soon as those six actors were dismissed and replaced by good Peronistas. This was done and the theater reopened; but the six who were dismissed could find no work on the Argentine stage.

At the end of 1947 José Espejo was made head of the C.G.T. and through him Eva had complete control of the syndicalized unions. There was no pretense of an election; he was nominated by a few officers of the C.G.T. at Eva's express command. He is a squat, swarthy little man with so little individuality that there have been times when he has not dared answer questions at his own press conferences. His career has not been notable; he was a chauffeur in a food-processing concern and joined the union of that industry, to become after a year or two a union official. It seems natural that it should have been said that he was once the doorman of the apartment building in Calle Posadas where Eva and Perón lived, as indeed he may have been at one time, for he showed himself to be one of Eva's most tractable servitors, always at her beck and call and more like an obsequious valet than the head, or even the figurehead, of a powerful organization that, Eva boasted, has a membership of over five million.

But the cornucopia of even so rich a country as Argentina could not supply indefinitely the means for Eva's largesse, and from the first Perón's five-year plan had encountered difficulties. Between 1946 and 1950 the gold reserve was reduced to one sixth and the national debt was more than doubled; the budget for 1943 was just over two and a quarter million pesos, for 1950 it was over eleven million; Perón, who had boastfully announced that Argentina needed nothing from abroad, had had to ask for a loan from the United States for a hundred and twenty-five million dollars, the granting of which did nothing to encourage the more democratic elements of Argentina. Perón had bought the railways from the British, but they ran at a loss of two million pesos a day, the service was cut by forty per cent and the fares went up fifty per cent; workmen complained that they could not get to work and trains sometimes were so crowded that the windows had to be slammed down as the train entered a station to prevent the crowds clambering in through the windows; the rolling stock was allowed to deteriorate shockingly and the press was forbidden to publish the accounts of accidents. Perón boasted he had bought up the tramway, telephone and electric power companies, all of which had been foreign-owned; but the streets are so ill-lit as to be dangerous, shops have to supply their own window lighting, trams are so crowded that

214

it is often impossible to gain foothold on the step, telephones—and Buenos Aires once boasted the most modern system in the world —are scarce and in such poor repair that to make a call to the suburbs often requires half an hour or more and is almost as frequently abandoned in despair. The cost of living was going up almost as fast as wages; in spite of the emigrants brought from Spain and Italy to colonize the interior the flow of migration continued steadily towards the cities; two years of bad droughts helped to diminish rural production, but industrial production had also begun to fall off, not to be wondered at since industrial and commercial workers had a hundred and twenty-two nonworking days in 1947. The Peronista revelation required a new almanac of feast days. A stew of meat and vegetables—the *puchero* which has for generations been the staple dish in Argentina—which in 1943 cost one peso for a family of four, cost two pesos, seventy-four centavos, in 1946 and has been on the way up ever since; the scraggy chicken that cost two pesos at the beginning of the decade cost six pesos in 1946 and ten or more in 1951. Since the peso was devaluated the price of imported goods has gone up even more sharply; silk stockings, they were real silk before the war, cost eight or ten pesos, imported nylons now cost eighty. The price of tea has gone so high that even the British have ceased to drink it. Perón has tried to turn the devaluation of the peso to his own account and in a speech he made in June 1951 he cited, as proof of Argentine prosperity, the fact that the trucks that had been imported in 1947 at eight thousand pesos[2] each were now worth a hundred and twenty thousand pesos each—an immense increase in the national patrimony that left the more simple among his listeners scratching their heads. But Argentina is the only country in the world where the number of automobiles has decreased in the last twenty years; in 1930 there were 296,990 cars and in 1950 the number had dropped to 219,870. All this in a country that had profited, not lost, by two world wars. But in the same speech in 1951 Perón announced that all social

[2]Eight thousand pesos in 1947 was worth about $1,900; 120,000 pesos in 1951 was worth less than $6,000.

problems were at an end; the workmen were comfortable and as for the employers—they were making more money every day! Far from giving the workers more than they asked for Eva was now declaring strikes illegal, and, instead of making working conditions more reasonable, was organizing a national working marathon. Every day the Peronista press carried stories of mechanics who worked for 106 consecutive hours, brewery workers who worked for 221 consecutive hours and metal workers who worked for 224 consecutive hours, and the telegrams of congratulations they received from Eva and Perón. And as yet not all the unions had joined the C.G.T.

In Tucumán the sugar workers, always among the poorest paid of Argentine workers, had, under Perón's encouragement, formed themselves into a union which had not become affiliated to the C.G.T. but which had in early days gained the workers an increase in wages. In 1949, the cost of living having soared, they demanded a further sixty per cent increase. Eva at once declared the strike illegal, as are all strikes now except those one-day strikes called by the C.G.T. as an expression of gratitude or loyalty towards Eva and Perón. The headquarters of the union were invaded by the police, the strikers imprisoned and beaten, and an *interventor* put in charge. The men continued to demand a raise and the return of their elected union leaders. The leaders of other local and independent unions met one day to decide whether they should call out their unions in sympathy. The police broke in on them, arrested them and beat them up. One of their number, Carlos Antonio Aguirre, secretary of the Waiters' Union and its affiliates, was not seen again. He was a man of high reputation, and his disappearance provoked an inquiry by his friends. When his body was discovered buried in the wilds of another province, the scandal reached such proportions that an official inquiry was forced. He had been beaten to death in the office of the chief of police in the provincial government house—the same one where Eva, a few years before, had been crowned Queen of the Sugar Crop—his body, hidden in a garbage can, had been taken off and buried in

216

that distant spot. The police officers involved were held under arrest for a few months and then released.

Meanwhile the strike was broken and when the sugar workers returned to work Perón made a special broadcast announcing that they were to have their sixty per cent increase. What they did not get was the return of their autonomous unions which continued under an *interventor,* for the destruction and discredit of which the Peróns had at first refused and then granted the increase.

The treatment of those unions who had been delivered over into the hands of the C.G.T. by their suborned officials and who tried to regain their independence was equally brutal. The Telephone Workers' Union had demanded that intervention in their affairs should cease and that a meeting should be called for the free election of their union officers. In 1949 on April 1—the date seems to have a hideous significance—officials from Special Section of Police in Buenos Aires broke into the homes of some forty telephone workers when they were still in bed or only just getting up and, without warrants, made twenty-one arrests and took the prisoners off to the Special Section. It is necessary to quote from only one of the depositions made later by these prisoners and presented before the Chamber of Deputies by members of the Opposition. Nelly Carolina Garlarde declares that on April 1, 1949, at 7:10 A.M. two plain-clothes policemen forced their way into her home saying that they had come to search for documents that had been misplaced at the office (of the Telephone Company or the union?). They seized her and took her off to the Special Section; her father tried to insist that he should be allowed to accompany her. After prolonged questioning they beat her and pulled her hair, threatened her with rape, stripped off most of her clothes, dowsed her in cold water and stood her by an open window with an electric fan turned on her—a treatment they call "scientific pneumonia." This in spite of the fact that they knew she was menstruating. Then they bandaged her eyes and took her into another room, where she judged from the talk and laughter some six or eight persons were present; they struck her, insulted her, snatched away the chair from

217

under her—all this while she was blindfolded and almost naked. Then they laid her on a bed, gagged her so that she could not scream and applied the instrument known in Argentina as the *picana electrica*—an electric goad would be the closest translation; it causes exquisite pain and leaves no mark. This they applied to her bare breast, her arms and legs, and to her groin. She was then locked for the night with six other women in a cell 5 by 10 feet 8 inches. The next day at 1:00 P.M. she was released.

One woman was dragged out in her nightgown; another, Nieves Boschi de Blanco, was submitted to an even greater brutality when it was discovered she was pregnant, one of her torturers threatening to make her child arrive before its time, which, with the *picana electrica,* he succeeded in doing, for the poor woman lost her child soon after her release.

The men and women of the Telephone Company who were arrested were employees of long and steady service; some of them had been with the Telephone Company for over twenty years. After their release they were suspended from work for three months; then they were dismissed. They have not been re-employed or received any compensation since.

It was not only the workers and the women workers whose champion Eva so loudly proclaimed herself to be that were subjected to such sadistic treatment, but even those who had been her intimate personal friends. Cipriano Reyes has been in prison since September, 1948. When the Peróns had lived in the apartment in Calle Posadas, Reyes had visited them informally almost daily; and it had been largely due to his efforts that Perón was returned from the prison island in Martín García. Reyes, as secretary of the Labor Party, had also been instrumental in getting Perón elected— he had then believed in the promises Perón had made for labor and, indeed, some of those promises had already been made good. Reyes' disillusionment came when Perón, as soon as he became President, decided to dissolve the Labor Party and create the Peronista Party. Reyes refused to countenance this and would not be intimidated, although half a dozen or more attempts were made

218

to assassinate him. He is a man of very great personal valor who is able to conduct a lucid and well-pointed argument even when he expects to be attacked at any moment. Many of the other members of the Labor Party had been seduced or bullied into the Peronista ranks. Seeing that he was not to be intimidated, Perón tried to bribe Reyes in 1948 by an offer of a ministry if he would come into the Peronista fold with the remnants of his party. It did not suit him to have Reyes, a man with so much standing among the shirtless ones, in the opposite camp. Reyes refused even to discuss the matter unless the vice-president of the Labor Party, his loyal friend Dr. Walter Beveraggi-Allende, were present and full publicity were given to the fact that the meeting had been sought by Perón. At first this request was refused and then Hector Campora, President of the Chamber of Deputies and Eva's errand boy, came to tell Reyes that Perón would agree to his conditions if Reyes himself would consent to one small formality—if he would make a courtesy call on the Señora de Perón.

Reyes, who strongly suspected that Eva had been behind the attempts on his life, refused in no polite terms to have anything to do with her.

That was in May. In September of the same year Reyes and Beveraggi-Allende were arrested, charged with an attempt on the lives of the Peróns. They were tortured—the *picana electrica* again and radios played *fortissimo* to drown their groans and cries—to force from them a confession that "North American Imperialists" had been behind the "plot," a confession that both courageously refused to tender. They were released in April of the following year by a judge whose integrity cost him his position. Reyes was shortly re-arrested; this time he was accused of violating the anti-gambling laws in his house, a charge that was patently ridiculous since he and his house had been under police surveillance. His friend Beveraggi-Allende evaded the police "protection" with his wife and infant daughter and escaped to Uruguay and from thence to the United States, where he placed a report of their imprisonment and torture before the United Nations. The indomitable Reyes is still in jail.[3]

These cases of police torture did not go without protest from the Opposition. A report was prepared from the depositions of the victims and read before the Chamber of Deputies in July, 1949, in spite of heckling and interruption from the Peronista bloc, and a commission of inquiry set up, headed by two Peronista deputies, José Emilio Visca and Rudolfo Decker, and one Radical deputy, Arturo Frondizi; but since only two were required to form a quorum the "investigation" was conducted without any reference to Dr. Frondizi. Visca and Decker, both toadies of Eva, ignored the question of police culpability entirely, and used their authority for investigating anti-Argentine—that is to say, anti-Peronista—activities. They became notorious for the severity with which they applied the law of *desacato*—in one week they closed down fifty newspapers for not carrying properly displayed at their masthead the words, *The Year of the Liberator, General San Martín*. It seems that they overstepped themselves and in May, 1950, the Commission was put under the authority of Miel Asquia, Eva's protégé; but by that time its original purpose had quite been forgotten, although arbitrary arrest, imprisonment without trial, and torture continued—and continue still.

It has been said in vindication of Eva and Perón that it may be that they did not know of the atrocities that were perpetrated in their name. This is not true. Eva herself was aware of all that went on in the Special Section of Police, which is accountable not to the chief of police but to the presidency, and whose torturers— Amoresano and Lombilla are the most infamous of these—boast of their immunity. In certain cases the police did overstep their instructions or acted on their own initiative: the blameless employee of a well-known firm of opticians was arrested and beaten for no other reason than that he had walked past the Special Section. Once

[3]On the eve of Perón's second inauguration in June 1952, Reyes, who had already been in prison nearly four years, was sentenced to five years' imprisonment.

the hydra of sadism is released it is impossible to control. But that Eva was aware of, condoned, aided and encouraged the atrocities committed by the Special Section was revealed by the Bravo case, by Dr. Caride's courageous report and the part that Eva's newspaper *Democracia* played in the affair.

In June 1951 there appeared scrawled upon the walls of Buenos Aires the words, *Where is Bravo?* and sometimes, *The police have assassinated the student Bravo!* Rumors ran wild through the city: a student named Bravo had been seized by the police and had disappeared; the bruised and beaten body of a young man had been picked up on the road to La Plata; Bravo's mother had asked to be allowed to see the body and had been refused. By June 11 *Democracia* had begun to deny the story. In headlines an inch and a half high they announced that International Communism planned to create disturbances by means of the university students. In headlines a little smaller they claimed that Wall Street and the Cominform were again arm in arm. Their story was that the student Bravo had been sequestered by fellow Communists as an excuse for dissension in the university; that he and two friends had been seen by the police walking near the Special Section—an odd place to choose for a constitutional if *Democracia's* story were true!—and that he had resisted arrest and shots had been exchanged before Bravo could be taken; and in proof of all this *Democracia* ran photographs of a police car with bullet holes in the door and of a pale but not disheveled Ernesto Mario Bravo under arrest. In proof of the importance they attached to the story was the amount of space allotted to it; by June 15, the whole front page and very nearly half of the eight-page newspaper was taken up with it; one article was entitled, *It will always be an honor to fight and die for Perón.* Behind this nefarious plot, so the stories in *Democracia* ran, were members of the Opposition, of the Democratic Union which included most of the exiles in Uruguay, of the Communist Party, Mr. John Griffiths, who was once cultural attaché to the American Embassy in Buenos Aires, and the "sinister shadow" of the former American ambassador, Mr. Spruille Braden. This inflammatory material continued to fill the pages of *Democracia* until June 18, when news of another story that was being circulated became generally known—it was the report made by Dr. Alberto Julian Caride at very grave risk to his life. Perhaps no one who has not lived under a dictatorship can realize the extraordinary sense of exhilaration, of exaltation almost, that the news of one courageous act can give. The mimeographed sheets of the report were passed from hand to hand, across the marble tops of café tables, in the shelter of a doorway, at cocktail parties, they were carried off to the provinces in the luggage of elderly men and the handbags of young girls, everywhere lighting the quick flame of courage in their wake.

Dr. Caride, who had in a private capacity attended members of the Special Section of Police in the past, had been called in by them on the case of young Bravo. Briefly his report is this: At dawn on May 18, 1951—it was, may it be remembered, in June that *Democracia* ran stories denying that the police had any knowledge of Bravo's whereabouts—he was called on the telephone by an officer of the Special Section, who told him that a police car was being sent round to pick him up. At the Special Section he was told that he would be given his passport—he had recently asked them to expedite the matter because he wished to take a holiday abroad—but that he must first attend to a prisoner who had been beaten up. He examined the prisoner, a tall, robust young man who was lying on the office floor in a semi-conscious state; he was very badly bruised all over his body—the doctor gives details of this—especially about his head and shoulders so that his features were distorted and his eyes closed; there was a deep and very painful wound in his head which made him cry out, even in his semi-conscious state, when the doctor examined it; a rib and two of his fingers were broken. When the doctor made his report one of the police officers replied that perhaps after all it would be better to eliminate the boy by throwing him under a truck; he said the boy had been beaten up by ten of his men without orders from him and that he could allow him to live only if he could be treated here in the Special Section.

Familiar as he was with members of the Special Section, Dr. Caride must have been aware of other such cases of brutality; perhaps his desire to take a trip abroad for "reasons of health" was evidence of his growing revulsion to the system under which he made his livelihood. He does not seem to have been a man of strong political conviction and certainly at this point he had no knowledge of his patient's political affiliation, or even of his identity. He saw Bravo only as a young man who had been brutally misused and from that moment he dedicated himself to the saving of the young man's life, regardless of the risk to himself and to his family. There had come a moment when his humanity raised him to heroic stature.

He goes on to report that from then on he and his house were under constant police surveillance; that he went nowhere except in a police car and accompanied by a police officer and was supervised even when he was visiting his private patients. The police warned him that any "indiscretion on his part would mean the prompt elimination of himself and the boy," and they boasted that they would have nothing to fear "from above" if this were necessary. The doctor continued to attend the boy and, after some insistence, had got him a bed and some blankets and in due course learnt the boy's name was Bravo. As soon as Bravo was conscious, not until four or five days later, his eyes were bandaged during the doctor's visits and the doctor was addressed by another name so that his patient would not recognize him at some later date. The doctor was told that a writ of habeas corpus had been issued and the police had reported that the boy was not and never had been under arrest and that no warrant had been issued for his arrest. They were now waiting for orders "from above" as to what should be done with the boy. The police had begun to fear that there might be an inspection of their offices; but they said quite frankly that there were only two judges whose inspection they feared since all the others had received orders not to visit the Special Section without previous advice that would give the officers time to remove any controversial prisoners through a rear entrance which gave conveniently onto the offices of Precinct 8. A few days

223

had been, courageously published the whole of the story, including the doctor's report and a report made by Bravo, on July 17. The protest aroused by the doctor's report forced the police to release Bravo and to put the officers involved under arrest. But before the end of July Amoresano, Lombilla, and the rest were comfortably lodged in the barracks of the mounted police in Palermo Park, under no supervision at all and entertained by their friends, while Bravo and Dr. Caride were still in hiding.

Bravo seems to have been arrested because of his activities in a Communist Youth Organization and this has shockingly been advanced by way of excuse for the treatment he received. His political affiliation cannot detract in any way from the brutality and injustice of the police and "those above," or from the shameless hypocrisy of the editorials in *Democracia* or from the heroism of Dr. Caride. Nor let it be comfortably supposed that the brutality of the Perón regime is directed only against communism; the only political party free from persecution in Argentina today is the Peronista Party. Radicals, as conservative as English Tories, Socialists, Conservatives and those who have no political opinions at all are equally vulnerable. Since the 1951 election eminent members of all parties have been imprisoned, including Ricardo Balbin and Arturo Frondizi, the Radical candidates, and Dr. Palacios. If they were not tortured it is only because they have too many sympathizers to be ill-treated with impunity. The policy of the Peróns is to ruin the wealthy, discredit the eminent, intimidate the foreigner and to maltreat the humble. They have used the bogey of communism as an excuse but in doing so almost invariably link communism with Wall Street and with the most reactionary members of the Opposition. By all accounts Bravo was an extremely courageous youth—he was beaten into unconsciousness and revived to be beaten again but he could not be made to sign a "confession"; he had an exemplary scholastic record and had been given the *Pro Patria* medal for merit during his term of military service; it is such as he, who have no open means of protesting the

225

injustice they see around them, whom the Peróns have driven into the arms of communism.

The references the police officers made to "those above" could refer only to the Presidency to whom the Special Section is directly answerable, and Eva is further implicated by the stand taken by *Democracia,* since *Democracia* insisted that the police knew nothing of Bravo after the police had received orders "from above" to remove him from the Special Section.

Those whom Eva did not charm by her glamour and her girlish air have remarked on the reptilian coldness of her eye. That she was pitiless and ruthless is self-evident; whether she ever gave direct orders that her fellow countrymen should be seized and tortured or whether she witnessed such brutality there is no proof. But that she was ignorant of the facts is impossible! And her knowledge of them, when she was in a position of such absolute authority, utterly invalidates any claim she could make of her compassion or sympathy for the working people. Her "love" for the poor people of Argentina was the sick love of an over-possessive mother; she loved them only so long as they were absolutely dependent on her and obedient to her wishes, as long as they expressed their adoration and devotion to her alone. Then she indulged them as the neurotic mother indulges an only darling child, giving them toys they were not allowed to touch, boasting of their mutual adoration before guests. But let them show a spark of independence, let them express an opinion contrary to her own, and she would turn on them as a psychotic mother turns upon her child and punish them in the most ruthless manner her sick mentality could suggest.

Fifteen

The watchword of the shirtless ones should be: Whoever
speaks ill of the government, give him what he deserves. Let's
not try to convince him. E. P.

In considering, and condemning, the methods used by the
Peronista police it should be remembered that there had
been many cases of police brutality in Argentina before the advent
of the Peróns—indeed, in what country have there not been isolated
incidents of police oppression? Such cases had been on the increase
since the beginning of the military regime in 1930; but the Peróns,
with their spies and their thugs, their early morning and midnight
arrests, their crowded prisons and their concentration camps, and
their torture, have far exceeded any brutality that existed in the
country since the days of the tyrant Rosas, the centenary of whose
overthrow in 1852 it is now illegal to celebrate; and this is not the

227

brutality of one or two sadistic police officers but a policy of terrorization directed towards the subjugation of an entire nation. The Peróns have introduced into South America their own version of a totalitarian dictatorship, on a smaller scale, less thorough, less efficient than the Nazi system it imitates, more capricious, more heavily disguised under a bland urbanity, but no less demoralizing, no less cruel. Cruelty seems almost more obscene when the sun shines so brightly and smiles are so affable.

To those who know and love Argentina the ruin that the Peróns have wrought is all the more shocking because on all counts it was unnecessary. This was not a country crowded and confined as Italy or Germany, not a country disrupted by revolution and war as Russia had been; it was a peaceful country on the threshold of great prosperity, one of the world's great storehouses of food with the majority of its resources as yet untouched. Buenos Aires is the third largest city in the Western Hemisphere, almost the equal in population to Chicago, and its streets, once washed and swept every night, were as clean and bright as any in the world. If there was a shocking disparity between life in the city and life in the more distant provinces yet Argentina was the most advanced of South American countries and the most literate—before the Peróns' day illiteracy had been reduced to sixteen per cent—and so prosperous that with a reasonably honest government there might easily have been achieved throughout the country a standard of living higher than any in the world, not excluding the United States. Had Perón treated the working people with honest liberality and given the advantage to rural communities rather than the cities, he would have had the strong support of Labor without having to resort to the methods of tyranny, and Eva might have had her forty thousand dollars' worth of dresses from Paris every year and her diamond clips and rings worth a few tens of thousands each without the country being measurably the worse for it. But there are no honest means for twisted minds and the necessities that drove both Eva and Perón had their source within.

Perón's specious program of reform was so dazzling in promise

228

that one is tempted to believe that had he not come under the influence of Eva he might have become a truly democratic leader and gone down in history as the great benefactor of his race; but while Eva did, without any doubt, encourage the corruption and the extravagance and the illiberality of the regime, Perón was trained in the Prussian school of militarism and had been inspired by the rantings of Mussolini and Hitler and was a believer in totalitarianism long before he met Eva. Eva, before she met him, believed only in herself. But it was she, with her insensitive, rough-shod autocracy, who created more enemies for the regime.

The hatred against Eva slowly spread from the oligarchs and the military, who were her first enemies, to the liberals and the labor leaders who blamed their disillusion with Perón on Eva's influence, and then to the more active of union members who had seen some of their companions disappear and had begun to recognize the price they had had to pay for higher wages. But the great majority of the working people were still behind Eva and Perón; few of them knew that their fellows have been tortured, for the Peronista press and the radio carried no word of it and those whose relatives had disappeared were often frightened into silence. To be found in possession of any literature criticizing the regime was proof of *desacato*.

Not a month went by without the rumor of a plot to overthrow the regime, but it is difficult as yet to say which of these rumors rested on fact, since anyone engaged in plotting was loath to talk and arrests and incarceration were no proof of guilt; many of these "plots" discovered so promptly and denounced with such passion in the Peronista press were certainly originated by the Peróns themselves, who used them to whip up the lagging enthusiasm of the shirtless ones or to put members of the Opposition in jail. No plot had yet approached success; they were no more than the sporadic attempts of separate groups—the students locking themselves in the universities, the ladies of the oligarchy staging a demonstration in Calle Florida, the railway workers calling a strike and blowing up bridges, a group of officers planning to seize Campo de Mayo; but none of these groups would co-operate in concerted rebellion.

In September 1948, radios and loudspeakers suddenly blared forth news of the discovery of a plot to assassinate Eva and Perón by means of a bomb at the gala performance in the Colón Opera House on October 12. The news was on the air and posters denouncing the plot were up all over the city a few hours after the arrests were made. It was an excellent opportunity to deflect attention from the failure of the regime to perform all it had promised, to stir up the people into a nationalistic frenzy, and to put Cipriano Reyes and others in jail. That Reyes and others who had become disillusioned with the regime held meetings to discuss its overthrow is certain; that they plotted to assassinate Eva and Perón at the opera house is improbable. The more responsible elements of the Opposition did not consider assassination as a method of ridding themselves of tyranny since it might well have thrown the country into civil war and have ended in another military dictatorship. Reyes had in fact become suspicious of certain Army officers who, pretending discontent under Peronista rule, had offered him their services, and he had called off the meetings with his friends; but they were arrested in their homes; a blind doctor, two priests and two women were among those arrested. As has been said the judge released them after six months, but Reyes was re-arrested on a trumped-up charge.

The arrests and the so-called plot were made the occasion for an eruption of hysterical denunciation and Peronista delirium. The C.G.T. called a one-day strike so that the workers would be free to demonstrate their indignant loyalty; thanksgiving masses were held in the churches; truckloads of shirtless ones, waving miniature gallows, were brought into Plaza de Mayo, and the crowds chanted, "Evita! Evita! Perón! Perón!" in a frenzy-inducing rhythm. From the balcony of the Casa Rosada Perón screamed accusation and threat, and Eva, working herself into an emotional orgasm, cried that she was ready to die a hundred deaths for the sake of the people, adding plaintively, "But why would anyone want to kill a simple woman like me?"

The Peronista newspaper *La Epoca* accused the United States of fostering and financing this plot. The "sinister" figures—they had by now become the classic bogeys of the Peronista regime—of Spruille Braden and John Griffiths were invoked. They were neither of them in the country; Mr. Braden had long since returned to Washington and Mr. Griffiths, no longer attached to the Embassy, had a few months before been accused of inciting bank employees to strike and, after a short spell in jail, had left the country; his arrest had been no more than a means of getting him out of the country, for he had worked closely with Spruille Braden who had so frankly censured the regime. In Montevideo, John Griffiths was awakened in the night by reporters clamoring for news of the plot he was supposed to have engineered; he would not listen to them at first, thinking that they were playing some fool joke on him.

On this and on similar occasions Perón did not hesitate to make suggestions of violence to the mob which are most shocking as coming from the country's chief executive. In August 1946, on another occasion, he said, "I will make a revolution a week earlier (than the Opposition). It is no more than a matter of providing each shirtless one with a few yards of twine—then we'll see who hangs whom!"

He has since improved on this by suggesting that the shirtless ones should carry lengths of wire in their pockets for the purpose. In September 1948, shortly after the discovery of the Reyes "plot," he said that his voice would not tremble when he ordered the hanging of his domestic enemies—under Argentine civil law there is no death penalty—and a few months later he enjoined his followers to be ready to "come forth and defend our cause. I shall say very soon what we are going to do."

When no scheming gave an excuse for rabble-rousing speeches, "plots" were manufactured from any small incident, some of them patently absurd. A cable sent to the parents of a new seven-pound baby congratulating them on the arrival of three and

231

a half kilos of dynamite led to a number of arrests, including that of the baby's father, before it could be proved that this dynamite came, as Argentines put it, from God. In a search for arms and ammunition—in a country where every rural household owns a sporting piece or two—an Englishman was imprisoned for having possession of a gun. That it was a museum piece and would have blown up in the hands of anyone rash enough to try to fire it made no difference. Foreigners in Argentina, Americans and English among them, were not free from arbitrary arrest and attacks by thugs but, as far as this writer knows, they were not inflicted with the attentions of the Special Section. Nor, on the whole, did they show themselves notably impervious to intimidation, although loud enough in their criticism of the regime and of Argentine flaccidity.

It was in the slow growth of anger among the working people that there lay the most serious threat to Eva and Perón. Strikes were more frequent than the country at large could know, for news of them was carried only in the underground papers brought out by the Radicals and Socialists. In the first six months of 1950 there were strikes, and sometimes repeated strikes, among airplane workers, dock workers, restaurant cooks, employees of the pasteurized milk industry, street cleaners, restaurant employees, sailors, construction workers and employees of the Swift meat-packing plant. There were slowdowns and protest demonstrations among municipal workers, employees of a shoe factory, train guards on one railway and peons on another, and employees of other meat packing plants. The strikes were declared illegal, strike leaders were arrested. Eva had some of them hauled before her and scolded them for behaving so badly when they had such a good government and ordered them back to work. But the strikes continued and grew worse.

Most serious of all was the growing dissatisfaction among the railway workers, the most powerful group of workers in the country. In November 1950, the railway peons went out on strike for higher wages—it should be remembered that the cost of living was constantly catching up with the boosts in wages; level-crossing guards, train and station personnel went out in sympathy. The raise was granted by the Minister of Transport, and the men went back to work. But in December they were out on strike again, protesting that the promised raise had not been forthcoming and demanding the resignation of their union officials; it was against them, especially against the secretary of their union, Pedro Lopez, rather than against the government that their protest was directed as yet. Again their demands were granted and Lopez resigned. But the C.G.T. appointed an *interventor* to their union and at the end of January, 1951, when the railway workers had still not been allowed to elect their own union officers and many of their fellow-strikers, whose release had been promised, were still in jail, they went out on strike again. Perón dismissed the Minister of Transport for having bargained with "illegal" strikers and, invoking an emergency decree, put the railway workers under martial law, dismissed two thousand of them and put some three hundred in jail. Eva, who takes any strike which is not in the Peronista interest as a personal insult against herself and Perón, flew around from one railway station to the next, haranguing the workers furiously; but now she was met with sullen silence and sometimes with hissing and boos. And chalked up on the walls of railway buildings there appeared the ominous words, *Viva Perón Viudo*—Long live Perón the Widower!

The strikers were forced to return to work; by the middle of the year twenty-seven of those arrested were still in prison and without trial. The strikes which had begun against the Peronista union officers, who, as the workers complained, went gadding around the country in special trains as if they were oligarchs, ended on a note of rising anger against Eva herself, which their forced return to work did nothing to conciliate.

It was as yet, early in 1951, only those workers who had become directly involved in strikes, who had felt themselves to be threatened by loss of employment or arrest, who had become seriously dissatisfied not only with their union officers but with the government, and many of them did not so much blame Perón as those who surrounded him, of whom Eva was one. The shortages that had been occasioned by Perón's policy did not as yet measurably affect the workingman who had never known much convenience or comfort in his life; the average workingman had never had a telephone in his home, owned a car or lived in a properly heated house, his wife had never used a gas range or an electric icebox. Kerosene was commonly used for cooking and heating and it was the shortage of this and the difficulty of getting to and from work by train or bus that inconvenienced the workingman most. Their diet was so simple that it was not greatly affected by any food shortage save that of meat or bread; the rise in the cost of living, which by 1951 had begun to rise steadily above the wage level, was offset in many cases by the fact that whereas in the past only adult males in the family earned a living wage—if their women took in washing at best they earned a dollar and a half a day—now the whole adult family were industrial workers and the women also benefited by the new wage scale. Their living quarters had never been so roomy or convenient that now they were greatly inconvenienced by the shortage of housing in the city; even those who came from the north and lived in shanty towns in the suburbs had lived under no better conditions at home. These inconveniences affected the white collar workers who had become used to modern conveniences in their homes and now had to fly around among their Peronista friends if they wanted gas laid on to a little house in the suburbs or a telephone installed.

But the Peróns themselves had been diligently undermining their own regime, for their policy of indulging the industrial worker to the detriment of the rural worker had begun to bring about a shortage in the two foodstuffs which would affect every man in the country—meat and bread.

ment; it certainly does not imply the moderation or stability of any central position. But to Eva *Peronismo* was a religion and she repeatedly declared herself its fanatical devotee. There is no doubt that if she had dared she would have set about disestablishing the Roman Catholic Church in Argentina as she disestablished or emasculated every other institution in the country; but the Church had a hold upon the mass of people as strong as Eva's own and she had to offer it at least a semblance of reverence. But the respect she showed the Church was not one genuflexion more than was absolutely necessary. True she put her own confessor, Father Benitez—as confessor his position was surely a sinecure—at the head of the Ecclesiastic Department of the Eva Perón Foundation; but Father Benitez showed himself to verge on heresy in the reverence he accorded to Eva herself. She supplied her hospitals and homes with chapels, but they were not always as large and never as luxurious as the rooms set aside for her own deification. She and Perón attended High Mass on public holidays but they sometimes took a part in the services more active than is usual for lay members, however august, of the congregation. This was as far as her piety would carry her and it is said that her lack of ceremony towards the clergy caused a considerable cooling between Cardinal Copello and the government during the last year or two.

In October 1950, when Cardinal Rufini, the papal legate, arrived in Argentina to attend the Eucharistic Congress in Rosario, Eva and Perón were not at the airport to meet him; they were spending the week end in San Vicente. It is said that the Peróns had sent a special plane to Rome to fetch the cardinal so that he might arrive in Buenos Aires before October 17, and appear with Eva and Perón on the balcony of the Casa Rosada for the celebrations on that Peronista anniversary, but that he refused the attention and arrived too late for the fiesta. The legate stayed at the house of an oligarch, a relative of the Pereyra Iraolas, whose property Eva had lately expropriated for her Home for the Aged; whether any reproof was meant by this choice of domicile this writer has no means of knowing; but Cardinal Copello administered a rebuke that sent the Peróns scurrying up to Rosario to pay their tardy respects to the legate there.

The incident had been accentuated by one that had occurred just before. On the eve of the Eucharistic Congress in Rosario the Basileo School of Scientific Spiritualists held their Congress in Luna Park, the indoor stadium where Eva and Perón first met. The posters announcing the Spiritualistic Congress bore the text, *Christ is not God*. This aroused a furious protest from the clergy and Catholic groups—among those who protested was Eva's friend, Ivanissevich—ending in a disorderly scene outside Luna Park on the evening of the Congress, which the police subdued with tear gas. Since today in Buenos Aires no ladies' cultural society may meet to discuss Jane Austen without previously notifying the police in detail, and very often admitting a police officer to the meeting, it is not likely that the authorities granted permission for the Congress without knowing of the text that was to be displayed; in spite of this Perón, who fancies himself as a patron of the sciences, sent a message to be read at the meeting by Colonel Ballofet; the hall was, of course, decorated with large portraits and medallions of the Peróns. It is inconceivable that the Peróns should not have realized that their expansiveness towards this unorthodox meeting would be extremely offensive to the Church. Cardinal Copello left them in no doubt, for he ordered special masses to be said in all the churches to atone for the blasphemy. It was at this moment that the Peróns chose to slight the papal legate. But the excuse given for the discourtesy in a letter written to the Supreme Court by Father Benitez throws a curious light upon Eva's relationship with the Church. He wrote to thank the judges for a donation they had made to the Eva Perón Foundation, and in eulogizing Eva he mentioned her profound study of spiritualism and that she was in constant communication with the immortals, San Martín among them, who guided her in her policy. The Church was opposed to these practices, Benitez went on, but the Vatican would one day recognize the real value of her studies. It was, he added, because of the Church's disapproval

237

that Eva had felt she could not, in all sincerity, extend a personal welcome to the legate.

That she and Perón should have shown an interest in the occult was to have been expected since the unease they shared in common with all dictators must have driven them to seek assurance of their future in this world as much as hope of life in the next. At one time, at least, they sought to discover their fate from Mr. Courtney Luck, an Englishman well known in Buenos Aires for his oracular demonstrations, whom Perón made Director of Psychic Research. And that Eva should have believed that she was in communication with the dead and endowed by them with supernatural authority came readily within the pattern of her fantasy.

Eva's only religion was *Peronismo* and its only tenet was faith in Perón. Whatever her personal feeling for him may once have been, it became lost in this extension of her fantasy; whatever her manner towards him in private, and she used her tongue just as roughly on him as on anyone, in public she never faltered in proclaiming her faith. There is no doubt that she saw him and herself canonized after death; but there was evidence in her speech and writing of more. She was building a myth around Perón—and in building it around Perón she was building it around herself—in which he was not only the wise and benign ruler but the semi-divine king.

"I sometimes think," she said, "that President Perón has ceased to be man like other men—that he is, rather, an ideal incarnate. For this our party may cherish him as our leader without fearing that he will disappear on that unhappy day when Perón in person is no longer here. Perón will always stand before the people as an ideal, a flag, a beacon, a very star to point the way through night to final victory."

"I cannot conceive of Heaven without General Perón," she said on more than one occasion; and, "But when we think that San Martín had his betrayers and Christ himself was denied, why should it not be so for Perón?"

"I see him [Perón] sometimes conceive an idea that to me seems

238

too close to the clouds . . . and then I see how that same idea begins to take form . . . and little by little his marvelous hands begin to convert it into reality." The points of suspension are her own. She used the word "marvelous" repeatedly in reference to Perón; she wrote of the day she met him as her "marvelous day," of his "marvelous humility" in stooping to her, and of his "marvelous ways" and his "marvelous heart."

The humble role she allotted to herself in this theocracy seemed in such direct contradiction to reality that it has been dismissed by many as propaganda and totally insincere; those who surrounded her closely certainly made full use of its publicity value. But to Eva herself it was more. It was an essential part of the fantasy with which she deluded and tried to reassure herself, and did not, in fact, contradict her inordinate ambition which, always overstepping what might have been the satisfactions of reality, had reached the limit of human aggrandizement. The next step was divinity, and by elevating her husband and humbling herself she had by no means renounced her own claims. She had been raised in the Roman Catholic religion whose God and whose saints preached and practiced humility; humility was the hallmark of the divine. And it is significant that it was not before God and the Church that she prostrated herself, but before Perón and the people. She referred to herself with an almost psychopathic insistence as a bridge over which the people must pass to reach Perón—and this is reminiscent of the part the Virgin plays in the Catholic religion. She prostrated herself before Perón—figuratively, of course—in an ecstasy. "I acknowledge," she wrote, "that I no longer exist in myself and that he [Perón] lives in my soul, lord of all my words and feelings, absolute master of my heart and life." She referred to herself as "a sort of slave" to Perón and as his shadow. "I know there is a great difference [between Perón and herself]. Where he gives a masterly lesson I barely stammer. When he can settle a problem in four words, it takes me sometimes a week. Where he decides I barely suggest. What he sees clearly I barely discern. He is the guide and I am only the shadow in his superior presence."

239

Her speeches and writings were repetitious to a tedious degree—or, perhaps, to a hypnotic one. She used the word "heart" so insistently—she was, in her speeches, forever opening up or giving away or leaving behind her heart—that Tristan, in the scathing cartoons he did for *Vanguardia,* made a pinchushiony little heart her motif; he has, of course, long since disappeared. But such persistent use of the words "heart," "abnegation" and "humility" cannot be dismissed altogether as the dramatics of demagogy or as the extravagance natural to the Spanish language, and there was a morbid note in her prostration that should yield study for the psychologists one day.

Perón himself has given no indication that his ambition exceeds his human nature nor, in spite of the freedom he allowed her and his remarkable loyalty to her person, that he thought of his wife as other than human; indeed there was sometimes a hint of patronage in his attitude towards her. He lent himself to her deification of himself since it suited his design admirably. In public he was the indulgent husband of a beautiful and talented wife; it was in private that he sometimes showed signs of being a little bit in awe of her. Eva was at times possessed of an incontrollable temper when "the lord of all her words and feelings" was as likely to come in for his share of abuse as anyone. When there was a witness to such scenes Perón shrugged his shoulders and explained apologetically, "My wife is so upset today." His attitude had the hallmarks of a henpecked husband. But along with this hint of timidity, and not at all discordant with it, was his obvious pride in her boldness and aggressiveness. When the Foundation was inaugurated he boasted, "Soon my wife will be handling more money than I do!" And when he once showed a favored guest her array of clothes and furs he said, with a smirk, "Not bad for a shirtless one, eh?" He has told how, when an elaborate buffet meal was prepared for Eva and a large party in the government house in Tucumán, she called in the little urchins from the plaza to stuff themselves, and he added with evident glee, "You can imagine the sensation that caused!"

But it is evident that he took her on his own evaluation and not on hers; she was a woman and not a saint to him, and *Peronismo* was no religion. At a dinner given in 1951 to British diplomats Eva broke out suddenly into one of her declamatory eulogies of *Peronismo* usually reserved for the mob in the Plaza de Mayo—that she should do this, almost mechanically as if a button had been pressed, it was said, on such an inappropriate occasion, shows the hold her "religion" had on her—and Perón shrugged his shoulders and grinned and made some apologetic remark about never being able to trust a woman at the dinner table, so that his guests laughed uneasily and Eva, disconcerted for once, was stopped short. It was Eva, not Perón, who had the fanaticism of a Hitler.

Only on very few occasions did Perón thwart Eva; he vetoed a grant of fourteen million dollars that both the Senate and the Chamber of Deputies had voted to the Foundation, and gave no public explanation of his veto; on occasion he censored her speeches before they appeared in print; it is said that he scolded her sometimes for interrupting some serious discussion. If he did not speak of her in public so gushingly as she spoke of him yet his tribute to her was always warm. "You see the extraordinary influence of the president of the Eva Perón Foundation—why is it? Because she dresses well and is pretty? No. She is loved and respected and honored by all the humble because she cannot eat or sleep or live for doing good."

Perón had not changed greatly during his first six-year term. He had grown somewhat fleshier and flabbier; he had, in some photographs, the rather dissipated look of an elderly and out-of-date actor, but possibly this was due to the suntan make-up he used to cover a scar or skin eruption on his cheek; in person he appeared larger, healthier and more genial than those by whom he is surrounded. In the past Eva had some hand in grooming him for public appearances; she insisted that he should have his teeth straightened while she was in Europe so that his smile became more expansive and dazzling than before; it was she who suggested that he should wear a white jacket to his uniform even in winter so that

241

in the poorly printed photographs of the Argentine press his figure should be clearly distinguishable; later, as he withdrew a little and she came forward in the public eye, he gave up this device, and she seemed to have lost her concern in his appearance. He was as industrious, if not as energetic, as his wife and his working day started at 6 A.M.; but his has been the more phlegmatic nature, and until her final illness he showed little sign of strain, unless his chain-smoking were the result of fatigue.

By 1951 Eva's schedule had become so exacting that the time she could spend with her husband had been reduced to a minimum and must have been absorbed by the necessary discussion of their policy. They could have had no time at all for private life. She herself admitted that there were days when she scarcely saw him and sometimes she got home in the early hours when it was time for him to get up and leave for the office; and she added coyly that he scolded her on those occasions. They no longer spent rural week ends in the San Vicente house; at one time she had shocked the more matronly Argentine ladies by her casual appearance in slacks on such occasions. They were no longer to be seen driving along the waterfront on hot evenings as they had once done. They did not have time now for those little democratic acts they had performed together which had done much to popularize them in early days; when the census was taken in 1947 Perón and Eva appeared in half a dozen workmen's homes and, while Perón took down the statistics, Eva distributed gifts among the goggling womenfolk and children; they appeared less frequently at sports events, the more popular of which they had once made a point of attending together. Yet before the world they continued to present an astonishingly united front; there appeared to be no change in their relationship, certainly no weakening of it, and their most bitter enemies were hard put to discover any slip in their sentimental duologue.

But Eva had changed and the change was profound.

The magnificently flamboyant creature of the middle of the decade, the Doña María Eva Duarte de Perón, had become the brusque, businesslike Eva Perón, as beautiful as and more elegant than she had ever been, in her severe tailor-made costumes with her diamond orchid almost as large as a real one in her lapel, her pale hair strained back into a heavy knot on her nape, her thinness accentuating her high round cheekbones and her youthful and rather bulging forehead. She could still look like a little girl at times, but she had lost all the fullness, all the softness of her womanhood; she had the perfect gloss of enamel. She was darting, brilliant, brittle as a dragonfly. She excited amazement and admiration and envy, but she no longer excited desire. When she was not smiling, and in public she wore an almost ceaselessly radiant smile, her mouth was arrogant, even a little cynical; she met strangers with a cold, distrustful, estimating stare but, once assured of their friendliness, melted to a sudden warmth that seemed to be sincere and even in its insincerity had a touch of pathos in it. She was still capable of moments of refreshing candor and would admit quite freely that she was what she called a "repentant brunette." Her complexion was exceedingly pale; it has often been described as having a greenish tinge; it was that matte white complexion that even under a photographer's cruel lights will show no flaw. She appeared to be utterly sure of herself and poised, but her hands betrayed her emotion and her true character; they were not the soft, white hands of a cocotte or the slender, limp hands of the visionary and saint; they were strong, dramatic, vulgar hands and the gestures she made with them were the strong, graphic gestures a countrywoman would use to punctuate her gossiping; they had none of the self-conscious elegance of affected gesturing. She would cross her arms over her chest like a washerwoman, wag a forefinger to emphasize an argument, brush aside all other arguments with a sweep of both hands, catch suddenly at her throat or at her diamond orchid as if a secret fear had caught at her heart, or spread out her fingertips on the table or balustrade before her to show her impatience with the slowness of the proceedings. Her hands were forceful, vulgar, impatient and, it is said, they were always cold.

Only for very formal occasions did she dress herself in her full

243

magnificence now, in those long wide skirts that she had begun to favor for gala affairs soon after her return from Paris and which made it necessary for her to stand a step or two ahead of the men with whom she was photographed—and she was almost always the only woman in the group. In this formal attire she often posed before a tapestry that hangs on the Residency wall and which made a somber and regal background to her pale beauty; she was more frequently photographed at her desk, at the microphone or with a group of union officers or government officials. There were very few informal pictures taken of her; there were very few informal moments in her life. For all the magnificence of her surroundings she was living a life of extreme austerity; she ate strictly according to her diet, drank sparingly, smoked not at all in public—Perón carried carmine-tipped cigarettes for her use in private. She had no purely social engagements, no pleasures beyond her work. She lived a dedicated life; but she was dedicated to a fantasy.

The voice with which she had harangued the mob was almost as harsh and ugly as the overstrained voices of the newsboys who used to cry the evening papers on the corners of Calle Corrientes; with almost every sentence her voice rose to the pitch of hysteria; she spoke rapidly, furiously, as if, it has been said,[1] she were always defending something. Perhaps it was herself she felt called upon to defend, for throughout her book[2] there is an angry, explanatory note. There was in her speeches and her writings an endless repetition of the same emotional phrases; she dealt in abstracts and used no facts or figures to substantiate her arguments. In arguing that the syndicalization of unions is necessary to the Peronista state she explained, "This is true, firstly because Perón says so, and secondly, because it is the truth." She used the same arguments that an ignorant mother uses to quiet the importunities of her child. She claimed proudly that she acted and spoke from the heart, which is to say that she acted and spoke under emotional compulsion. But emotional as her speeches continued to be, their violence had al-

[1] By Milton Bracker in the New York *Times*.
[2] *La Razón de mi Vida.*

244

ready begun to abate; she was less of a virago and more of the prophetess. She had begun to prepare for her final metamorphosis.

Eva had no intimate friends; she had enemies, disciples, lovers, protégés, but no friends. She had women who played the part of confidante in matters such as clothes and jewelry, but she treated them as ladies-in-waiting rather than as intimates and her confidence in them did not last. When she first came into power her confidential secretary was Isabel Ernst, Mercante's friend, who was always at her elbow to guide her in her official acts; but Eva drove the young woman so ruthlessly, often in the press of work not giving her time to eat, that Ernst became ill and had to retire. One of Eva's first and closest friends was the wife of Alberto Dodero, the shipping magnate, who, for a while, went everywhere with Eva. But Eva expected her companions to be at her beck and call at any moment of the day, she allowed them no life of their own, and Mrs. Dodero, who was an American and had been in the show business herself, was not ready to surrender her independence; and they quarreled and parted. For a while Eva had the Señora Largomarsino de Guardo to dance attendance on her, but the two ladies fell out on the European trip and on her return Eva switched her patronage to Hector Campora's shy, pretty wife. Eva was too demanding to allow friendship to survive, and she could no more tolerate a woman's competition in what social life she led than she could tolerate the rivalry of any man in her political life.

Eva carried her family along with her into affluence; she had to do so to assure their loyalty but she did not allow any of them to rival her. Their photographs were seldom seen in the press and their names seldom appeared. Her brother Juancito was the only one she allowed a measure of publicity and for whom she seemed to have had some affection or respect; it is said that he was able to quiet her in her tantrums and that he used no gentle methods to accomplish this. Among many notorious reputations in Buenos Aires his has been conspicuous; there are endless stories of his dealings on the black market and of his brawls with women in public places. So sinister did his reputation become that, so the story goes, the father of one aspiring young actress, seeing that his daughter had caught Juancito's eye, whisked her out of the country overnight. Yet Juancito Duarte continued as close as ever to the Presidency. Eva's eldest sister Elisa became something of a political boss in Junín, but since Eva never returned to the scene of her bitter childhood Elisa's activities in no way trespassed on her own. Blanca was made Inspector of Schools, no very exalted post under the circumstances, and gossip has it that Eva set a watch on her sister to make sure that she left for work by 7 A.M. but that the less energetic Blanca slipped home again to bed.

Eva's mother, the redoubtable Doña Juana, lived modestly in the apartment in Calle Posadas where Eva used to live. A policeman guarded the door but there was no other sign of her residence. Sometimes she returned to Junín for a visit to old friends and while she was there she occupied a house that was no more spacious and very little more up-to-date than the one she occupied when Eva was a child. She liked the comforts and indulgences of a woman growing old and spent her money on massage, beauty treatments and at the roulette tables in Mar del Plata. It is said that she suffered from insomnia and that she used to beg her daughter to allow her enough money to settle her old bones abroad before the crash, but that Eva, infuriated by such croaking, refused. It seems that Doña Juana also consulted the occult sciences and it is probable that the old lady lived in mortal fear of retribution falling on the family.

By the beginning of 1951 Eva Perón had reached what was to be the zenith of her career, although at the time the potentialities of her influence seemed alarmingly unlimited. She was thirty-one and in those thirty-one years she had achieved a world-wide notoriety, she had been decorated by a dozen different nations, had had ships, schools, parks, subway stations, housing projects and a star named after her,[3] she had the title of First Samaritan and was called the Lady of Hope and the Standard Bearer of the Workers

[3]In 1952 it was announced that the Pampa Province was to be known as the Eva Perón Province. Perón has had an equal number of schools, parks, etc. and a province named after him.

246

—and now it seemed that she was to have the added authority of an official status in the government. But her ambition had outgrown the honors of this world and she was losing touch with reality. The one man with whom she had achieved a close and lasting relationship had become a symbol in her life of fantasy. All the honor and the glory enclosed an emptiness in which she lived alone.

which Perón was not anxious to have advertised; Eva did not show herself so sensitive to alien criticism. *Democracia* had been foremost in branding *La Prensa* and *La Nación* as organs of a "degenerate" oligarchy, which was true in so far as one was the property of the Paz family and the other of the Mitre family, both families of great wealth and both names illustrious in Argentine history. *Democracia* accused them also of being subsidized from abroad, an accusation that was totaly untrue since they derived the greater part of their incomes from classified advertisements and were justly renowned for the independence this allowed them; *La Prensa's* first seven or more pages were once devoted to small advertisements. They had presented the news with honesty and conservative dignity and *La Prensa* in particular had been outspoken in its criticism of unconstitutional decrees. In 1931 *La Prensa* had been instrumental in forcing General Uriburu to hold elections, for, when he had threatened to have it closed for criticizing his dictatorial methods, old Señor Ezequiel Paz, owner and publisher of the paper, had retorted that he would continue to publish it in Paris with daily headlines explaining the reason for its exile. In October 1945 *La Prensa* had called for the Supreme Court to take over the government and thus had earned for itself Eva's personal enmity; her resentment against those who did not demand Perón's reinstatement seemed to become more bitter with the years. No sooner was Perón in office than the campaign against the free press became intensified; *La Prensa* was denounced as an enemy of the people; the Newsboys' Union, incited by the C.G.T., demanded that home deliveries of the paper should cease and, later, that they should be given a percentage of the income from classified advertisements; stocks of newsprint were confiscated and permits for import were cut until its forty-odd pages were reduced to sixteen, to twelve and less. At the beginning of 1951, when *La Prensa* continued to publish news of the railway strikes, the C.G.T. instigated a boycott of the paper; truckers and airline employees refused to handle it, telephone and other public services were not extended to it and its photographers were refused entrance to sports stadiums. After the paper had been forced to remain closed for a month some twelve hundred of its employees, many of whom had a sense of personal loyalty towards the paper, determined that it should be published. As they entered the plant they were attacked by a band of Peronista hoodlums who fired on them, killing one and wounding fourteen others. Although police protection had been promised none was forthcoming and the employees had to defend themselves with sticks and stones. However, when they did drive their assailants off and it became evident that they would succeed in bringing the paper out, police arrived to take six hundred of the employees themselves off to the police station.

Because *La Prensa,* which had once prided itself on printing more foreign news than any other paper in the world, had refused to give up the services of the United Press and make use of those offered by the Argentine Ministry of Information, it was accused of being part of an international publicity medium and prejudicial to the national interests. Señor Gainza Paz, who had succeeded his uncle as publisher, had to flee the country to escape arrest, and the baroque old building of the newspaper was taken over by Peronista officials, adorned with pictures of Eva and Perón, while the Peronista press proclaimed jubilantly that it would be turned over to the C.G.T. for the use of the people. Eva announced, with a cynicism of which she was perhaps unaware, that the Foundation would be responsible for the salaries due to those who had so suddenly lost their means of livelihood; it is said that she offered a compensation to the family of the man who had been killed but that it was refused. Only a very few of those who had been employed by *La Prensa* were kept on; the rest have found it difficult or impossible to find work elsewhere. When *La Prensa* was finally turned over to the C.G.T. in November, Eva sent a message of congratulation in which she said that now a page of truth would take the place of each page of lies.

As the year advanced the uneasiness in the city was aggravated by the signs of economic crisis which were becoming obvious to the man in the street, by the flux of rumors both of violence expected daily and of Eva's ill-health, and by the approach of the elections which were scheduled for February 1952. Perón's assurances that he did not intend to run for a second term had carried little weight since he himself, in the reform of the Constitution, had made a second term possible. It seemed likely that Colonel Mercante would take Quijano's place as vice-president; of all the officials whose careers had rocketed with the Peróns he had retained their closest confidence. When he ran for the governorship of the province of Buenos Aires, Eva and Perón had personally campaigned for his election. "To support Mercante is to support Perón," Eva had said. There was as yet no talk of Eva running for the vice-presidency, an eventuality which seemed almost unthinkable in a country where women had not yet had an opportunity to vote. But it is very possible that Eva herself had had just such a contingency in mind from the first years of Perón's presidency when she began to canvass for women's suffrage. Her ambitions were always a leap ahead of events and it is likely that she was already visualizing herself in office before she was well settled into the Residency, just as now, when her election became possible, she was seeing herself canonized.

There had been no general outcry in Argentina for women's suffrage; the majority of women themselves considered politics beyond their sphere and a sense of social responsibility had not been fostered among them; those who advocated votes for women were among the liberal and intellectual elements of the Opposition. But with Perón to abet her Eva had no need of popular support in such a project and although all the Peronistas themselves did not approve of the innovation Eva had no difficulty in persuading the Senate to incorporate the measure in the reform of the Constitution.

The matter of whether or not a woman's age was to appear on her voting papers seems to have caused more discussion than the actual granting of the suffrage. Eva, who spoke before the Chamber of Deputies on the matter, insisted that she had received thousands of requests from women all over the country begging that their age should be allowed to remain secret—a sorry comment on the mentality of the women were it true. Radical Deputy Pastor remarked that he could very well understand gallantry towards one woman but that he found gallantry towards four million women alarming. It is this gallantry that in part produced Eva and, in part, gave her her advantage, for while it allowed a woman no mature independence and made it necessary for an ambitious woman to use guile to gain her ends, it also restrained the more honorable of the Opposition from attacking Eva as they would have attacked a man in her position. It is possible that Perón was clever enough to have foreseen this and that it was a further reason for allowing Eva so much prominence.

Eva herself, for all her frustrations, was no feminist. If she advanced the feminine cause in Argentina it was by chance in advancing her own career and Peronismo. She ridiculed feminist leaders in general and insisted that their "failure" was due to the fact that they tried to imitate men; women's place, she said as firmly as any Victorian, was in the home, and she asserted her belief that men were "in a certain way" superior to women—a belief that in no way limited her own activities.

As Eva advanced in her public career a great number of women, more interested in their own advancement than in women's rights or social aid, were drawn into her train. They came in numbers from that class of women whose only opportunity had until now been in teaching or in some minor civil service post. Perhaps because of the frustrations and difficulties besetting a woman in Argentina who was determined on her own career these señoritas had developed into what was almost a standard type, the female bureaucrat, whose very appearance was almost uniform; their neat dress and elaborate hair are defensively respectable, they wear pince nez pinned to their bosoms and they are too whitely powdered and too pinkly rouged, and they wear their clothes and their make-up as if they were an armor with which they never allow themselves to dispense. They are often women whom intelligence as much as circumstance has driven to choose the independence of a career; but insecurity in their careers has pressed them into a conventional pattern from which all originality and spontaneity have been squeezed by the necessity to appear obviously and above all respectable. The Eva Perón Foundation and the Peronista Feminine Party have offered these women great opportunities for earning better salaries but they offered no greater independence of spirit; more than ever before their careers depended on their absolute conformity. In 1949 a congress of the Peronista Feminine Party was held at the Teatro Cervantes in Buenos Aires at which some fifteen hundred of these women from all over the country acclaimed Eva with an enthusiasm that verged on hysteria; Mercante was the only man present and he was almost ignored. Among these women there were certainly a number who were fanatically devoted to Eva but the majority of these señoritas—many of them are señoras but they all have a somewhat inviolate air—were too close to her regime to retain their illusions and, if they admired her at all, it was not as an evangelist but as a hard-headed career woman. It was not these women who were ready to fall on their knees at her approach and strew her path with roses, and they had nothing but scorn for those who did.

However, although they get their share of good wages, pensions and bonuses, and perhaps of cars and washing machines as well, they were not allowed to share a scrap of the publicity. Under the tens of thousands of pictures that were published of Eva there was seldom mention of any name other than her own or Perón's; sometimes the name of Mercante, Aloé, Espejo or some other favored Peronista appeared, more rarely the name of one of their wives was mentioned; but the women who worked for Eva in the Peronista Feminine Party had to remain anonymous.

The organization of the Peronista Feminine Party remained entirely independent of the male Peronista Party; Eva herself was its president and it had its own headquarters scattered throughout the country. As the election approached, offices of the Peronista Party were opened on every few blocks in Buenos Aires and these

254

were duplicated by the offices of Eva's party—as the Feminine Party might well have been called. They were readily recognizable, by day because of the blue and white decorations, the Peronista coats-of-arms and the multiple portraits of Eva and, by night, because they were a blaze of electricity in streets that were dangerously ill-lit. The posters of Eva were almost all identical; her head graciously inclined, a fixed benevolent smile on her lips, they were reminiscent, but for the sanctimonious expression, of poorly produced advertisements for chewing-gum or toothpaste, and did justice neither to her beauty nor to her elegance. Smaller portraits were cut out in the shape of a heart and arranged, Valentine-like, in the form of a larger heart.

Once women's suffrage became law it was compulsory for women to register—voting is obligatory in Argentina; they were issued with small voting books, as necessary for identification for work or business as the man's *libreta de enrolamiento,* and equally useful as a further means of control. On these *libretas* the women's age does not appear but they are classed according to the year of their birth! Since a good number of women had failed to register within the proscribed time Eva declared an amnesty for them just before the elections; those who took advantage of this amnesty were questioned severely as to their failure to comply with the law before. The registry offices did not proclaim themselves as offshoots of the Peronista Feminine Party, but it needed no stretch of the imagination to believe that those officiating there were, to a woman, active members of the party.

If, on registering, the new voter was not immediately impressed into the party she was not allowed to enjoy her independence for long. Early in the year Eva had organized a door-to-door canvass that was almost as thorough as a census taking, and if no actual intimidation was used on those housewives who had no party card to show, a threat was implicit in the repeated visits and questionings, and it was generally understood that action would be taken against those who continued to prove stubborn. How much this understanding grew from the attitude of the inquisitors and how much from the fear-sharpened imaginations of those who were questioned it is hard to say; but certainly no one could expect to put through any small official business, renewing a business permit or claiming some annuity, while they remained obdurate. It required a high temper of courage for the housewife to resist the pressure put on her, since she was often interviewed when she was alone in the house with her children and gossip had done so much to enlarge the threat of retribution; yet some continued to resist, although their courage was further put on trial by relatives and friends who, far from commending them, told them they were fools not to comply. The ends of tyranny are unhappily furthered by those who, ashamed of their own lack of fortitude, belittle the resistance of others.

With the rumors of expected revolt and the rumors of Eva's ill-health there began to circulate the rumor of her candidacy for the vice-presidency. Early in the year the C.G.T. had begun to organize demonstrations calling for Perón's re-election; daily there were meetings in every part of the country and delegations of workers who called at the Casa Rosada or at the Ministry of Labor to express their "total adhesion" to Perón; Eva herself, at the head of a delegation of the Peronista Feminine Party, called at the Casa Rosada to present her husband with a gold watch and to implore him to continue as the head of the government; and the personnel of the Ministry of Public Works made a pilgrimage to Luján to pray for Perón's re-election. But in all this there had been no official mention of Eva's candidacy. No one seemed to know where this rumor sprang from but it became suddenly an accepted fact, almost welcomed by the Opposition who saw in it the possible downfall of Perón.

Eva's own intentions were revealed in the speech she made on May 1 from the balcony of the Casa Rosada. May 1 is celebrated in Argentina as Labor Day and the Plaza de Mayo was packed with crowds bearing banners proclaiming allegiance to Perón.

"My beloved shirtless ones," Eva began, "on this traditional

ing to nominate a candidate would be dissolved. In this way Perón had not only made it impossible for the Opposition to unite openly against him but he had made it improbable that any party would be willing to withdraw their candidate and privately urge their members to vote for some other and more popular opposition candidate. The Radical Party, always the strongest of the Opposition, was again divided among themselves; one faction favored candidates of the old school and the other faction called for new and more energetic leadership. Eventually the names of two of the younger deputies were agreed upon; Ricardo Balbin and Arturo Frondizi were both men in their forties who had been unknown in politics before the advent of Perón but who had distinguished themselves by their forthright and courageous opposition to him in the Chamber of Deputies; they represented the more liberal element among the Radicals. But theirs was a lost cause; they were allowed no opportunity of speaking on the radio— officially Perón announced that they could have as much time on the air as they had money to buy but, in fact, no station would sell them time; only *La Nación* and an occasional clandestine sheet carried news of their meetings; no printing house would accept work for them and they could bring out handbills and posters only by keeping their own press one step ahead of the police who closed any shop they operated. Since any criticism of the government, however well supported by documented proof, could be considered as *desacato,* members of the Opposition were likely to find themselves in jail after every meeting; Balbin was in and out of jail throughout the campaign. And their homes were marked with the infamous red crosses. Dr. Palacios, who was running on the Socialist ticket, announced that he would withdraw from the campaign as a protest against these impossible conditions, but his party members persuaded him to continue since without a candidate the party would find itself dissolved. In spite of these difficulties the Radical meetings in the city and the province were well attended and in some remote pueblos the Peronista party had to impose fines on those who absented themselves to assure a full attendance at

258

their meetings. But it seems not so much that the people had any intention of voting against Perón as that they were tired of the constant demands made on their time and their pockets. One country postman voiced what may have been the feelings of many. "I'm not a Peronista," he said. "But what happens to the pension he has promised me if I don't vote for him?"

In Buenos Aires the Peronista posters were frequently defaced; the New York *Times* reports how one wag, tired of seeing *Viva Perón!* written up everywhere, changed the phrase to *Viva yo!*— Long live I!—which was soon to be seen scribbled everywhere in the streets.

The Opposition were further embarrassed by the sudden announcement that the election was to be advanced to November 11, a move which seemed at first designed solely for their discomfiture but which later appeared to have been made so that the elections would take place before the country had to be rationed.

At the annual military dinner given on the eve of July 9, Independence Day, Mercante's absence seemed confirmation of the rumor that Eva was to take his place as candidate for the vice-presidency. There was talk that he was becoming altogether too popular in La Plata, capital of the province of Buenos Aires and seat of much of the discontent brewing against the regime.

During these months the railway workers had grown no more reconciled with the situation; twenty-seven of their companions, arrested earlier in the year, were still under arrest without trial. An unusually heavy rain had uncovered the bodies of ten or twelve men who had been killed and buried in a garbage dump; the police announced that they had no clue to their identities and advanced the unlikely theory that they were bodies stolen from cemeteries for the sake of their shrouds; they were all men in the prime of life and all marks of identification had been destroyed. Their identities were never discovered, or, at least, they were never published, and the story circulated that they were the bodies of strikers who had been murdered.

On July 31, at midnight, the railway workers declared a general walk-out and at three-thirty next morning there were eighteen explosions on the various railway lines, and a bridge was blown up. There would have been more if the authorities, evidently warned, had not set guards at strategic points. For a day or two Perón seemed very little disturbed by this outbreak which was, in fact, more violent than any before; it seems that he felt that he had the situation well in hand, for no especial measures were taken until August 3 when, perhaps because the engine drivers were not returning to work as quickly as he had expected, Perón invoked his emergency powers and mobilized the railway workers again.

The strike had been inadequately organized and the workmen had not had the support of the students who had recently agitated over Bravo's disappearance, or of the military who must have been planning their own insurrection at this time. The Peronista press blamed the outbreak on international plotters, and the man in the street knew very little of what was going on until it was all over.

Since the middle of the year José Espejo, head of the C.G.T., had been making preparations for a giant rally to be held on August 22, in the 450-foot-wide Avenida 9 de Julio which bisects the city as if a hurricane had cut a swathe through the buildings. Everyone understood that this was to be the occasion for the announcement of Eva's candidacy. Already the well-marshaled chorus of the shirtless ones were adding her name to their prayers for Perón's re-election. The hysteria was mounting but it was a hysteria artificially engendered; not only were there daily pilgrimages of provincial government officials—and these were certainly sincere, if self-interested, in the desire to see Perón re-elected—and of union delegations to the city and demonstrations of workers all over the country, but now the children were impressed into the campaign and meetings of schoolchildren were organized so that eight- and nine- and ten-year-olds might make their political affiliation clear to others, however muddled the issue was in their own excited little heads; and it is to be understood that for the sake of children themselves their parents dared not encourage their truancy. A children's rally was held in Luna Park with Eva's and Perón's personal appearance and the promise of bicycles and other prizes to persuade a maximum attendance. Thousands of children, inadequately supervised and wildly excited at the thought of the prizes, many of them fighting to approach Evita so that they might deliver into her hands some begging letter entrusted to them by their parents, brought about a minor riot in which, according to one report, two hundred and fifty children were injured and two killed.

Yearly rallies had been organized for the celebration of Labor Day and Loyalty Day but none on such a scale as the rally of August 22; it was said that two million shirtless ones were expected, most of them from out of town. A stage was set up in the avenida, house-sized portraits of Eva and Perón were displayed, loudspeakers were on every lamppost and stickers, posters, streamers and flags were everywhere. The most extravagant gestures of loyalty were performed, many of them doubtless in the hope of attracting Eva's attention and gaining for the performer some recompense in proportion to the absurdity of his feat. The faithful set out to walk to the city from provinces hundreds of miles away, one couple carried their infant daughter, one man came with a sack of wheat on his shoulders, all bore with them the two talismanic names; one man drove his car backwards to Luján and back, another came two hundred miles on top a rolling barrel; the whole country had turned itself into a circus, and *Democracia* announced jubilantly that all calculations for the rally were to be surpassed. August 22 had been declared a holiday throughout the country, but many of the provincial towns declared a holiday of several days to allow the people to make the trip to the capital and back. For forty-eight hours before the rally all public conveyances, trains, planes, buses, river boats, were reserved for the free passage of those who came to join the demonstration. From Rosario alone there were twelve special trains, twenty-four buses of the Rosario transport system, nine private buses chartered by the C.G.T., and six hundred trucks. Caravans of fancifully decorated private cars invaded the city and, according to *Democracia,* tens of thousands of telegrams were received daily at the Casa Rosada from those who were unable to attend.

For blocks around the Avenida 9 de Julio no traffic was allowed; passage on subway and tramcars was free for those who could find a footing on them. In the plazas barbecues were set up to feed the crowds which were as noisy as the crowds at carnival; for most of them this was just a spree. It was not a brightly colored throng, for the Argentine is sober in his dress and only in the costumes of the Andean provinces is there a touch of Incan coloring; the countryman was usually to be distinguished by the rustic cut of his clothes. Some wore the horseman's wide cotton breeches and here and there some Beau Brummell of the plains sported a belt of silver coins, boots concertina-creased and a vicuña poncho flung cavalierly over one shoulder. Some wore their ponchos, which to the countryman is both blanket and overcoat, draped over citified clothes. Only the younger and bolder among the women wore the harsh pinks and blues that seem like a gesture of rebellion against the drabness of their lives; the older women wore black, and clutched small children and paper bags of food or sat placidly nursing their babies on a doorstep or a bench—for fecundity causes little embarrassment in Argentina. Half-nomad women and girls— who seem, like gypsies, to appear only for such gala occasions— carried their meager bodies thrust forward, like women of medieval times, to balance the trays of glutinous sweetmeats they carried swung from their necks; street salesmen set up easels stuck all over with flags, buttons, emblems, rosettes, pins, bows, all with the two magic names, or touted portraits and postcards of the pair. Peronista songs and marches resounded from the loudspeakers on every side and the crowds, marching in groups with banners proclaiming their origin and their "adhesion" to the cause, cheered and chanted their new battle cry, *Perón! Eva Perón!* But although the vast avenue seemed packed from wall to wall, the expectations of the C.G.T. had not been fulfilled and by most counts there were no more than a quarter of a million of the two million expected there.

262

They called it the *Cabildo Abierto,* or open assembly, after the
famous *Cabildo Abierto* of 1810 when the people of Buenos Aires
voted to depose the Viceroy. Soon after five in the afternoon Perón
appeared on the stage with José Espejo and other officers of the
C.G.T. and Admiral Tessaire, president of the Peronista party.
There was no sign of Eva, and Espejo, who was the first to speak,
commented on her absence.

"My general," he said, "we note one absence, the absence of
your wife, of Eva Perón, she who is without peer in the world, in
history, in the love and veneration of the Argentine people. Companions, possibly her modesty, which is perhaps the greatest of her
merits, has kept her from this gathering, but the *Cabildo Abierto*
cannot continue without the presence of the Comrade Eva Perón."

An escort of C.G.T. officials was dispatched to fetch her and
in a very little while they returned with Eva, hatless and dressed
with that simple elegance which only the expenditure of money and
time can achieve. The crowd roared their acclaim and Eva and
Perón raised their arms in acknowledgment. After the Anthem
had been played Espejo spoke again, first asking Perón to stand
for re-election and then begging Eva to accept the nomination for
vice-presidency.

Eva's reply was in great part a bitter denunciation against the
oligarchs—and anyone, she had said, who was not Peronista was
oligarch—who were still plotting, so she said, to overthrow the
country; she herself, she insisted, had never been disturbed by their
calumny or their attacks against "a weak Argentine woman"; on
the contrary, she would be profoundly happy if her breast would
serve to shield Perón from all attack, for "it is not Eva Perón they
attack, but Perón." Her reply and her hesitation in accepting the
nomination—she had said no more than that she would be willing
to do what the people wanted—showed that she was fully aware
of the strong opposition to her candidacy. After Perón had spoken
speciously of the doctrine of *Justicialismo* and of his own sacrifices
for the people, Espejo urged Eva to give a definite reply. There followed a curious little scene of diffidence, persuasion, hesitation, and

263

final capitulation. Eva begged them not to force her into doing what she did not want to do and asked for four days in which to think the matter over. The crowd, at Espejo's instigation, shouted for her to give her answer, "Now! Now!" She looked helplessly towards Perón and begged to be allowed a few hours' grace, but the people, who had, most of them, been on their feet since dawn, demanded an immediate decision. With tears in her eyes and in a broken voice she gave them her reply, "I shall do as the people wish."

Shouting and singing, the crowds went off to enjoy the free theaters and movies which had been thrown open at midnight; all actors and entertainers had been ordered on duty from eleven-thirty. It was one way of solving the sleeping accommodation for such a crowd.

Later in the evening the Peronista Party announced the official nomination of General Perón and Eva Perón.

The great jamboree was over but the city could not settle back in peace.

The rumors were at boiling point now and some demonstration or revolt was expected from day to day; each gossip had his own theory but all were agreed on one point—Eva's nomination could not go unchallenged. But the announcement she made over the radio was the least expected of all developments.

On the night of August 31, at ten-thirty, Eva made a surprise broadcast over the whole Argentine radio network. She spoke in a low voice, broken by emotion. "It is my irrevocable decision," she said, "to refuse the honor which the workers and the people of my country wished to confer upon me at the historic *Cabildo Abierto* of August 22. I declare that this decision was born in my inner-most consciousness and is therefore perfectly free and has all the force of my final will."

She spoke of her great happiness in living and working by the side of General Perón and of the vow she had taken to serve the country and its humble working people.

264

"I had not then, nor do I have now, more than a single ambition, only one great personal ambition, that it should be said of me when the marvelous chapter will be written which history will dedicate to Perón, that there was by the side of Perón a woman who had devoted herself to bringing before the President the hopes of the people, which Perón converted into beautiful reality, and that this woman was lovingly called by the people: Evita."

She added that now no one would be able to say that she was guided by petty or egotistical personal ambition. "I know that every one of the shirtless ones who really loves me would also wish that nobody could disbelieve my words after this, nobody who is not wicked will be able to doubt the honesty, the loyalty, and the sincerity of my conduct. That is why I wish my shirtless ones to remain calm. I have not renounced either work or struggle, all I have renounced are honors."

The announcement, dramatic as it was in itself, coming as it did so soon and so unexpectedly after the hysterical acclaim given to Eva only ten days before, was made more impressive by the broken and almost inaudible voice in which it was made. It was evident that she was under some tremendous pressure and on the verge of collapse.

Eighteen

*From that day I thought that it would not be difficult to die
for a cause one loves. Or simply: to die for love.* E. P.

It was the Army whose pressure had at last forced Eva
into retreat; it is evident that they threatened Perón with
the withdrawal of their support or perhaps with a general mutiny
if Eva's candidacy were not withdrawn. They found it intolerable
to be faced with the possibility of having to acknowledge a woman
as their commander-in-chief—for should the President die that
command would fall to the Vice-President. Yet it is likely that the
intrigues of the military would have continued unsuccessful had
circumstances not lent force to their arguments. The growing discontent among the people and especially among the working people
had weakened Eva's position and the falling off of their support

267

had been made apparent to all at the *Cabildo Abierto* at which the attendance, full and enthusiastic as it seemed, was so much less than had been expected. It seems evident from her speech on May 1, when she had called upon the people to invest her with authority, that Eva had expected the whole country to rise up as one and demand her nomination. There was some talk after the *Cabildo Abierto* of Espejo's dismissal and of a general reorganization of the C.G.T., which no doubt would have taken place had Eva remained active.

The center of insubordination was in La Plata, capital of the province of Buenos Aires, whose authorities had never become so subservient to the regime as those of the federal capital; one judge of the La Plata courts had recently dismissed as an impertinence the demand of the C.G.T. that he reverse the judgment on a case. Colonel Mercante had gained some reputation for himself as governor of the province; his headquarters were in La Plata where the military and a faction of the Peronista deputies favored his candidacy for the vice-presidency. It was reported that a contingent of two thousand Peronistas had set out from La Plata to attend the *Cabildo Abierto* carrying banners that bore Mercante's name, and that they had been forced to turn back.

Before Eva's renunciation there had been a split among the Peronista deputies in the provincial legislature, the twenty-seven who supported her candidacy had walked out of the session, leaving twenty-five who favored Mercante. What took place in the closed meeting they held with Eva and Mercante present soon after was, of course, not disclosed; it is said that Eva used all her dynamic powers of persuasion into urging the Peronista deputies to stand solidly behind Perón. Whatever arguments were used both Eva and Mercante withdrew their claims and it was announced that Dr. Quijano would run again for the vice-presidency. Dr. Quijano[1] was in hospital undergoing a series of operations that, for a man of his age, were serious; he seems to have been the only candidate

---

[1] Dr. Quijano died on April 3, 1952, before the inauguration of his second vice-presidential term.

268

sufficiently ineffectual to please both factions. Perón took no overt part in these proceedings but maintained a strategic aloofness from his party's bickerings. It was Eva's first major defeat and it was immediately after this meeting that she made her speech of renunciation over the air.

It was announced in the Peronista press that Eva's withdrawal had been necessitated by a technicality: presidential and vice-presidential candidates had to have passed their thirtieth birthday and Eva, they said, was only twenty-eight. This was not very consistent with her claim of self-sacrifice and had it been true— she was, of course, thirty-two—was a somewhat ridiculous excuse to put forward; the matter of her age could hardly have been overlooked for so long, especially since her birthday had been lavishly celebrated in May as the Day of Love and Gratitude with a great many flowery speeches and gifts. Immediately after her renunciation Raul Apold, Secretary of Information, issued a statement that Eva was suffering from anemia and that she was confined to bed with influenza. Eva, who must have been on the point of collapse when she made her broadcast on August 31, had a nervous breakdown immediately after and had to be kept under restraint for a week. The frustration of her ambition had to resolve itself in a collapse and the humiliation of her defeat could be reconciled with her fantasy only by investing it with martyrdom to which her very real physical illness lent verisimilitude. For the past year she had been attended by Dr. Zarwarski, a Polish blood specialist, for anemia; her blood count was down to 3.500 as against the 5.000 normal, and rumors exaggerating her condition had credited her with the proclivities of a Dracula. With amazing obstinacy and fortitude she had continued her exhausting schedule, refusing to pander to her physical weakness or even to allow the matter to be discussed. At a dinner at the Residency, when Eva noticed Dr. Zarwarski in earnest conversation with Perón, she demanded to be told what it was that they were discussing. The doctor replied that he had been warning His Excellency that her condition was serious and that she must not continue to work so hard. In a rage she whipped her table napkin across the doctor's face, crying, "I told you you were not to discuss my health with the President!"

It was perhaps during her collapse, when she was under sedation and Dr. Ricardo Finochietto, director of the Policlínico Presidente Perón, was called in, that she received her first internal examination and cancer of the uterus was suspected; she had until then refused to allow any thorough examination of herself. Later in September, Dr. George T. Pack, cancer specialist of the New York Memorial Hospital, flew to Buenos Aires to speak before a conference of cancer specialists; he was not then called in to see Eva. She was as yet, and probably until after her operation, kept in ignorance of her condition. It was without her knowledge that Dr. A. Canonico consulted Dr. Pack on her behalf. She seemed to have shared with the simplest of her fellow countrymen a dread of doctors and of alien doctors in particular. In October, Dr. Pack was called back to Buenos Aires to examine Eva; she was already under anesthesia when he saw her and was almost certainly unaware that he was to examine her at all. All this was, of course, kept from the public who were unable to account for Perón's sudden demand for a protracted leave of absence which, in consequence, gave rise to the rumor that he and Eva were about to skip the country before its economic collapse.

But for the time public attention was diverted from Eva's dramatic disappearance from public life. At 11:10 A.M. on September 28, it was announced over the radio that the Army was in revolt; a few minutes later Espejo called a country-wide walkout of the C.G.T. in protest against the revolt. For a short while the radio continued to broadcast announcements that mutinous officers would be shot, and just before one o'clock it was announced that the rebellion had been quelled. The attempt seems at best to have been a half-hearted affair. Early in the morning rebel planes from the military air base at El Palomar and from the naval base at Punta del Indio flew over the city dropping leaflets announcing the uprising; by Peronista report there were only two rebel planes over the city but according to an eyewitness there were thirty or forty.

270

At Campo de Mayo, General Menendez had seized one of the gates leading to the noncommissioned officers' school where, later in the morning, Perón was to make the presentation of a flag. According to the reports in the Peronista press, whose front pages were devoted to the belittling of the attempt, Menendez seized the officers arriving for the ceremony, but two loyal guards galloped off on horseback to warn their superior officers who arrived on the scene shortly after with reinforcements; a few shots were exchanged and one Peronista sergeant died shouting, "Viva Perón!" According to other reports Army officers noticed unusual activity at El Palomar air base, which is contiguous to Campo de Mayo, and hastened to the city to warn Perón. A report brought out recently by the Radicals in the clandestine paper *El Cuidadano* claims that members of the C.G.T. had already been organized into shock troops and it was their prompt answer to Espejo's broadcast that foiled the attempt. *El Cuidadano* carried copies of contracts made with an Argentine firm later in the year for the delivery of five thousand automatics and two thousand carbines to the Eva Perón Foundation which, according to the editor, were for those shock troops that had proved themselves so effective in September. Menendez and his followers contacted the co-conspirators in El Palomar but seem to have got no further on the road to Buenos Aires; their failure seems to have been due as much to their own vacillation and lack of organization and perhaps to their mistrust of one another—and doubtless there were spies and traitors among their ranks—rather than to strong action on Perón's part. They had made no effort to engage the co-operation of disaffected groups among the civilian population. It was the old story of each man for himself; and the enthusiasm of some of the rebels may have been cooled by Eva's withdrawal and her illness.

By two in the afternoon Army jet planes were skimming the rooftops in a demonstration of loyalty—and force—and the shirtless ones again were flocking into the Plaza de Mayo to punctuate their *Lider's* speech with cries of, "To the gallows! To the gallows with the traitors!"

Eva was not told of the commotion until it was all over. She had had another blood transfusion that day and was very weak. When she heard of the crowds gathered in the Plaza she wanted to rise up and speak to them—to find herself so suddenly and utterly removed from events in a moment of crisis must have been intolerable —and when this was manifestly impossible she insisted on speaking over the air from her bed. In a voice weak and trembling with emotion she begged the people to follow their happiness with Perón as they had done this day, until their death, because Perón deserved it, because he had won it, because they must atone to him with their love for the infamies of his enemies, who were the enemies of the *patria* and of the people themselves.

"To all of you I give a great embrace from my heart," she ended. "For me there is nothing in the world but the love of Perón and my people."

So ineffectual had the attempt been that many believed it had been manufactured by Perón as a further excuse for arresting his opponents and to whip up national feeling on the eve of the elections with the perennial bogeys of American imperialism and Mr. Spruille Braden, in spite of the fact that Menendez was known as a strong nationalist and anti-American. Many of the rebels escaped over to Uruguay in commandeered planes. It was reported officially that some two hundred arrests had been made but according to unofficial reports as many as two thousand were sent in chains to the concentration camps of the south. Among those arrested were General Menendez and General Rawson, both retired from the Army and both of whom had been under recent investigation for subversive activities, which seems to bear out the theory that Perón had allowed the plot to ripen and had used it for his own ends. General Rawson was that same rash and gallant general who had replaced President Castillo for two days and later was imprisoned for an attempted uprising against Farrell and Perón; he was cleared of participation in the plot but seems to have been kept under arrest. According to official reports, the officers arrested received relatively light sentences; General Menendez was given fifteen years of prison and the others were given sentences of three to six years. Congress passed a law giving Perón power to promote, demote or retire any officer, which he at once used to make drastic changes in all services.

The story is told of one fashionable girls' school whose pupils all raced excitedly to the windows at the sound of the rebel planes, shouting, *"Viva la revolución!"* Unfortunately for the nuns who ran the school, Major Aloé's daughter was among their pupils and she reported the incident to her father. The school was closed and has remained closed since.

Eva's withdrawal from the campaign and her illness, which had at first given encouragement to the opposition, proved to be Perón's strongest cards. As a candidate Eva had had a disrupting influence on the party; as a sick woman she became the center of an emotional exhibition in which her suffering and the "sacrifice of her health for the sake of the people" were squeezed for the last drop of their sentimental appeal. Her name, far from disappearing from Peronista propaganda, was in evidence everywhere so that to the stranger it seemed as if the ticket were still Perón-Perón. Perón had canceled his nationwide tour, but the country was flooded with propaganda—it is said that Peronista publicity was costing a million pesos a day—in which Eva's picture and name appeared as largely as Perón's. Down the length of Calle Florida a scaffolding was erected on either side of the street bearing the legend, *The New Argentina of Perón,* with portraits of Eva and Perón and the Peronista coats-of-arms at either end. This obstruction to traffic was paid for by levies on the shops whose entrances and windows were obscured by the scaffolding and who, as one observer pointed out, were cut off from the approach of fire trucks. Masses were held, not only in all the churches across the land but at altars erected in plazas and on the highroad so that passers-by might add their prayers for Eva's recovery; the endless pilgrimages on foot to Luján of small groups carrying images of the Virgin and scrolls of prayers for Eva's recovery, the hysterical offerings of blood for transfusion, the innumerable delegations, demonstrations, meetings, held by groups of all sorts all over the country, served admirably as publicity for Perón's cause. That the Opposition continued to hold meetings was regarded by Peronistas as inconsideration towards a sick woman.

After Dr. Pack had examined Eva in October—and presumably after the inevitability of an operation became evident—the matter of Eva's illness seemed to eclipse the campaign altogether and the demonstrations of public sentiment took on the conspiratorial tone of a Christmas arranged previously with the collusion of press and the general public for the indulgence of a dying child. It was announced that this year Loyalty Day, October 17, would be dedicated to Evita and in preparation for the event television sets were installed in all public schools in and around the city.

The Plaza de Mayo was as crowded as it had been in 1945; both October 17 and 18 were holidays and again all theaters and movies were free. On the balcony of the Casa Rosada Eva appeared and was seated in an arm chair; she was hatless and wore a close-buttoned dark red suit; her face was wan and haggard, both illness and fantasy casting her for the role of *religieuse*. Perón hovered over her and grouped fondly around were the élite of the Peronistas, Espejo, Freire, Campora, Apold, Aloé, and even Colonel Mercante who had returned to the fold for the celebration. The crowd applauded thunderously and chanted the party's marching song, "The Peronista Boys." Espejo made a speech in which he eulogized her abnegation, and presented her with the Laurels of Grateful Distinction, First Class, a decoration that seems to have been expressly designed for her. She was too overcome to answer him at once—the doctor had advised against her appearance. Then Perón pinned on her breast the Grand Peronista Medal, Extraordinary Class, in recognition of her selflessness in renouncing her candidacy. He embraced her and for a moment she clung to his shoulder weeping.

"This marvelous people," said Perón, "whom we have already qualified as being the best in the world, has decided that this October 17 should be dedicated to Eva Perón. There could be no homage more just, more deep, more honorable than this dedication of October 17 to Eva Perón. She is not only the guide and the standard-bearer of our movement but in Argentine history the figure of Eva Perón will be seen as one of the greatest women of humanity." Then he begged for absolute silence so that the Señora Eva Perón might speak without strain.

That Eva could make such a speech as she did in the condition in which she was is another proof of her astonishing resolution. In the utter stillness of the crowd she began:

My beloved shirtless ones, this is a day of great emotion for me. With all my soul I have desired to be with you and with Perón on this glorious day of the shirtless ones. I could never miss this appointment that I have with the people on each October 17. I assure you that nothing and no one could have prevented me from coming, because I have a sacred debt to Perón and to you, to the workers and the boys of the C.G.T., and it does not matter to me if in paying it I must leave shreds of my life by the wayside.

I had to come and I came to thank Perón and the C.G.T. and the shirtless ones and my people. To Perón, who has just honored me with the highest distinction that can be given a Peronista, I shall never finish paying my debt, not until I give my life in gratitude for the kindness he has always shown me. Nothing that I have, nothing that I am, nothing that I think is mine; it is Perón's. I will not tell the usual lie and say that I have not deserved this; yes, I deserve it, my general. I deserve it for one thing only that is worth all the gold in the world. I deserve it because all I have done is for love of this country. What I have done is of no value; my renunciation is of no value; what I am and what I have is of no value. I have only one thing of value and that is in my heart. It burns in my soul, aches in my flesh, stings in my nerves; it is love for the people and Perón. And I give thanks to you, my general, who have taught me to know you and love you. If the people asked for my life I would give it singing, because the happiness of one shirtless one is worth more than my life.

275

I had to come to give thanks to the C.G.T. for the Laurels with which they have decorated me which are for me the dearest memento of the Argentine workers. I had to come to thank the workers and the C.G.T. who dedicated this glorious day to a humble woman.

I had to come to tell you, as I told the general, that it is necessary to keep an alert watch on all sides in our struggle. The danger is not past. The enemies of the people, of Perón and of the patria do not sleep. It is necessary that each Argentine worker keeps on the lookout and that he should not sleep, for the enemies work in the shadow of treason and sometimes they hide behind a smile or an outstretched hand. I had to come to thank all my beloved shirtless ones from every corner of the patria because on September 28 you knew how to risk your lives for Perón. I was sure that you would know, as you have known before, how to act as a trench for Perón. The enemies of Perón and of the patria have known for a long time that Perón and Eva Perón are ready to die for the people. Now they know that the people are ready to die for Perón.

I ask just one thing of you today, comrades, that we all swear publicly to defend Perón and to fight for him and we will shout our oath aloud for the space of a minute so that the sound of it may reach the furthest corners of the world.

At this the crowd set up a tremendous roar of "My life for Perón! My life for Perón!" which, if it did not reach the furthest corners of the world, might almost have been heard in the prisons of Villa Devoto and San Miguel. When the shouts had given way to silence Eva continued:

I thank you, comrades, for your prayers for my health. I thank you from my heart. I hope that God hears the humble people of my patria so that I may soon return to the battle and continue fighting with Perón for you and with you for Perón until death.

I have wanted and I want nothing for myself. My glory is and always will be the shield of Perón and the banner of my people, and even if I leave shreds of my life on the wayside I know that you will gather them up in my name and carry them like a flag to victory.

I know that God is with us because he is with the humble and despises the pride of the oligarchs, and so the victory will be ours. Sooner or later we will reach it, cost what it may and fall who must.

My shirtless ones, I would like to say many things to you but the doctors have told me I must not talk. I leave you my heart and I tell you I am sure, as it is my wish, that I shall soon be in the fight again, with more strength and more love, to fight for this country that I love so much, as I love Perón. I ask only one thing of you: I am sure that I will soon be with you, but if because of my health I cannot, help Perón, be loyal to Perón as you have been until now, because this is to be loyal to the patria *and to yourselves. And all those shirtless ones of the interior, I embrace them very close to my heart and I hope that they realize how much I love them.*

One has only to look at the pictures taken of Eva during this ceremony to be convinced of her sincerity; she had utterly convinced herself that she was the Lady of Hope and of Compassion, loving and beloved of everyone. But the love of which she boasted must have been a bitter love, for it ached and stung and burnt her soul.

When she had spoken and the clamor had died down Perón declared that October 18 was to be "Santa Evita's Day."

On November 5, Dr. Pack was back in Buenos Aires; he was kept in absolute seclusion and was not permitted to communicate even with the American Ambassador, Mr. Ellsworth Bunker, who was a personal friend. It became known that on November 3 Eva had been taken to the Policlinico Presidente Perón, the second floor of which had been cleared, so it was said, for her reception; a few months before the hospital had still been to all intents and purposes unoccupied, so that it was probably a matter of fitting it with suitable luxury. Crowds began to gather in the streets outside to pray for her recovery; but not all their fervor was spontaneous or sincere, for some Buenos Aires firms reported that they had been ordered to supply so many employees, with the necessary transport, to pray outside the hospital. All Peronista rallies and official functions had been called off, hourly masses were said for her recovery, telegrams were sent to the Pope begging for his intercession, senators and deputies and the entire staffs of governmental offices prayed as if the whole city were threatened with the plague. But much of this tenderness for Eva was no more than a part of the Peronista campaign and her illness was turned into a gross piece of election propaganda, so timely that one is tempted to wonder if her operation had not been delayed until its impact on the emotions of the voting public would be to the greatest advantage to Perón. Her very fantasy of martyrdom, as much a part of her sickness as the cancer for which she was to be operated, was encouraged and exploited with as little consideration for her mental health as in medieval days the visions and ecstasies of demented girls were exploited by unscrupulous priests.

On November 6, Eva was operated for cancer of the uterus. Again it was said that as she went under the anesthetic she cried, "Viva Perón!" Dr. Ricardo Finochietto, director of the Policlinico, Dr. Jorge Albertelli, a gynecologist of reputation, and Dr. Roque Izzo, director of the Medical School of the University of Buenos Aires, were present while Dr. Pack performed the operation. It seems that the Argentine specialists had been unwilling to operate on her when the outcome was so uncertain. The operation lasted three hours and twenty minutes and the cancer pronounced to be reasonably confined. Again Eva was, almost certainly, unaware that Dr. Pack was to be present, for she was already under the anesthetic when he saw her, and she was certainly unaware that he was to perform the operation. When Dr. Pack returned to Buenos Aires in December he was decorated for his researches in the study of cancer and the presentation made to Dr. Finochietto at the same time was worded in such a way as to make it seem possible that he had performed the operation. This ambiguity may have been designed to hide from the public the fact that a foreign specialist had been

278

called in; but it is very possible that Eva did not know to the end by whom the operation was performed.

The elections were held five days later, on November 11, and Perón was re-elected with a majority of sixty-six per cent. A special ballot box was carried to Eva's bedside so that she might register her vote, one of the four million women in Argentina who voted for the first time in their lives. Before Eva was taken to the Policlinico she recorded a speech which was broadcast on the last day of the campaign.

"Not to vote for Perón," she said, "is for an Argentine—I say it because I feel it—to betray the country." She would, she said, be with each voter in spirit on every step they made on November 11. "I will follow you like a shadow, repeating in your ears and your conscience the name of Perón until you have deposited your vote in the urn as a message of love and of faith and of loyalty towards the *Lider* of the people." And she ended, "May every Peronista vote on November 11 be a silent cry from an Argentine heart, 'My life for Perón!' "

Epilogue

I will return and I will be millions. E. P.

Eva Duarte de Perón died on July 26, 1952, less than a year after the throng in the Avenida Nueve de Julio had demanded her nomination as candidate for the vice-presidency. It had been a year of suffering for her. After her operation she had made a few public appearances: the first when Perón's victory had been announced and the boys of the C.G.T. had marched in a torchlight procession from the Plaza de Mayo, down Calle Florida and along Avenida Libertador General San Martín—once known as Avenida Alvear—to the presidential residence where Eva had made a brief appearance in a wheelchair on the balcony. Her last public appearance was on June 4, 1952, at the inauguration of Perón's second term.

Although the public had been urged to pray for her recovery, no mention was made in the press of the seriousness of her condition, but it was evident to those who saw her that she was desperately ill. In front of a battery of cameras she would straighten up in a gallant attempt to appear her old driving dynamic self, but when they were gone she would slump back into exhaustion. She hardly had the strength to play the role of martyr.

After her death the Peronista press reported that in spite of the pain she had cried to the doctors that she did not want to die, that Perón and her people needed her, and that at the end she had called for Perón and had made him swear that he would never forsake their "shirtless ones." This may have been Peronista propaganda but it may as easily been true, for she had long abandoned the world of reality for that of fantasy, and believed as implicitly as did the most devoted of her followers that she and Perón had been destined to be the saviors of mankind.

A few days before her death Perón presented her with the collar of the Order of San Martín, a decoration reserved for chiefs of state and which entitled her, who held no rank, to the honors of a presidential funeral. There were seven hundred diamonds, emeralds and rubies in the gold and platinum collar. It was the last treasure to be added to her hoard.

Her mother, her brother, her three sisters, Perón and the members of the cabinet were at her bedside when she died. That evening the radio stations in Buenos Aires interrupted their programs while the Sub-Secretary of Information performed the "very sad duty of announcing that at 8:25 the Señora Perón, the Spiritual Leader of the Nation, passed away." The bulletin was repeated every fifteen minutes, the interludes filled with religious music. The cabinet met to announce

280

that all political activity would be suspended for two days. There were to be thirty days of official mourning. Church bells were to toll throughout the country and a five-minute silence was to be observed.

It had already been decreed that a mausoleum of marble and bronze, larger than the Statue of Liberty, was to be built in Palermo Park, and that replicas of it were to be erected in all the provincial cities. Members of the C.G.T. had been asked to contribute their wages for August 22—henceforward to be known as Renunciation Day—toward the cost. The white sarcophagus was to be carried through the mourning crowds to the Ministry of Labor where Eva had reigned for six years. The throng that gathered on the first day was so great that at least three were killed and two thousand or more injured. Hysterical women flung themselves forward to kiss the glass of the coffin and troops were called up to control the crowd. Perón announced that the funeral rites would be postponed until the line outside the Ministry of Labor had ceased to form.

For three days no business was conducted in Buenos Aires, no shops or restaurants were open, there were no taxis on the streets and no news on the air except that of mourning. In the elegant Plaza Hotel the guests had to make their own beds and be content with one meal served a day—it was impossible to buy food elsewhere. The florists alone did a thriving business, and their shops were soon denuded to supply the wreaths which overflowed the Ministry of Labor and lay a dozen deep around the building in the rain.

In the Senate and over the air she was eulogized: Martyr of Labor, Protector of the Forsaken, Defender of the Worker, Guiding Light of the Children, she was called. It was decreed that for evermore July 26 would be a day of mourning, that for evermore Peronista party members would wear black ties at all official functions, that on every school day of the year a delegation of school children would lay flowers on her sarcophagus, and that her tomb was to have a guard of honor of twenty workers for evermore.

Evita was thirty-three years old when she died, and her early death seems to have a classical inevitability. No other end would have suited her so well. She had always believed in her own destiny—it was this belief that had been her greatest strength. Years before she had announced that one day she would be the greatest actress in the world. It was a dream shared by many girls, but chance and opportunity, her own indefatigable energy and ruthlessness, had provided her with a role which far outstripped her dreams. She had become the most loved and most hated woman of her time, the most powerful and the most notorious and perhaps the richest woman in the world. There was no other honor left but canonization. The Pope refused her this, but Eva died believing herself a saint.

Evita's story did not end with death. More than a quarter of a century later she still haunts the country. The passionate words she cast upon the air so generously have risen up like dragons' teeth in strife, and her name is still enough to set Argentinian against Argentinian, Peronista against Peronista.

There was in Juan Perón's character a touch of that apathy, philosophical rather than physical, which affects so many South Americans, the shrug that seems to say, "so what!" He was no gambler to risk his all on a single throw but, rather, a wily poker player, and one who would keep the ace of spades up his sleeve. In 1945, while he had grumbled about the discomforts of prison life on the island of Martín García, it had been Evita who had aroused the *descamisados* to his support. Almost until her death she had been the dynamo which had supplied him with energy. Once she was gone his resolution faltered.

Before the mausoleum which was to house Evita's body in perpetuity had been completed, Perón was forced into exile. In 1955, three years after Evita's death, the army, appalled by a policy which had brought the country to the verge of bankruptcy, staged a coup. It was supported by the Catholic hierarchy, whose churches had been vandalized and looted by the Peronista thugs. Students were rioting and even the CGT, that vast armed mob on which Perón relied, failed to rally to his support. There was no Evita to whip them into action. After five days of fighting, with the navy, always an enemy of Perón, threatening to shell the city, he was allowed to go into exile on a Uraguayan gunboat. That he was neither imprisoned nor shot was less a measure of his enemies' humanity than of their conviction that his cause was lost forever. In Buenos Aires the people poured into the streets, rejoicing at his downfall. All but the most fanatical Peronistas believed they had seen the last of him. So it might have been if it had not been for the inefficiency and corruption of the regimes that followed, and for that ace of spades he kept up his sleeve—the body of Evita.

Her body had lain in state, first in the Ministry of Labor, then in the Senate, and finally in a chapel in the headquarters of the CGT. While it was there it underwent further embalming at the hands of Pedro Ara, the famous Spanish pathologist. The job is said to have cost Perón a hundred thousand dollars, but it was money well spent, for now that body was virtually indestructible.

When General Aramburu seized the headquarters of the CGT, the body was found, not in the chapel, not even in its coffin, but lying on a makeshift altar in a locked office. It was not the least of the problems the general had to face.

The Peronista feminists, whose party had been dissolved, were clamoring to be given the body for Christian burial, but, wherever it was buried, it was bound to become a Peronista shrine, a rallying point for political dissent. The navy had refused to have her in their cemetery on the island of Martín García, and her family, exiled in Venezuela, ungratefully washed their hands of her. The body disappeared and was not heard of again for sixteen years.

Rumors ran riot through the city. In restaurants and expresso coffee bars, in boudoirs and on park benches, conjectures as to its whereabouts were exchanged: Aramburu had had it thrown into the river; disguised as the body of a nun, it had been spirited off to Rome for burial; twenty-five prominent citizens, sworn separately to secrecy, had each been given a coffin for clandestine burial, each believing his coffin to contain the remains of Evita. What happened to her body for the next two years is still uncertain, but in 1957 a Señora Iroldi, a lay sister of the Order of St. Paul, arrived in Milan with a coffin which she believed to contain the body of Maria Maggi, an Italian widow who had died in Argentina. It was buried in Milan's Musocco cemetery, and lay there undisturbed for fourteen years.

Perón had fled to Paraguay, and from there to Panama City and to Santo Domingo—Ciudad Trujillo as it was called then—and at last to Madrid. It was no easier for him to find a permanent resting place.

Perón was a true Argentine *macho;* he could no more do without women than without food. After Evita's death he had affronted her devotees by his goings-on with teen-age school girls in the *quinta* of the presidential residence in Olivos. In Panama City he met a young Argentine cabaret dancer, María Estela Martinez, who traveled with him to Madrid and, in 1961, became his wife.

Even if the rumor were true that, after Evita's death, the number of her Swiss bank account could not be found, when Perón left his country he was an enormously wealthy man. He and Isabelita, as his third wife came to be called, lived in princely style in a luxurious, well-guarded villa in the elite Puerta de Hierro district outside Madrid. There he continued to receive the faithful, delegates from labor unions and the Peronista party. As one disastrous regime followed another—in the seventeen years after Perón's departure there were five military and three civilian administrations in Argentina—the steady stream of visitors to the great house in the Puerta de Hierro became a flood. The euphoria following Perón's downfall had quickly dissipated. Prices had continued to rise, corruption was as prevalent, and repression increased as violence became a way of life. As Perón himself once cynically remarked: "It was not that we were so good, but those who followed us were so bad it made us look better than we were."

Even if the more conservative elements had begun to believe that Perón, who had left the country in chaos, might be the only one who might restore tranquility.

Perón was a master of guile. The *justicialismo* he preached was, he said, a middle way between capitalism and communism. The word was, in fact, so meaningless it allowed him to embrace anyone who came to see him, each left believing he had Perón's sympathy. To the military and businessmen he promised a return to law and order; to a younger generation, who could not remember how oppressive his

283

regime had been, he promised justice and a new social order. It was a political ambiguity which was to release a Pandora's box of trouble on his countrymen.

Perón himself seems to have been in no hurry to leave the comfortable life in the Puerta de Hierro, where Isabelita fussed over his diet and protected him from too exhausting an influx of visitors. He tired more easily. He was in his seventies and, so his enemies insisted, was growing senile. There were still many who wished him dead. It was that body lying in the Musocco cemetery that would not let him rest.

The mystery of Evita's disappearance had added enormously to the legend of her name. The poor remembered only the kisses she had blown them and the promises she had made. She had become a cult figure to a new generation who chanted: "Evita lives!" The Montoneros, a youthful, far-left terrorist group claimed her for their own: "If Evita were alive she would be a Montonera." In the increasing chaos, even those who had most hated Evita had begun to look back on the Perón era as a time of comparative stability.

More than once Perón had asked Generalissimo Franco for permission to bring Evita's body to Madrid, but Franco, who had not been overeager to receive Perón himself, refused. In 1971 he relented. It is possible that General Alejandro Lanusse, the latest to seize power in Argentina, had found himself under pressure from the Peronistas and had used his influence. Perhaps Franco, with his finger to the wind, had sensed the coming change. In June of that year a man, representing himself as Carlos Maggi, brother of the fictitious Maria Maggi, received permission from the Milan authorities to exhume and transport the body. The outer wooden casing had rotted, but the coffin itself, said to be of silver, was in excellent condition, as was the body, whose face could be seen through the glass window in the lid. The man calling himself Carlos Maggi escorted the body in a funeral van around the coast of France to the villa in the Puerta de Hierro.

We have no account of its arrival there, but it seems that Isabelita, whatever her private feelings may have been, received the body of her predecessor with as much reverence as if it had been a holy relic.

The military themselves had become disillusioned with their attempts to restore order in the country. Inflation was running at nearly seventy percent and still rising, foreigners were withdrawing capital from the country, and the numbers of bombings and assassinations continued to increase. Lanusse announced the elections would be held in 1973—the first to be held in a decade. It had become obvious that no peaceful transfer of power would be effected without the cooperation of the Peronistas, who seemed incapable of cooperating with each other. As businessmen and Maoists, military men and terrorists, gathered under the Perón banner, the dissension in the Peronista ranks became violent. Lanusse, in an attempt to pacify them, announced reluctantly that Perón would be welcome if he came home. No mention was made of

Evita's body. Its potential was too dangerous.

Perón's return with Isabelita in 1972 was a disappointment both to him and his followers. The tired old man who stepped from the chartered Alitalia plane into the rain waved briefly to the crowd and hurried to a waiting car; he was no longer the flamboyant *caudillo* who had shouldered his way into the cheering mobs with outstretched hands. Nor was there a mob to greet him. Barely six hundred, mostly newspaper reporters, had gathered at the Ezeiza airport. The thousands, with their banners and their drums, promised him by the Peronista party, had been held back on the way by troops. The city was deserted. Lanusse, in order to avoid demonstrations, had declared it to be a day of enforced inactivity, and the CGT had called a general strike to allow the *descamisados* to welcome their hero home.

Perón has dawdled so over his return that he had missed the August deadline that would have allowed his name to appear on the ballot for the March elections. Indignant because Lanusse would not change the rules for his convenience, feeling himself slighted by officials, and disappointed at his welcome, Perón left the country again after six weeks, with very little more ceremony than when he had fled into exile in 1955. He and Isabelita returned to Madrid to await the outcome of the elections.

If Perón's presence had lost much of its charisma, the names of Evita and Perón had lost none of their old magic. Their portraits covered the walls as if it were they who were running for office. The candidate Perón had endorsed, Héctor Cámpora, was an obscure politician with nothing to recommend him but a servile devotion to Perón. He won under the slogan "Cámpora in government—Perón in power." He resigned fifty days after his inauguration, and Perón, who had returned triumphantly in June, was elected for a third term in September, with Isabelita as his running mate.

Seen at a distance on the balcony of the Casa Rosada, Perón was still a fine figure of a man; *un buen pedazo de pan,* as Argentinians say. Handsome, erect—he was over six feet tall—his hair dyed black, buoyed by his recent victory, he could still give an impression of vigor. Visitors to the presidential *quinta* in Olivos could still be impressed by the warmth of his manner and disarming smile. He seemed to play the role of wily elder statesman, and there were many who still believed he could unite the country and bring the peace and prosperity he had promised; but Perón was seventy-seven years old and already there were rumors of his failing health. On July 1, 1974, nine months after he had taken office, Perón died of pneumonia followed by cardiac arrest, leaving Isabelita to become the first woman head of state in the Americas.

It is ironic that it should have been Isabelita and not Evita who eventually filled this role, and there is something pathetic in her attempts to model herself after her predecessor. There was a certain similarity in their backgrounds, although Isabelita's was perhaps the more conventional. Her father had died when she was young, and she had left the province of La Rioja to join a group of folk dancers in Buenos Aires. She was no better educated than Evita. She, too, had her ambitions, but she was totally lacking in the drive, the daring, the political opportunism, and the overwhelming belief in her own great destiny which had carried Evita forward with such irresistible impetus; and she was faced with a situation before which Evita herself might have quailed.

Perón had done nothing to heal the rift in Peronista ranks. When he had returned triumphantly after Cámpora's election, the thousands gathered to greet him at the airport had come to blows. There had been a pitched battle, and a hundred had been left dead and hundreds more wounded.

He had surrounded himself with a group of advisers distinguished chiefly for their anonymity. One of these, José López Rega, an astrologer and a sinister Svengali-like figure, had been constantly at Perón's elbow, and was now at Isabelita's. His influence was mistrusted equally by those on the right and those on the left. Isabelita herself was mistrusted, not only for her lack of experience but because she was a woman. Old-time Peronistas resented her attempt to imitate Evita: She wore her hair pulled tightly back into a bun as Evita had at the end.

The country was in chaos: Inflation had risen to three hundred percent and was still rising; foreign businessmen, faced by threats of kidnapping and murder, were withdrawing their assets from the country. Political assassinations had reached an average of three a day. Isabelita played the only card left to her: the ace of spades Perón had kept up his sleeve. She sent López Rega to Madrid to bring Evita home.

Some say she did so to save López Rega, whose life had been threatened; others that she hoped to divert attention from taxation and rising prices. The most bizarre explanation, and yet the most credible, was that the Montoneros had bargained for an exchange of bodies. Four years before, the Montoneros had murdered General Aramburu, that same Aramburu who had spirited Evita's body out of the country in 1955. Recently they had stolen his body from the family vault, and now they offered to return it if Evita was brought home. As the plane carrying her coffin landed at the air force base, they phoned the newspapers telling them where Aramburu's body might be found in a parked van on a Buenos Aires street.

Only a few had been there to welcome Evita. Her return had been conducted with such secrecy that the public was not aware of it until her body lay beside Perón's in the mausoleum in Palermo Park. Evita had returned but she was not, as she had boasted she would be, millions; and yet that one poor shrunken little corpse still held the potential for destruction.

286

Isabelita had been appearing less and less frequently in public. She was a thin, brittle, nervous woman of forty-three, whose shrill voice sometimes became hysterical. The city was full of rumors: that she would resign, that López Rega was under arrest or had gone into exile, that the bodies of the Peróns had vanished and that a wax figure lay in Evita's place. Isabelita retreated to the hills of Córdoba, for the sake of her health, she said. She returned to Buenos Aires and almost at once went into a hospital. There was some safety in ill health, and she was like a hare, doubling this way and that. Yet she continued to cling, with foolhardy desperation, to her brief spell in the Argentine sun.

The end came as a surprise to no one but Isabelita herself. She was totally unaware of the carefully planned coup until the helicopter, which was to have taken her to the presidential *quinta* in Olivos, was diverted and she was unceremoniously informed that she was under arrest. Later she was put on trial for having diverted a hundred thousand dollars of relief funds to her own use. Even in larceny she was but a poor shadow of Evita who had refused to account for the hundred million dollars a year which, in the name of the Eva Perón Foundation, had passed through her hands and disappeared.

History must judge how much blame should be laid on Evita and Perón for the destruction of a country which, for the first three decades of this century, was the most stable, the most advanced, the richest and most promising in South America. Some blame must fall on the Argentine people themselves, on a patriarchal system which allowed vast wealth to flourish beside abject poverty, on a *machismo* which not only kept women in subjugation, but made it impossible for men to subject themselves to the common good, and for a social order which laid on Evita the dual burden of poverty and womanhood.

In a more open society she might have been given the opportunity to put her superabundant energy and undoubted talents to a better purpose. In a later generation she might well have taken the lead in the liberation of women. Dubious as her methods and her motives were, she must be given some credit for what independence Argentine women have achieved. It was due to her that divorce was made legal and that women were given the vote at last. This latter amendment to the Constitution was passed as a concession to the Señora Evita; women were expected to vote as their husbands did, and the only serious discussion it provoked was whether or not a woman's age should appear on her registration card, a discussion in which chivalry prevailed.

Evita was the first fashionable Argentine woman to appear in public wearing pants, a gesture which may have had more symbolic significance than she was aware of. For all her expressions of abject humility and cloying adoration of her husband, her very presence was a flamboyant challenge to the traditional inferiority of women and to the authority of men. Those who derided her for her ignorance and despised her for her immorality feared her as much as they hated her, for she had broken down old barriers. To the women of the Peronista party she was an inspiration not as a saint, although they gave lip service to her as such, but as an example of what any woman might achieve. To the poor she offered hope, and to those too young to remember how an earlier generation of students had been beaten, tortured, and imprisoned under the Peróns, she seemed to have opened the way to the future. The tragedy is that she herself had helped to initiate the tyranny which was to crush the hopes she had kindled in women, in the young, and in the poor.

After the last of the Peróns was gone, political and economic chaos continued and increased. Not only were foreigners leaving the country, but Argentinians themselves left in droves, young professionals and artisans who saw no future for themselves at home, older people who feared for their lives and those of their children. Violence had become an undeclared civil war. Montoneros murdered government officials, army officers, or any they suspected of collaborating with the police. Police squads, often unable to find the terrorists, arrested and tortured their families or anyone who might have had the remotest connection with the dissidents. There are signs now that economic stability may be reestablished under President Videla but such stability will have been achieved at an intolerable cost. The present regime is as repressive as any in the past. Terror has all but eliminated opposition, and yet the midnight arrests, the disappearances, the tortures and the murders continue. There is scarcely a family in Buenos Aires that cannot count a *desaparecido* among its ranks. To make inquiries about a husband or a son is to risk disappearing into that limbo which lies just below the surface in the Argentina of today.

The bodies of Evita and Perón no longer lie in state in the mausoleum on Avenida Alvear; Perón has been buried in his grandfather's tomb in the Chacarita, a cemetery in the suburbs of Buenos Aires.

There is another, more exclusive, cemetery which lies in the most fashionable part of Buenos Aires. Here, in the Recoleta, the wealthiest and most famous families in Argentina lie crowded together in tombs of alabaster, marble and bronze. In one of her gestures of defiance toward the oligarchy, Evita had bought a tomb in the Recoleta intended for the Duarte family. Five meters below this Gothic structure there is a vault made of steel. It was built by a firm whose business it was to make safety vaults for banks. The locks are of the latest and most burglar-proof design, and an alarm system connects, it with police headquarters. There Evita lies, hidden from the eyes of those who believed her to be a saint and might claim her body as a source of miracles. There she lies, out of reach of those who might use her body for political propaganda. There she lies, among the tombs of the oligarchs she hated and who so hated her.

288